14 DAY BOO
This book is due on or befo...

D0151548

WITHDRAWN

3 0700 10793 3649

French Cinema in the 1980s

Nostalgia and the Crisis of Masculinity

PHIL POWRIE

CLARENDON PRESS · OXFORD
1997

Oxford University Press, Great Clarendon Street, Oxford OX2 6DP

Oxford New York

Athens Auckland Bangkok Bombay
Buenos Aires Calcutta Cape Town Dar es Salaam
Delhi Florence Hong Kong Istanbul Karachi
Kuala Lumpur Madras Madrid Melbourne
Mexico City Nairobi Paris Singapore
Taipei Tokyo Toronto Warsaw

and associated companies in
Berlin Ibadan

Oxford is a trade mark of Oxford University Press

Published in the United States
by Oxford University Press Inc., New York

© Phil Powrie 1997

All rights reserved. No part of this publication may be reproduced,
stored in a retrieval system, or transmitted, in any form or by any means,
without the prior permission in writing of Oxford University Press.
Within the UK, exceptions are allowed in respect of any fair dealing for the
purpose of research or private study, or criticism or review, as permitted
under the Copyright, Designs and Patents Act, 1988, or in the case of
reprographic reproduction in accordance with the terms of the licences
issued by the Copyright Licensing Agency. Enquiries concerning
reproduction outside these terms and in other countries should be
sent to the Rights Department, Oxford University Press,
at the address above

This book is sold subject to the condition that it shall not, by way
of trade or otherwise, be lent, re-sold, hired out or otherwise circulated
without the publisher's prior consent in any form of binding or cover
other than that in which it is published and without a similar condition
including this condition being imposed on the subsequent purchaser

British Library Cataloguing in Publication Data
Data available

Library of Congress Cataloging in Publication Data
Data available
ISBN 0–19–871118–2
ISBN 0–19–871119–0 (pbk)

1 3 5 7 9 10 8 6 4 2

Typeset by Cambrian Typesetters, Frimley, Surrey
Printed in Great Britain on acid-free paper by
Bookcraft Ltd., Midsomer Norton, Somerset

For Nanou, whose laughter whenever I mentioned masochism or nostalgia helped me keep a sense of proportion

Preface

ALTHOUGH this book focuses on films which appeared in the 1980s, it is not strictly a history of French film in the 1980s. There are a number of histories of French film which cover the period very well and often exhaustively (see Frodon 1995, Hayward 1993*a*, Prédal 1991, Siclier 1991), making a further history unnecessary. This book is rather a set of critical essays on a number of films which help to focus on a particular theme whose roots are in the 1970s, and which extends beyond the 1980s into the 1990s: the crisis of masculinity in contemporary French culture, and its interrelationship with nostalgia.

I have chosen to concentrate on films from three genres. The first of these, the nostalgia film, emerged during the 1980s, and it vehicles the same crisis of masculinity, in my view, as the other two more popular genres, the *polar*, or police thriller, and the comic film, have nearly always done. My concern is less to ground the crisis of masculinity in a socio-political context (although I have done so briefly in the Introduction) than to investigate the crisis insofar as it positions the spectator. In that sense, the theoretical context for the work in this book is spectatorship theory, which, it could be argued, reached its apogee, but also a dead end, during the 1980s. Thus, although the book is not a history, its theoretical framework is historically located. This is all the more the case since the spectatorship paradigm is complemented by two theoretical paradigms developed during the 1980s: the interference between cinema and painting, developed mainly by critics associated with the *Cahiers du cinéma* as part of the 'valorization of a particular model of French auteur cinema' (Darke 1993: 374), and the considerably more robust paradigm of star studies whose impact has had the opposite effect of dismantling auteurist perspectives in favour of a cultural studies approach to film.

The book is structured around the three genres mentioned above. After an introduction, which gives a brief overview both of the crisis in the French film industry during the 1980s, and of the socio-political crisis of masculinity in the wake of feminism, each of the sections devoted to the three genres begins with a brief preface which attempts to highlight the major issues underlying the genre during the 1980s, and my approach to the films to be discussed. Thus, the preface to the nostalgia film attempts to define the genre and its ideological function as an affirmation of either vanishing or high-cultural values, before outlining the theoretical context of spectatorship, which informs the whole book. The preface to the *polar* similarly discusses the genre's ideological function as a vehicle for negotiating national identity, before using it to discuss the crisis of the film image during the 1980s. Finally, the preface to the comic film reviews different types of comic film, with a particular emphasis on the type which came to the fore during the 1980s, *café-théâtre*.

Work on the films in the first two sections of this book has either been previously published, or given as papers at conferences:

- *Un amour de Swann*: Burn Conference, Stirling (1989); subsequently published in *Film Criticism*, 12 (1988 [*sic*]) and *French Cultural Studies*, 1 (1990).
- *Un dimanche à la campagne*: Conference on French Cinema, Nottingham (1994).
- *Jean de Florette/Manon des Sources*: Conference on Popular European Cinema, Warwick (1989); subsequently published in *French Studies*, 46 (1992).
- *Vivement dimanche!*: *Modern & Contemporary France*, 43 (1990).
- *Diva*: *Nottingham French Studies*, 32 (1993).
- *Subway*: Film Culture History Conference, Aberdeen (1996).
- *Mauvais Sang*: *Modern & Contemporary France*, 4 (1996).

Most of these have been substantially reworked for this book. I gratefully acknowledge the permission of the periodicals concerned to allow these chapters to appear here. The remaining chapters are here published for the first time.

The reader will find that there is an emphasis in the discussions of the films in the book on views and reviews by French commentators. These and other material originally in French have been translated by me unless otherwise indicated. Translations of film dialogue are usually modified versions of existing subtitles. The referencing system used in this book is the Harvard reference-within-the-text; this is to avoid constant reference to notes. Indeed, the reader should not be surprised by the absence of notes, which too often, in my view, disrupt concentration on the argument. The filmography does not give information such as the cast list, director of photography, etc. This information is now readily available elsewhere, e.g. in Tulard (1990), or in electronic form in the BFI's *Film Index International*, available on CD-ROM, or in the Internet Movie Guide at location http://www.cs.cf.ac.uk/Movies/search.html. The filmography does, however, give information which is as yet difficult to locate, namely the number of weeks a film ran in Paris, and the number of spectators it attracted.

I wish to thank students at the University of Newcastle upon Tyne during the 1980s and 1990s, whose often critical comments have I hope made once obscure material more transparent. I also wish to thank conference colleagues who have helped me refine the work which appears here; Jean-Marc Vernier of the Centre National de la Cinématographie for supplying statistics for many of the films mentioned in this book; and, finally, my most particular thanks go to Keith Reader, who has given me invaluable advice at all stages.

P.P.

Contents

LIST OF PLATES   xiii

1. Introduction   1

2. The Nostalgia Film   13

3. *Un amour de Swann*: Nostalgia and Sexuality   28

4. *Un dimanche à la campagne*: Nostalgia, Painting, and Depressive Masochism   38

5. *Jean de Florette* and *Manon des Sources*: Nostalgia and Hysteria   50

6. *Coup de foudre*: Nostalgia and Lesbianism   62

7. The *Polar*   75

8. *Vivement dimanche!* Or How to Take Away with One Hand What you Give with the Other   84

9. A Fistful of *Polars*: Chronicles of Discomfiture   96

10. *Diva*'s Deluxe Disasters   109

11. *Subway*: Identity and Inarticulacy   121

12. *Mauvais Sang*: The Flight of the Female   130

13. The Comic Film   141

14. *Trois hommes et un couffin*: Hysterical Homoeroticism   147

15. *La Vie est un long fleuve tranquille*: Fallen Angels and Men Overboard   159

16. *Tenue de soirée*: The 'Suffering Macho'   171

17. Conclusion   183

xii Contents

FILMOGRAPHY   187

BIBLIOGRAPHY   190

INDEX   199

List of Plates

(*between* pp. 114–115)

1. Édouard Vuillard, *Window* (1914; collection of Mr and Mrs Alex M. Lewyt, New York); cf. the opening shot of *Un dimanche à la campagne*

2. Édouard Vuillard, *Self-Portrait* (1925; collection of Ian Woodner, New York); cf. M. Ladmiral's morning wash in *Un dimanche à la campagne*

3. Édouard Vuillard, *Monsieur et Madame Feydeau Sitting on a Sofa* (1905; private collection); cf. Édouard/Gonzague's post-prandial admission of failure in *Un dimanche à la campagne*

4. Pierre-Auguste Renoir, *Dance at Bougival* (1882–3; Museum of Fine Arts, Boston); cf. the shot of the waitress and the fisherman just before Irène and M. Ladmiral dance at the *guinguette* in *Un dimanche à la campagne*

5. Irène and M. Ladmiral dance at the *guinguette* in *Un dimanche à la campagne*

6. Jean returns to Mother Earth in *Jean de Florette*

7. The elegance of closeted lesbianism in *Coup de foudre*

8. Framing the woman who wants to do and know too much in *Vivement dimanche!*

9. Dédé's self-inflicted disfigurement in *La Balance*

10. Françoise comforts Jim in his tiredness (*Détective*)

11. The detectives in *Diva* overwhelmed by postmodern disaster

12. Fred with 'le gros Bill' and 'le roller' in *Subway*

13. The flight of the predatory *femme fatale* in *Mauvais Sang*

14. The 'pregnant' new man who resurfaces in Jacques's drunken confession in *Trois hommes et un couffin*

15. The Le Quesnoys in *La Vie est un long fleuve tranquille*

16. Depardieu and Blanc camp it up in *Tenue de soirée*

Je me souviens de la première fois, et alors seulement le souvenir de la douleur me donne du plaisir. Après coup.

I remember the first time, and it's only the memory of the pain which gives me pleasure. Afterwards.

(*Noir et blanc*, 1986)

Celui qui est parti pour rien était parti pour le seul plaisir de rentrer; c'est le plaisir de rentrer qui l'avait fait partir—le plaisir de rentrer et d'anticiper sur le plaisir du retour, et de raconter ensuite son voyage; le voyageur imagine à l'avance ce retour plus doux que le miel, et il s'ingénie, en flânant sur la route, à faire durer le plaisir. Mais rassurons-nous: on ne revient jamais.

He who left for no particular reason left for the pleasure of returning; it is the pleasure of returning which made him leave, the pleasure of returning and looking forward to the pleasure of returning, and of subsequently recounting his travels; the traveller imagines in advance this return so sweet, and he contrives, as he idles on the road, to make his pleasure last longer. But let us reassure ourselves; one never returns.

(Jankélévitch, 1974: 382)

Introduction

THIS introduction will give a context for the chapters which follow by focusing on two parallel crises: the crisis of the cinema, and the crisis of masculinity.

THE CRISIS OF THE CINEMA

French cinema in the 1980s was in crisis, although retrospectively it can be seen more as a continuing decline. The perceived reasons for a crisis were as follows:

- a crisis of frequentation with more spectators for US films than French films from 1986 grafted on to the continuing decline in spectators;
- a crisis of production with the dissolution of auteur cinema and the gradual integration of cinema within the audiovisual, particularly television;
- a crisis of genre as the traditional genres flagged and American-style super-productions began to appear;
- a crisis of style with the appeal by younger directors to advertising in their *mise en scène*.

It is perhaps understandable that the first three reasons should give the French cause for alarm, since they undermine the specificity of a national cinema most forcefully. The 1980s saw a gradual decline in admissions corresponding to 32 per cent over the decade, with a particularly serious loss of some 31 million spectators from 1986 to 1987. The decline in admissions occurred at the same time as admissions for American films shown in France overtook admissions for the home product. We need only recall how ferociously the French remain attached to the notion of national sovereignty in the face of general US hegemony (for example, by the maintenance of a nuclear deterrent independent of NATO structures in the political arena, and in the cultural arena by the periodic attempts to outlaw Anglicisms) to appreciate how galling it might be for US films to be more popular than French films. The increase in admissions for American films is partly due to the decline in the number of French films distributed for the first time in France, whereas American films remained relatively constant over the decade as a percentage of the total films distributed for the first time. It might be thought that a second reason would be that fewer French films were being made, but in fact production remained steady, reaching a plateau of some 130 films per year in the last few years of the decade. There were, however, significant changes in production.

The major change was an increase in co-productions by the end of the decade, accounting for just over 50 per cent in 1989. One reason for this was the escalating costs of film production during the decade. The average cost of a film almost tripled (if we take 100 as the 1980 base, by the end of the decade the index in constant francs had risen to 197.9). Films had bigger and bigger budgets. There was an increase of 17 per cent to 32 per cent in middle- to high-budget films (i.e. costing 20–50 million francs), at the expense of low-budget films (i.e. costing less than 8 million francs), whose number dropped from 43 per cent to 19 per cent of the total number of films over the last five years of the decade.

This was partly due to one of the many strategies introduced by the Minister of Culture, Jack Lang, from 1981 onwards, to counter the trends discussed above. These have been documented elsewhere (Hayward 1993*b*), but it is worth briefly recalling the main strategies here. An anti-trust measure loosened the grip of Gaumont-Pathé on distribution, which meant more competition and therefore more likelihood that an auteur cinema might thrive; funds were provided to help distribution as well as the building of new film theatres. In production, various improvements were made to existing loans systems, and a new source of investment was made available, the SOFICAs, or *sociétés pour le financement de l'industrie cinématographique et audiovisuelle*. These agencies administer private investment in cinema and TV; up to 25 per cent of taxable revenue can be invested over a period of five years benefiting from tax relief. The SOFICAs' contribution to production costs became substantial; in 1988, for example, this amounted to 187 million, or 9 per cent, of the 2,104 million francs invested in French or mainly French films (Virenque 1990: 92). The problem with this type of investment is that these agencies tend to invest in the more prestigious big-budget films, thus increasing production costs, and, correlatively, squeezing out the low-budget auteur film (see Hayward 1993*b*: 384).

The 1980s saw the development of the prestigious big-budget film, or 'film-événement' as the French dramatically call it. Initiated by Annaud's *La Guerre du feu* (1979), the media saturation strategies used have since become familiar: the public is constantly reminded of the development of the film at its various stages, with copious interviews of director and stars; the launching of the film is a media splash, accompanied by the book of the making of the film. Other films by Annaud (*Le Nom de la rose*, 1986; *L'Ours*, 1988), as well as Berri's *Jean de Florette* (1986) and *Manon des Sources* (1986), Besson's *Le Grand Bleu* (1988), and Nuttyens/Adjani's *Camille Claudel* (1988), followed the same pattern, which did not necessarily always bring success in France, and even less abroad, as was demonstrated by Joffé's *Harem* (1985) or Glenn's *Terminus* (1987).

The development of the American-style big-budget film may well have been helped by the investment strategies of the SOFICAs, but it was largely a response to audience demand. Audiences in the 1980s and beyond want such films because they go to the cinema less, and when they do, they want high production values. They go to the cinema less because of the development of the video culture on the one hand, and the increasing number of films on TV on the other. The increase in the number of films on TV is due to two factors: more TV channels and TV's increasingly important role in film investment. In the 1980s, three public channels (TF1, A2, FR3) turned into two public channels (A2, FR3), three commercial channels (TF1, privatized in 1986, La Cinq, later replaced by a Franco-German channel called Arté, and La Sept), and a subscription channel devoted almost entirely to films (Canal Plus in 1985). The number of films shown on TV went up from 950 in 1986 to 1,330 in 1988 (of which 709 were French). The increased number of channels made control by exhibitors more difficult. Secondly, there is TV investment, a phenomenon seen in West Germany in the 1970s, and in the UK in the 1980s as well. Investment increased by 156 per cent between 1985–1989, comprising an increase of 35 per cent in the funding of co-productions and a massive 267 per cent increase in broadcasting rights. The major player in this respect, as might be expected, was the film channel, Canal Plus, whose total investments in film production relative to the other channels doubled in only three years (from 21 per cent in 1986 to 40.4 per cent in 1988). Canal Plus could show films it had co-produced after only eleven months, other channels having to wait two years; but all channels had to wait three years to broadcast films they had not co-produced. The obvious effect of this arrangement was to encourage the TV channels to co-produce, hence encouraging a televisualization of the cinema: films were made with a view to eventual transmission on the television (for a more detailed view of the relationship between television and cinema, see Kermabon and Shahani 1991. In particular, Serge Daney, *Libération*'s film critic, wrote a series of articles in the newspaper in 1987, which were later published (Daney 1993)).

The various factors mentioned so far—increased production costs, the development of big-budget productions, TV co-productions—led to a crisis in the notion of the auteur, a key concept for post-war French cinema, established by the young critics of the New Wave during the late 1950s, and operative to this day. As Toubiana says, the televisualization of cinema 'prevents what is basic to cinema: the encounter between an auteur and a subject. The cinema must have its own temporality: a tempo which is different from the one dictated by media "culture" ' (Toubiana 1991: 48). The key figure for French commentators was François Truffaut, upon whom centred the notion of the auteur. It was the French who gave the film world the *politique des auteurs*, even if the original idea was then adapted by an American, Andrew Sarris, in a rather mechanistic fashion. It was the French cinema which had consistently produced directors who had, we were told, a personal vision, who made the industry seem a little more like a seventh art (a French phrase) than an industry. Both for Prédal, who wrote for *Jeune Cinéma*, and for Toubiana, editor of the *Cahiers du cinéma* during the 1980s, Truffaut's death in 1984 marked the watershed which now divides auteur cinema and big-budget commercial cinema (see Prédal 1991: 395–7; Toubiana 1991: 43). Truffaut was adept at both auteur cinema and commercial cinema, even if his budgets were not on a large scale. 'Since his death the two tendencies have been growing further apart', wrote a contributor in the *Cahiers du cinéma* in 1989 (quoted by Prédal 1991: 395). According to Toubiana, the problem is that the auteur as the controlling origin of a particular voice or style associated with a critical view became, in his caustic phrase, 'a brand-name' (Toubiana 1991: 46):

There has been a profound change during the 1980s: auteurs, real and false, have been caught up in the free for all of the cinema. The idea of the ghetto (which did not only have disadvantages, because it protected those film makers who did not have access to the system) has more or less fallen into disuse ... This is thanks to the triumph (both cultural and commercial) of the notion of the auteur, which is spilling out of its legitimate arena (a critical, and often minority arena: that was how we saw it in the 1970s). The *politique des auteurs* has become reduced to the promotion of 'signatures'. (Toubiana 1991: 46)

Curiously, though, French commentators are still wedded to the notion of the auteur as a defining characteristic of their cinema. Thus, in a retrospective dossier in *Revue du cinéma*, François Chevassu gave a gloomy view of the state of French cinema in the 1980s, and suggested that a two-pronged strategy was required: the cultivation of the *film-événement* for quantity, and the *cinéma d'auteur* for quality, or, as he put it, 'to differentiate from televisual ready-to-wear (prêt-à-porter)' (Chevassu 1988: 58). He began his section on the auteurs on a positive note by saying that readers should not forget that 'there are still auteurs to maintain a personal, often striking cinema, which is far removed from the banality of the rest' (Chevassu 1988: 63). He then listed some eighteen directors (none of them women), and suggested that the reader might be surprised that there were so many, only to point out on the one hand that he had been generous in the way he had interpreted an auteur, and on the other that, as he put it, 'auteur does not mean masterpiece' (Chevassu 1988: 66). When, in the same dossier, his colleague Marcel Martin listed the same eighteen but added a further fifty-five, in a list which he claimed he wanted to be 'exhaustive but far from complete' (Martin 1988: 72), we can see that the idea of what an auteur is, is problematic. The most that can be said, perhaps ungenerously, is that it allowed French film critics to position themselves (are you for or against Carax . . .?), as well as giving them the possibility of contrasting, as we have seen, a deliberately commercial cinema with one that was not so commercially oriented, but whose objectives were various, usually subsumed under the idea of the 'personal style which remains coherent over a period of time'.

Whether we consider new developments such as the super-production, or more typically French, and certainly more popular, genres such as comedy or the police thriller, the view of French film critics at the end of the 1980s was pessimistic. I shall consider all three of these genres in more detail in the following chapters, confining my comments here to a very brief overview.

The super-productions tended to be nostalgic period reconstructions. Those directors who had made a mark in the *polar* or police thriller (Arcady, Boisset, Granier-Defferre), as well as relative newcomers (Bral, Béhat, Perrin), were considered to be using tried and tested strategies rather than progressing the genre. On the other hand, a more interesting development was the attempt to tackle the *polar* by a number of directors not normally associated with the genre (Deville, Godard). Where comedy is concerned, the same view obtains: formulaic repetition, particularly of the male couple of comics, relieved by a few successes, distributed abroad (unusually, given the 'unexportability' of comic genres), such as Zidi's *Les Ripoux* (1984), Serreau's *Trois hommes et un couffin* (1985), or Blier's *Tenue de soirée* (1986). The one new development in comedy, *café-théâtre*, despite some promising beginnings, did not, it was considered, fulfil its potential.

Finally, there was a crisis of style. Debate during the 1980s centred on the youth-oriented cinema of directors such as Beineix and Besson, in what became known as the *cinéma du look*. These young directors were seen by some during the 1980s as a new direction in French cinema. They rejected, or appeared to reject, the values of the New Wave, which had been predominant until the 1980s and had inaugurated a new style of film-making closely associated with advertising. During the mid-1980s, this caused considerable debate in the film press, although by the early 1990s the *Cahiers du cinéma*, who were the most strongly critical of this new direction, could adopt a more distanced view, as the directors in question seemed to have lost their way. Beineix's *Diva* (1980) and *37°, 2 le matin* (1986) may have achieved cult status both in France and on the Anglo-American markets, but his later films did not. Toubiana sees them firmly as a phenomenon of the 1980s, already 'overtaken', as he puts it, by Caro and Jeunet's *Delicatessen* (1991):

The end of artisanal film-making, the fear of the telefilm—or what was seen as being vaguely related to a televisual esthetic—the relative ease with which expensive films could be made, the crisis in good subjects, and of course what was in the air, advertising, pop videos, short films, zapping, were all elements which pushed cinema towards 'the image and nothing but the image' . . . [This] has the advantage of being a third way between the return to the French quality cinema of some directors from the 1970s, and the marginalized auteur cinema. (Toubiana 1991: 47)

If one is a critic wedded to the notion that the cinema should reflect some kind of truth, rather than merely purvey doubtful pleasure, then the cinema of the 1980s is disappointing. Both Chevassu and Toubiana, for example, make the same point, that in the 1980s the cinema tended to avoid 'reality'. A few films engaged with contemporary conditions or issues, for example, the Beur film (i.e. films centring on the lives of second-generation Arab immigrant families); but the overwhelming tendency in the 1980s was to go for nostalgia, as can be seen by the uncritical adherence to familiar genres, as well as by the development of the nostalgia film proper, or indeed by the many films in the 1980s which dealt with childhood (see Chevassu 1988: 61–2, and Brisset 1990: 119–36). It is almost as if the cinema was attempting to escape reality by a double movement of nostalgia and return to childhood. Toubiana is scathing in his overall judgement:

You could say that the French cinema has not taken reality on board very much. What were its subjects? 'Decent' images of the Arab immigrant or the unemployed nice guy, essential characters to spice up a few well-meaning fictions. Youth-speak, middle-class angst, a return to caricature or parody, a new parochialism: these are the tendencies of today's ready-made cinema. (Toubiana 1991: 47)

And yet, even with the short amount of hindsight that we may have from the mid-1990s, it is clear that Toubiana's view, if it is broadly right in its appraisal of 1980s cinema, is overly pessimistic when projected into the 1990s. Nostalgia films in the 1980s and early 1990s are more often than not constructed on regressive stereotypes, or peddle 'sentimental tourism' as Guy Austin calls it (Austin 1996: 162), even when they wear their liberal credentials ostentatiously, such as the various films which apparently function, at least in part, as a critique of war (e.g. Tavernier's *La Vie et rien d'autre*, 1989) or of colonialism (Corneau's *Fort Saganne*, 1984, or Wargnier's *Indochine*, 1991). But in the 1990s the nostalgia film became grittier, more brutal, and can be seen as an allegory of contemporary concerns in a way which is not true of it in the 1980s. Berri's *Germinal* (1993) is clearly an attempt to create a popular heritage cinema by linking an icon of national literary culture (the Zola novel) to contemporary circumstances (the recession). Chéreau's *La Reine Margot* (1994), with its graphic rendering of the St Bartholomew's massacre, was marketed (by the director, the star, Isabelle Adjani, and reviewers) as a reflection of ethnic cleansing in Bosnia (see Austin 1996: 167–8). Rappeneau's equally gory *Le Hussard sur le toit* (1995) could be seen as an indirect, although highly melodramatic, reference to AIDS.

In the 1980s, however, such socio-political concerns are generally not apparent in the nostalgia film. But rather than seeing these films as regressive by their reinscription of the past and past values, I would like to focus more on the way in which they allow, along with the police thriller and the comedy, a reworking and rethinking of the past, albeit indirectly, by the crisis of masculinity which they vehicle.

THE CRISIS OF MASCULINITY

During the 1980s, the crisis of masculinity which had begun in the 1970s with the advent of feminism became more acute, largely due to social factors. As Yvonne Tasker points out, in the 1980s men became 'more overtly targeted as consumers of lifestyle. The invitation extended to western men to define themselves through consumption brings with it a consequent stress on the fabrication of identity, a denaturalizing of the supposed naturalness of male identity' (Tasker 1993: 110). She associates this shift with the emergence of the women's movement, and it is this which brought about the first of several commonplaces concerning women and work in France which it is worth repeating here.

The first is that despite the economic crisis the number of French women at work had increased rapidly after 1968, going from below 7 million in the early 1960s to around 10 million in the late 1980s (6,741,000 in 1961 to 10,321,000 in 1988; INSEE figures quoted by Artinian and Boccara 1992: 13). This represents an increase of approximately 2 per cent per year, or 150,000–200,000 additional women at work, while at the same time the number of men at work was decreasing by a similar amount per annum. During the 1980s in particular a battery of measures were introduced by the Socialist government to improve the condition of women at work. These included, for example, a law on equal pay for equal work in 1983, an obligation for companies to present equal opportunities strategies, reimbursement for abortion (1982), recovery of maintenance payments by absent parents (1984), training for women returners, and so on (all mentioned in Matignon 1985: 2–3).

Statistics do not necessarily indicate changes in perception, nor indeed in attitude, as we shall see. Where perceptions are concerned, however, it is clear that the general public was aware of these changes, as can be gauged by publications in general circulation, such as for example a special number of the *Monde dossiers et documents* on women at work in 1980, or Gérard Mermet's popular *Francoscopie*, in which the section on work dwells principally on the increase in women at work and unemployment. Mermet makes the important point concerning the type of work undertaken by women, and it is the second commonplace, namely that changes in the workplace were favourable to women, particularly the increase in service sector employment and part-time employment (Mermet 1985: 246).

Mermet also covers the third commonplace, that the increase of women at work had an impact on the nature of couple relationships and sex roles. Domestic tasks were more equally shared, at least notionally, and the 1980s saw the arrival of the French equivalent of the 'new man'. Popular works such as Badinter's *L'Amour en plus* helped fuel the vociferous debates on the new man by the demythologizing of maternal love, and the notion of the maternal male was discussed both at the academic level (see Saint-Marc 1988; note especially the title of the special number in which the article occurs), as well as being vehicled in popular magazines and in publicity images. An article in the women's magazine *Avantages* in 1988, for example, discusses the 'nouveau père' represented in a multitude of commercials by companies such as Philips, Volkswagen, Danone, the pregnant male of Cadum (whom we shall encounter in *Trois hommes et un couffin*) or the interestingly named 'mâle aimé' of Dim underwear (a pun on 'badly loved'/'the male who is loved', as well as referring to a well-known poem by the early twentieth-century poet Guillaume Apollinaire; see Vidal 1989: 112–13).

I mentioned above that statistics do not necessarily affect attitudes, and this constitutes the fourth commonplace: despite huge demographic and social changes, attitudes to women at work did not keep pace with those changes. Women remained ghettoized in certain jobs (secretaries and the caring professions), earning 15 per cent less than men despite equal pay for equal work legislation. Although the proportion of the French population believing that a woman should work when she chooses increased from 29 per cent in 1978 to 43 per cent in 1989, the same figures cannot hide that one out of two French people believed that she should not be allowed to choose, and some 70 per cent believed that young mothers should be given incentives to stay at home rather than benefiting from additional childcare provision (only 30 per cent in favour; figures quoted in Cordero 1994: 164–6). Where equality in domestic chores is concerned, Mermet pointed out in 1985 that a hierarchy seemed to operate, with men participating more in shopping than in the more menial chores of ironing and cleaning (Mermet 1985: 86; it is worth pointing out that more recent studies, such as those by Kaufmann (1992 and 1994), suggest that the division of labour is considerably more complex, and is determined more by the need for territoriality).

Despite the evidence of a double standard, it is clear that sex roles changed during the 1980s, and that this led to a crisis of male identity. Basing her work on the Anglo-American phenomenon of Men's Studies, the popular sociologist Elizabeth Badinter exemplifies interest in this crisis in France with the publication in 1992 of her *XY: De l'identité masculine*. While admitting that the crisis of masculinity is apparently less obvious in France than in the USA and the UK, she nevertheless maintains that it exists in France, and that it is directly consequent upon the women's movement. This has always been the case, she maintains in a special issue of *Sciences humaines* on gender, for example in the seventeenth century in France and England:

There is a crisis in masculinity when women begin a movement of protest. The crisis is a response to the recriminations of women. What causes the crisis of masculinity is not so much the change of roles, but the questioning of male authority. (Badinter 1994*b*: 33)

The central tenet of her book is that social changes, in particular those consequent upon feminism, have caused men to repress traditionally masculine traits without anything to replace them, hence the crisis of masculinity. Men have to repress not only their femininity under the edicts of patriarchal values, but also, under the impact of feminism, their masculinity: 'The feminist critique of the patriarchal male makes the division of the male (into a repressed femininity and a dominant masculinity) impossible to bear. To the traditional ban on showing one's femininity is added that of expressing a virility which has been challenged' (Badinter 1994*a*: 186). Badinter characterizes the man of the 1980s as a 'sick man' ('homme malade'; ibid.). Social change, particularly the increasing number of women in employment, coupled with changes in mentality consequent on the women's movements of the 1970s and 1980s, means that the conditions for a new type of male are ripe. But as Badinter points out, 'it is not because you question the identity of your fathers that you are psychologically ready to reconcile yourself with your femininity' (Badinter 1994*a*: 272), and it is clear that social attitudes, as mentioned above in relation to the changes in women's employment, are not conducive to rapid change.

That the *polars* and comic films I shall be examining in this book exemplify the crisis of masculinity is hardly surprising. The crisis of masculinity is, of course, like the crisis of the cinema, not a new concept. The *polar* is linked to film noir of the 1940s and 1950s, and a standard interpretation of film noir is that it reflects the malaise of American men in the post-war period in the face of women who had become more confident and independent. Similarly, the French comic film has nearly always relied on male incompetence as a source of humour, although clearly it is questionable to what extent such humour is subversive of traditional norms. What is perhaps more surprising, however, is the fact that the nostalgia film also seems to vehicle the crisis of masculinity as a social phenomenon. And it will be my contention, as I examine the three genres, that they do not simply vehicle a social crisis, but place the spectator firmly within that crisis by processes of identification. It is this repositioning of the spectator which makes the films of the 1980s which I shall examine less regressive than the nostalgia film in particular might have led one to expect.

However, it must be said that although the films studied may be less regressive in their repositioning of the spectator, it does not necessarily mean that they encourage positive reconstructions of masculinity. For a start, the crisis of masculinity which they vehicle is in psychoanalytical terms masochistic. This may well afford some pleasure to the spectator, but it does not necessarily encourage positive reconstructions of gender identity (whatever the reader may understand by the term 'positive'), although it must be remembered that I shall be examining successful mainstream films in the following chapters, and that, as I shall explain in my conclusion, art-house films with limited distribution and success may bring about a more disruptive and more meaningful repositioning. My exploration of the cinema of the 1980s therefore does not lead me to the kind of apocalyptic despair expressed by Toubiana, but then it does not pretend either that the crisis of masculinity is anything other than relative and partial.

It is partial in the sense that it is unresolved; the crisis of masculinity as a social phenomenon continues. It is partial in another sense, that as a theoretical position in film studies it is relative to spectatorial position, raising a final question-begging problem. I have so far used a non-gender-specific notion of the spectator, but clearly the crisis of masculinity I wish to explore will impact differently on female and gay spectators, rather than the 'male spectator' of the mainstream spectatorship paradigm. Arguably, the crisis of masculinity as a theoretical paradigm could be seen as the last gasp of the hegemonic spectatorship paradigm which has endured successive theoretical batterings almost since its inception in the mid-1970s, and has gradually been exiting the centre of the theoretical stage with its phallus between its legs since the end of the 1980s. I am of course aware that the theoretical gesture I have just sketched out is in itself problematic, since it could be construed as masochistic self-indulgence in this theoretical crisis, an ostentatious wearing of the withering phallus on the sleeve. However, my view is that spectatorship theory is a useful tool for film analysis, and that it is all the more appropriate to use it since the debates of the 1980s raised key issues to do with identification. In the next chapter, therefore, I shall review the debates concerning the 'spectator', after placing the nostalgia film within the ideological paradigm developed in Andrew Higson's work on the British heritage film.

2

The Nostalgia Film

ONE of the most successful types of film in the 1980s in the UK was the quality costume drama, labelled heritage film by Andrew Higson. This trend was inaugurated early in the decade by the TV series *Brideshead Revisited* (1981), and the film *Chariots of Fire* (1981). Subsequent years saw a series of such films, often based on novels by E. M. Forster, doing extremely well at the box office (*Another Country*, 1984; *A Passage to India*, 1985; *A Room with a View*, 1986; *Maurice*, 1987; *A Handful of Dust*, 1987; *Little Dorrit*, 1987; *Where Angels Fear to Tread*, 1991; *Howard's End*, 1992). In France, a similar type of film did well at the box office during the same period, sometimes extremely well, although its manifestations were arguably more diverse than the costume dramas in the British tradition; indeed, not all the films about to be mentioned are necessarily nostalgia films as I would like to define them. The prevalence of such films during the 1980s in France is due to much the same reasons as their prevalence in the UK. The 1980s saw, as in the UK, the end of period of economic boom, initiated by the oil crisis in 1974, combined with increasing unemployment, and a change of government in 1981 with which the French became rapidly disillusioned. Disillusion and failure of a sort are the appropriate conditions for nostalgia, which could be defined at its simplest as an escape from reality and the attempt to return to a presupposed golden age. Both in the UK and in France such films were often based on well-known literary texts, or attempted to recreate specific historical periods; but whereas the British heritage films were almost exclusively located in the Edwardian period, the French films ranged more widely.

One strand of 'historical' film, for example, is the film adaptation of the French literary classic, likely to appeal to schoolchildren and students as well as a more general public. Thus Coggio adapted a number of Molière plays in the course of the 1980s (*Les Fourberies de Scapin*, 1980; *Le Bourgeois gentilhomme*, 1981; the former was the fifteenth most popular film in France in 1981); Hossein provided yet another adaptation of Hugo's *Les Misérables* (1982; the ninth most popular film in France in 1982). Pialat adapted Bernanos's modern classic *Sous le soleil de Satan* (1987), booed at Cannes when it received the Palme d'Or, and judged considerably less successful than the internationally successful Proust adaptation *Un amour de Swann* (1984). Clearly, all of these films are nostalgic in the sense that they are literary adaptations, and therefore play upon the replay of real or imagined pleasures connected with the act of reading (or viewing in the case of theatre). However, I would argue that only the last of these, *Un amour de Swann*, is 'nostalgic' in the sense I wish to define it. This is first because it attempts to recreate a very particular period, the *belle époque*, and in so doing depends on very high production values; it is in this sense the French counterpart to the Edwardian heritage film (it is significant in this respect that it won prizes for décor and costume at Cannes). The second reason is because the subject of the novel, as of the film, is the past.

Another strand of historical film is the film set in the medieval period, for example Tavernier's *La Passion Béatrice* (1987) or Delvaux's *L'Œuvre au noir* (1988), the latter based on the well-known novel by Marguerite Yourcenar. The two most successful examples of this type of historical reconstruction were the international co-production *Le Nom de la rose* (1986), based on Umberto Eco's best-seller, with almost 5 million spectators in France, and, more surprisingly, *Le Retour de Martin Guerre* (1982) early in the decade, directed by an unknown, Daniel Vigne. This was a Depardieu vehicle, and, indeed, reputedly the actor-star's favourite film. Again, I would suggest that only this last film is nostalgic, principally by virtue of its narrative, which, as the title suggests, is the return from the past. The early 1990s saw a development of this trend in films set in the pre-modern period. The early 1990s saw the immensely successful *Cyrano de Bergerac* (1990) and the almost as successful *Tous les matins du monde* (1992), both starring Depardieu and Anne Brochet. Both are nostalgic with narratives of lost love, the nostalgic potential of each being redoubled, in the case of the first because it is a nineteenth-century play of a seventeenth-century writer; in the case of the second, because of the haunting baroque music from the French tradition. Music, as we shall see, plays an important part in any theory of nostalgia.

The dramatic potential of war clearly accounts for the numerous films located during the Second World War in the course of the 1980s, of which Truffaut's *Le Dernier Métro* (1980) is probably the best known. Most of them have not been distributed outside of France; the other successful film of this type, both in France and abroad, was Malle's *Au revoir les enfants* (1987), and it is the only one which could be called nostalgic by virtue of its combination of historical reconstruction and evocation of childhood and its traumas. A similar point could be made about several 'colonial' films. These are more convincingly nostalgic because they focus directly on loss, the loss of the colonial lifestyle, for example Tavernier's *Coup de torchon* (1981), or indeed a double loss, childhood in the colonies in the case of the newcomer Claire Denis's *Chocolat* (1988). Denis's film is presented as autobiographical, a factor which is further likely to increase the sense of nostalgia. Diane Kurys's *Coup de foudre* (1983) combines autobiography with a wartime and immediately post-war setting, introducing a further complication, a lesbian subtext, which gives the film an edge which the later, equally autobiographical, but considerably more sentimental, *La Baule-les-Pins* (1989) by Kurys was unable to sustain.

Finally, three films which are unequivocally 'nostalgic' in my view are all historical reconstructions, and all literary adaptations of relatively minor writers: *Un dimanche à la campagne* (1984) and *Jean de Florette* and *Manon des Sources*. Tavernier said that his aim in making *Un dimanche à la campagne* was 'to rediscover the things of the past, of my past, my cultural, affective, and emotional roots' (Maillet 1983: 84); this unashamedly nostalgic project clearly touched a nerve with the French public. An extract from a review, although the style of writing is most inappropriate for it, from *Télérama*, the equivalent of *Radio Times*, suggests how strongly spectators were affected by the film:

That Sunday, I do not know where I was. All I know is that I was young and innocent. There was a garden, for sure, and wild perfumes, leafy nooks and crannies, worrying little creatures whom it must have been essential to control, fruit which had an incomparable taste no doubt because it must have been forbidden to pick it . . . That Sunday . . . seems so far away, so elusive that all that remains are the sensations. It is only now that I have the (mistaken) impression that I am tasting the pith. Remembering from these odd snatches of childhood only the pleasures, the regrets. Like a supreme, tardy recompense, a nostalgic tearing asunder because I wasted opportunities of biting into the apple of life more violently, of loving myself a little more. (Douin 1984: 20, reprinted Douin 1988: 59–60)

The second film, or diptych, was one of the most successful films of the 1980s. Fifteen weeks after its initial release on 27 August 1986 *Jean de Florette* had been viewed by over 6 million people, and only three weeks after release on 19 November 1986 *Manon des Sources* had already been seen by over a million. Indeed, the films were so successful in France that they spawned another successful Pagnol-based diptych directed by Yves Robert, *La Gloire de mon père* (1990) and *Le Château de ma mère* (1990).

Several of the films so far mentioned in this survey of the genre will be examined in more depth in the following chapters. The remainder of this introduction will attempt to lay the ground for a theory of the nostalgia film in France. I would like to do so by exploring two functions of the nostalgia film. First, I shall turn to the socio-historical point of view to explore its ideological function as, broadly speaking, a conservative attempt in both social and cinematographic terms to return to a golden age. Second, I would like to relate its psychological structure of loss to the psycho-analytical paradigm used in film theory since the mid-1970s.

THE NOSTALGIA FOR RURAL COMMUNITIES

Nostalgia has a venerable history which it is not my intention to chronicle here, since it has been well covered elsewhere (see Lowenthal 1985 and Starobinski 1966 for the socio-historical aspect and Lerner 1972 for the literary aspect). It is perhaps worth mentioning, however, that the word was coined from two Greek words meaning to return home (*nostos*) and pain or longing (*algia*) by Johannes Hofer in 1688 to describe what he saw as a medical condition suffered by Swiss mercenaries who longed to return home. It was only as late as the twentieth century that it was seen less as an organic malady and more as a state of mind, coinciding in the UK during the first half of the century with a general return to the past; 'by the turn of the century all Britain seemed bent on nostalgic quest' (Lowenthal 1985: 9).

If it is correct to see the modern phenomenon of nostalgia as a yearning for a complex which includes an amalgam of the innocence of pre-industrial communities and the return to a 'childhood divested of responsibilities' (Lowenthal 1985: 25), then it is understandable that in France nostalgia should be a relatively recent phenomenon. France's industrial revolution occurred in the thirty years 1945–74. In that time of rapid socio-economic change, France's peasantry left the land for the burgeoning new cities where the factories fuelling France's economic boom could be found; that, and the development of the professional classes in the same period, led to the gradual dislocation of the extended family. In such conditions, it is hardly surprising that nostalgia should be predicated on the family and childhood, and the countryside, as in *Un dimanche à la campagne*, where the pace of life, as we are frequently reminded in this film, is distinctly slower than the city. The conversation between the father and his son in the pavilion stresses this point. Ladmiral mentions that a road is being built nearby. This leads to a discussion on how photography is taking over from painting. Ladmiral comments: 'I always promised myself to live with my times . . . but day after day come up against little nothings. If it's new, I tremble.' To a contemporary French audience the setting locates the film in the period before the rural exodus, which brought about the gradual dislocation of the traditional extended family network. These two factors—family disintegration and the shock of the new—are embodied for the most part in the figure of Irène, the daughter. The film shows the fissure between the certainties of the past, and past values, represented by the son, Gonzague, and his father, and the shock of new values, represented by Irène, exemplified in the quarrel over their dead mother's clothes which Irène has brought down from the attic with a view to selling them. As this incident suggests, the ideological value of childhood is paramount in the film; children figure throughout, and the film is clearly intended to evoke a lost childhood. Apart from the obvious fact that the film chronicles a typically family Sunday in 1912, there is the combination of soundtrack and location in a country house which is calculated to evoke nostalgic feelings in the audience, as Tavernier himself admitted in an interview: 'It's true that I brought out all my childhood memories. And it's true that the notion of the family is for me embedded in the décor. The shutters being closed, the noises

you hear coming from outside are things which I find touching'
(Douin 1988: 134). The film is nostalgic then in the literal sense of
the pain generated by a loss of origins, although it is by no means
simplistically nostalgic, since Gonzague is a figure of fun and Irène
clearly a figure to be admired. A similar contrast between old and
new in a rural setting can be seen in *Jean de Florette*, where
Depardieu plays an overly trustful city-dweller returning to his
'roots', only to be outwitted by the wily French peasants who are in
fact, unbeknownst to any of them until the dramatic denouement,
members of the same family.

THE AFFIRMATION OF EUROPEAN CULTURE

Un amour de Swann, although set at the same time as *Un dimanche
à la campagne*, 1912, and sharing the same costume designer,
Yvonne Sassinot de Nesles, is clearly nostalgic for reasons other
than a rural setting and an emphasis on traditional family values.
Un amour de Swann is part of one of the great novels of European
culture, Proust's *A la recherche du temps perdu*. The classic nature
of the novel is one of the crucial aspects of its nostalgic function:
'the adaptation trades upon the memory of the novel, a memory
that can derive from actual reading, or, as is more likely with a
classic of literature, a generally circulated cultural memory' (Ellis
1982: 8).

The film's 'Europeanness' is at the heart of its nostalgic function.
A 'classic European novel' signifies nostalgia for the past. The last
great spate of literary adaptations occurred in the 1950s in both
France and West Germany. Eric Rentschler points out that in West
Germany prestige productions in the 1950s signified nostalgia for
an idealized and less problematic past. Such films were a vacation
from history, writes Rentschler, 'tours through the lost bourgeois
past, pictures that found a receptive audience in a country seeking
to re-establish ties with a shattered tradition' (Rentschler 1984:
138). One can say the same about the prestige productions in
France at the time, usually based on Stendhal. Just as the
adaptations of the 1950s were a throwback to pre-war ideologies of
vigorous nationalisms, so *Un amour de Swann* is a throwback to
the 1950s when the Common Market seemed to be about to resolve
European conflict and absorb the nationalism of nation-states into

a European nationalism. *Un amour de Swann* is a vacation from old (economic) conflicts which have arisen in new forms (the European Parliament), a fantasy of European solidarity.

The use of music in such films is of considerable importance, since it supports their 'classical Europeanness'. Painting has the same effect, although I do not wish to consider it in detail here, as I shall use it as a focus in the chapter on *Un dimanche à la campagne*. None the less, three of the films I wish to consider in the following chapters could not have more different types of music: period music by Fauré for *Un dimanche à la campagne*, a modernist rendering by Hans Werner Henze of the famous 'petite phrase' in *Un amour de Swann*, or the melodramatic reworking of Verdi's *The Force of Destiny* in *Jean de Florette* and *Manon des Sources*. Their common factor is that they represent the European classical music tradition, thereby adding ideological value on three counts: the legitimization of high culture (it is alright for the middle classes to applaud these sorts of films, because they are not 'popular' entertainment); the legitimization of an inscription of the otherwise popular medium of film within a central high European culture; and, finally, the legitimization of tradition, which overlaps with the nostalgic inscription of the film.

This is partly because the history of nostalgia is grounded in music. Starobinski, citing a dissertation from the early eighteenth century, explains how Swiss mercenaries would fall prey to sadness, often leading to desertion, upon hearing 'certain rustic cantilena, to which the Swiss drive their herds to pasture in the Alps' (Starobinski 1966: 90). Throughout the eighteenth century, music became the focus for the study of what was seen as a disease. Rousseau, for example, called such music a 'memorative sign' in his *Dictionary of Music*, prefiguring Proust's notion of the involuntary memory activated by the 'petite phrase'. As Starobinski comments, 'exile, alpine music, sad, tender recollections, golden visions of childhood: this conjunction of themes leads not only to an "acoustical" theory of nostalgia; it also leads to the formation of the romantic theory of music and even to the definition of romanticism' (Starobinski 1996: 93). In the modern period, theoretical discourse on music in film has tended towards the psychoanalytical paradigm, where music returns the spectator to a sense of plenitude associated with the mother, which is merely an extension of what commentators on nostalgia were already saying in the eighteenth century. I shall discuss this point in more detail below, and it will resurface in the chapters on *Diva* (1980) and *Subway* (1985).

Just as the use of classical music guarantees at one and the same time 'Europeanness' and nostalgia, so too does the status of the director. In the face of American hegemony, the nostalgia film must have a director embodying two contradictory functions. On the one hand, the director must bring the auteurist stamp associated with European art cinema generally, but at the same time, the director must not be so individual as to obscure the other function discussed previously, namely the 'historical' text at the origin of the film, bolstered by its status as a classic European text, and authenticated by the use of classical European music.

In the case of the films I wish to discuss in the following chapters, this can be seen to work in a variety of ways. The promotional discourses surrounding *Un amour de Swann* frequently repeat the fact that the director, a German, Volker Schlöndorff, is primarily a literary adapter (ten films out of nineteen before *Un amour de Swann*, in fact). More importantly, though, he carries the image of an honest craftsman, essential if the collective European image of the film is to survive auteurist consecration. Schlöndorff 'must inevitably strike one as a compromise, no one's initial choice, an expert technician bereft of any strong directorial impulse, be it thematic, stylistic or formal' (Adair 1984: 112); he has 'no substantial style of his own, no controlling design to impose on the material' (Borger 1984: 16). The emphasis on Schlöndorff's 'absence of style' is essential to the marketing of the film. Schlöndorff's transparency allows the supposed 'truth' of the film's spectacular visual nature to shine through. Indeed, the photographer is as highly profiled as the director in many, if not most of the reviews. Similar criticisms were made of Claude Berri's style, the director of *Jean de Florette* and *Manon des Sources*, better known as a producer than as a director. For many reviewers, whether the prestigious *Cahiers du cinéma* (Toubiana), or more widely read magazines such as *Télérama* (Murat), *Jean de Florette* was a laboriously faithful adaptation; 'academic' is the word most frequently used.

The case of Bertrand Tavernier, the director of *Un dimanche à la campagne*, is slightly different. He is associated with a previous style of film-making; hence the excoriating review the film received in *Cahiers du cinéma*. Accusing Tavernier of being thirty years late on the New Wave, Lardeau punctured Tavernier's avowed aim to make a film close to Jean Renoir, impregnated with 'the vitality and cinematographic freshness of Impressionism' (Lardeau 1984: 36), saying that all that was left of this aim, despite 'big production values, good taste, the respectability and preciosity of culture, is a bloated, rheumatic, potbellied sign of age, a film which amounts to little more than a rancid windbag artificially pumped up with steroids' (ibid.). *Un dimanche à la campagne* was based on a novel by Pierre Bost, a deliberate reference to the films of the 'tradition de qualité' of the 1950s, when many films were scripted by Bost and his collaborator Jean Aurenche, a team whom Truffaut singled out in an article of 1954 in the *Cahiers du cinéma* as typical of everything he hated about the films of the 1950s (Truffaut 1976). Tavernier worked with both Aurenche and Bost. The team scripted his first feature, *L'Horloger de Saint-Paul* (1974), and Aurenche scripted three of the six films Tavernier made before *Un dimanche à la campagne* (*Que la fête commence*, 1975; *Le Juge et l'assassin*, 1976; *Coup de torchon*, 1981). Just as in the UK the association of Merchant and Ivory with films of the novels of Forster has come to epitomize the heritage film, so too, for a French audience, the film of a novel by Bost would have been a factor in its nostalgic appeal.

The final case I shall consider is Diane Kurys's *Coup de foudre*. This film is slightly marginal compared with the others I have so far considered, not because its director is a woman, but because it is not a literary adaptation, and yet it functions at least partly as a nostalgia film. I think that the reason for this is its biographical nature (the film is based on the life of the director's mother). Biography replaces the 'classic' or not so classic ur-text, returning the spectator to a past revisited through the sensibility of the director. The film, like all the others, is not in any sense radical cinematographically. Indeed, the final issue concerning the nostalgia film I wish to consider in relation to its ideological function is its conservatism.

Higson makes points about the British heritage film in this respect which apply equally to the French nostalgia film: 'By turning their backs on the industrialized, chaotic present, they nostalgically . . . offer apparently more settled and visually splendid manifestations of an essentially pastoral national identity and authentic culture' (Higson 1993: 110). He warns us, however, that such films do not necessarily subscribe to Thatcherite political values, and that, indeed, they 'propose more liberal-humanist visions of social relations, at least at the level of dialogue and narrative theme. It is this tension between visual splendor and narrative meaning in the films that makes them so fascinating' (ibid.). We can see how this tension works in the first of the films I shall be considering, *Un amour de Swann*. Reviewers were harsh in their assessment of the film in part because of the expectations generated by Schlöndorff earlier, more radical films. Proust's novel is an acute observation of the decaying social hierarchies at the turn of the century, dwelling on the affairs of two major social classes, the upper middle class and the aristocracy. The witty observations of individual performers in the social kaleidoscope with which the novel is studded are turned into caricature by the film, as I have shown elsewhere (Powrie 1988). There is no sense of historical context or process, and this, together with the virtual impossibility for the film to suggest motivation for social behaviour as the novel does, means that the secondary characters remain isolated eccentrics, at best a sequence of colourfully spectacular vignettes, at worst a tedious list of some of Proust's favourite characters. The overall result is vacuous spectacle, as Higson points out in relation to the British heritage film. Le Fanu pointedly says of *Un amour de Swann* that 'we surely go to films like this in the same way that we flip through the pages of *Vogue* and *Harper's Bazaar*: at its simplest, to see beautiful women in elegant costumes in the interiors of houses to which we, the public, would not normally gain access' (Le Fanu 1984: 38). Nowhere is this clearer than in the piece written for the fashion page of *The Times* with its telling title, 'a priceless parade of props', where we are told that 'the decolleté necklines ... are decorated by Cartier's most priceless pieces' (Menkes 1984: 10). The evacuation of history leaves merely a showcase for commodity fetishization, tinged with a nostalgic trace of radicalism in the insistence on including servants and domestics in crowded boudoir scenes where the protagonists are surrounded by mute domestics tending their masters and mistresses as they might children or dolls. Clearly, a point, however mild, is being made by these codes, 'a hint of a social message about the brutality of the 19th-century rich towards the lower orders' (Tomalin 1984: 39), but it is immediately neutralized by turning them into traditional comic types. More-over, the insistence on servility is disingenuous. Combined with the spectacular 'period' nature of the context, it suggests that this sort of servility no longer exists. In fact, the very insistence of this visual code blinds us to its present relevance. The image makes present the past, and makes past the present, so that the spectators live at the moment of watching the film in a self-congratulatory and illusory image of a classless society.

The nostalgia film is an attempt to return to a golden age, where all the trappings of high culture, whether it be the adaptation of a classic novel, or the use of classical music and/or painting, or the insistence on the director's credentials (a typically European auteur, but not so auteurish as to obscure the transmission of the memory which the film is supposed to evoke via its source-text), are shackled to cinematographic conservatism. My analysis is so far no different from Higson's analysis of the British heritage film. In the following section, however, I would like to move on from a purely ideological analysis to begin to suggest how the nostalgia film positions the spectator.

THE POSITION OF THE SPECTATOR

I would like to start by returning to music, which we saw was at the origins of nostalgia in the form of the Swiss cantilena. I do so because work by Flinn suggests how important the theorization of music has been in the psychoanalytically based work of French theorists, such as Barthes and Kristeva. We therefore need to start here to begin to suggest a theory of the nostalgia film in relation to the spectator.

From early on commentators have linked music to a function of plenitude and compensation for loss, whether they considered it as compensation for the lack of natural sound or as compensation for the overly technological and supposedly dehumanizing aspect of the film apparatus in silent films. In more recent times Barthes linked music to the notion of loss, and particularly the loss of the mother, in a variety of texts written in the 1970s, as did Kristeva with her notion of the rhythmic pre-Oedipal space, or *chora*, where mother and child are in symbiosis. Basing her analysis on the work of Barthes and Kristeva, Flinn shows how 'coinciding with its ability to reconstitute the maternal object and to simulate the primordial pleasure of the subject's unity with her, music simultaneously reminds the subject of its present separation from her'

(Flinn 1992: 63). I would like to extend this notion of maternal loss from the strictly musical nostalgia examined by Flinn to the nostalgia film generally, to suggest that the nostalgia film functions psychologically in exactly the same way, gratifying the spectator by the pleasure of reunion with the mother, while at the same time, and paradoxically, threatening the spectator precisely by reminding him of that loss.

The problem with this theorization, as Flinn points out, is that the spectator in question can only be male, since woman, as is so often the case, is in the position of negation, seen as a threat, in the same way that in visual terms woman as a fetishized object on screen, to recall Mulvey's view, is a castration threat for the male spectator. As Flinn says, some psychoanalytical critics evoke the anxiousness that music can create specifically in terms of the Freudian *unheimlich*, or uncanny, and she reminds us that the German term 'invokes the familiar idea of the absented original space (or "home", as the German tells us), returning the male subject repeatedly back upon the threat of feminine castration' (Flinn 1992: 67).

There have of course been significant developments in theories of spectatorship since Mulvey's key paper of the mid-1970s (Mulvey 1975). Obvious lacunae were pointed to. Quite apart from the fact that Mulvey's view took little or no account of films which overtly question traditional narrative cinema (e.g. the films of Chantal Akerman or Yvonne Rainer; for an analysis of the latter's *Journeys from Berlin/71*, see Silverman 1984), or even of films within mainstream narrative cinema which might call into question the position of woman as object (e.g. Ridley Scott's *Thelma and Louise*), her article raised important theoretical problems, which Mulvey herself began addressing in a later article (Mulvey 1981). The ones which interest me here focus on the position of the female spectator, and the overlapping but more general problem of the nature of identification. If 'woman' could only be the object of the male gaze, then what was the position of a female spectator? Did she identify with the male 'subject' leading to her defeminization? Or did she identify with the female 'object' leading to a masochistic or alienated position? More generally, Mulvey's view assumed that identification was unchanging, but spectators could well have different reactions before, during, and after watching a film. During the 1980s film theorists developed this notion of multiple points of identification, using Freud's paper on masochism, 'A Child is Being Beaten':

Freud demonstrates the possibilities for the subject of fantasy to participate in a variety of roles—sliding, exchanging and doubling in the interchangeable positions of subject, object and observer. He does this by engaging with different forms of the fantasy in terms of the linguistic pronouns they imply: 'My father is beating the child,' 'I am being beaten by my father,' and 'A child is being beaten' (I am probably looking on). During the three stages of this fantasy, the subject (a woman) takes the place of the father who is doing the beating, the child being beaten, and the viewer of the scene. The subject of the fantasy thus becomes a mobile and mutable entity rather than a particular gendered individual. (Stam 1992: 154)

The most significant advance on Mulvey's view combined the notion of fantasy, bisexuality, and masochism with a critique of the impasse in the identification structures for the female spectator. Where Mulvey had founded her view on Freudian Oedipal structures, Studlar dismantled those Oedipal structures by privileging the pre-Oedipal. In other words, whereas Freud's analysis of masochism privileged the father (fear of castration leads the boy to be passive to win father's love), Studlar focused on Deleuze's analysis of the work of Sacher-Masoch, showing how a masochistic economy privileges the mother, who becomes all-powerful because she possesses what the male lacks (the breast and the womb). As Studlar pointed out, the relative unimportance of castration in this analysis offers an alternative (the powerful pre-genital oral mother) to the dead end of the phallic Freudian model based on control and mastery. (I am, of course, aware that Studlar's work has been criticized by Rodowick 1991: 142–3, and Silverman 1992: 417.)

One of the more important points to emerge from Studlar's work, and one which I shall return to throughout these essays, concerns identification. According to Studlar, the cinema places the spectator in the pre-Oedipal position, thus allowing the fluid identifications afforded by infantile perversions, as had been presaged by the work done by other theorists using Freud's paper 'A Child is Being Beaten', discussed above. This might allow opposite-sex identification, for example, which has repercussions on the problems of identification for women spectators (the problem discussed above). Whereas the masculinization of the female spectator was focused on by Mulvey, and others, Studlar's analysis reverses this view, pointing to the possibility of the feminization of the male spectator by identification with the female character, or even a feminized male character. Indeed, work done by Steve Neale on masculinity reaffirms this point, that the male spectator does not necessarily identify with the male character as Mulvey states, since identification is fluid in the cinema (Neale 1983: 4–5). Neale's analysis of the western suggests that male characters can be the object of the voyeuristic sadistic gaze both of other male characters and of the spectator, as well as objects of fetishistic gazing, a position reserved for women characters in Mulvey's analysis. However, he makes the important caveat that male eroticism is never as obvious as female eroticism; it is repressed and disavowed, except possibly in the feminization of the male in some melodrama and in the musical, examples of which will be discussed in the following chapters, particularly those concerning *Jean de Florette* and *Subway*.

The point of this brief review of the principal theories of spectatorship is to ground the analyses of the films which follow. I began this section obliquely by considering the way in which music signals a return to the Mother(land), suggesting that this could be extended to the nostalgia film generally. The nostalgia film at one and the same time returns spectators, both male and female, to Mother while reminding them of the loss incurred. The discussion of the problems theorists have had with Mulvey's work has highlighted several points which I would like to stress in developing this idea of nostalgia as maternal loss. These concern spectator identification. In the essays which follow, I shall be suggesting that the French nostalgia film shows signs of a crisis of masculinity. The films present the spectator with images of masculinity which profoundly undermine heterosexist male mastery. The characters in these films are often weak, misguided, close to failure. In so far as male spectators are likely to identify with the male characters on screen (what film theory calls secondary identification), this already positions male spectators differently. But where primary identification is concerned, there is also, as I shall try to show in my essay on *Un dimanche à la campagne*, a placing of the male spectator in a masochistic position, a position which is made explicit in *Noir et blanc*. I should perhaps stress that when I speak of the 'male spectator', I am referring to the heterosexist male spectator of mainstream spectatorship theory. My examination of the films in this book will show how that conception of the male spectator is

questioned and destabilized by the masochistic position developed
in many films. This does not resolve the issue of how female or gay
spectators relate to on-screen characters, this being more of a 1990s
debate, developed in the work on stars by Stacey (1994), and on
queer theory by Dyer (1990), amongst others. It does, however,
make identification for such spectators considerably easier, if only
because the pre-Oedipal structures associated with masochism
undermine the heterosexist male position. Destabilized spectator
positions make playful fluidity more possible, encouraging cross-
gender identification. As mentioned at the end of the Introduction,
this does not necessarily mean positive reconstructions of masculinity; but it does mean a productive questioning of masculinity and
the male spectatorial position.

The studies which follow will attempt to demystify the films as
spectacle and to concentrate on the films as process. To use a
medical term which might recall the strongly medical view of
nostalgia at its origins, I shall study the films as operations which
attempt to cure loss and failure by embodying them. The readings
are therefore symptomatic and critical. My purpose is to show how
a decentred/destabilized masculine subject is created: a narcissistic
homosexual subject in *Un amour de Swann*; a hysterical, feminized
subject in *Jean de Florette* and *Manon des Sources*; a masochistic
failure in *Un dimanche à la campagne*. The chapter on *Coup de
foudre* will explore how a difficult female subjectivity is articulated
in the nostalgia structure.

3
Un amour de Swann:
Nostalgia and Sexuality

A LA recherche du temps perdu is a manual of self-discovery (it is also, of course, an acute social analysis). It is a many-stranded narrative; it is indeed a stranded narrative, losing itself/myself purposefully so as to (perhaps) find itself/myself. *Un amour de Swann*, on the other hand, is relentlessly literal, reinforcing dominant narrative by its typically voyeuristic, narcissistic hero, with whom I, the male spectator, am supposed partially to identify, or at least partially to empathize. Moreover, *Un amour de Swann* unsubtly caricatures what it clearly represents as 'deviant' sexuality—homosexuality, male and female—upholding a brutalist heterosexuality and punishing dominant women characters for the reckless expression of independence.

I shall start with the most obviously, indeed crudely, visible: (explicit) eroticism, which paradoxically draws a veil over 'deviant' desire. Some reviews comment on what is clearly seen as an admirable/admirably faithful eroticism in the film:

The film's episode showing Swann making futile, fatal attempts to lay bare Odette's past as he undresses her establishes a motif to which the novel constantly devotes half-appalled, half-ironic attention. Repeatedly ruffled by fears of infidelity, these scenes are steadily faithful to Proust's work— which they accurately reflect, too, in being tinged with an eroticism that stems from the tension between passion and protocol. Reminders of the book's potent interplay of social formality and private licence are here given in moments where kid-gloved fingers fondle flesh or an elegant clothes brush is sensuously stroked along a naked spine. (Kemp 1984: 51)

In the novel, however, we never read directly about sexual, or even sensual, contact between Swann and Odette of the type mentioned here. It is certainly implied in the novel that Odette's sexuality is bound up with Swann's difficulties in 'possessing' her, or more precisely possessing her identity. But this is nowhere literalized in the way that is suggested by Kemp. In *A la recherche du temps perdu*, the emphasis, both in general terms, and in literal terms, is more on homosexuality.

Homosexuality is, of course, stressed by the film. Swann's brutal questioning of Odette over her supposed lesbianism, for example, is lifted directly from the text. But the theme of homosexuality in *A la recherche du temps perdu* is part of a general inquiry into the nature of identity, and finds its most extraordinary, and lengthy, expression in the first section of *Sodome et Gomorrhe* where the narrator observes Charlus seducing Jupien, the waistcoat-maker, and launches into a deconstruction of the notion of gender by discussing 'hommes-femmes', men who are also women. In the film, Charlus is presented as a caricatural eccentric, much loved by reviewers, who almost without exception praise Delon's Charlus at the expense of the other actors. This is an ideological displacement. Homosexuality (male and female) is the key issue in determining identity for Proust. The emphasis on Charlus's quirkiness in the film displaces the centrality of homosexuality; the purely formal aspects of the actor's work are highlighted at the expense of their signification. A second aspect of displacement is that if male homosexuality is marginalized (paradoxically) by exaggeration, both by the caricatural eccentricity of the Charlus figure, as I have just indicated, and by Swann's 'brutalism', illustrated in the 'gross' brothel scene, as one reviewer labels it (Robinson 1984: 15), female homosexuality is dwelt on at length in the film. And yet, even for the film, male homosexuality, I would contend, is the crucial issue, displaced, hidden, disgraced, but the essential machine which produces the film's ideological cohesion.

THE BROTHEL

The brothel scene is one of two scenes in the film which amalgamate as many as three different scenes from the novel. In the novel we are told that Swann visits brothels regularly, but only to talk with the prostitutes. It is in this scene of the novel that the manageress (and not the prostitute) says to Swann that 'the society ladies are so flighty; a real scandal, I call it' (Proust 1983: i. 373). This scene is amalgamated with an episode much later in *A la recherche du temps perdu* when the narrator asks Aimé, the head waiter at the Balbec hotel, to make enquiries about the narrator's lover Albertine, whom he suspects of lesbian tendencies. Aimé writes two letters to the narrator. In the first he reports the comments of a public-bath attendant on 10-franc tips given to her by two women (Proust 1983: iii. 515–16). In the second, Aimé reports that he went to bed with a washerwoman, out of a sense of duty (this is intentionally comic), who had spoken of caresses and love-bites between two women (Proust 1983: iii. 524–5). The major feature of these three scenes is that sex is kept at a distance by dialogue. In the film, explicit sex occurs in the context of what amounts to an interrogation. The condensation and tonal shift shown here is symptomatic of the way in which sexuality is used in the film, as I shall show by considering what Carrière, the scriptwriter, had to say about it in an interview:

A.S. [Avant-Scène]: A scene which seems somewhat shocking, in the context of Proust, is the brothel scene. Proust is so elliptical in this description, so refined.

J.-C.C. [Jean-Claude Carrière]: There are two answers to that. First, we are expressly told that Swann is a womanizer, really into sex (*un baiseur*), who screws (*saute*) chambermaids in carriages. This side of the character exists, I don't see why we should have minimized it. In the scene you've just mentioned, there's a sort of conflict between the physical pleasure which Swann usually takes, and carries through, and the mental obsession which prevents him from taking it that day. It's that dichotomy which we wanted to stress. It didn't seem to us that we should make Swann a prudish character. On the contrary, the fact that he seeks physical pleasures besides Odette (he'll still seek it after his marriage) needs to be stressed.

As for Proust's writing, which people like saying is elegant and refined. I think there are several possible readings. For me, Proust is perhaps the most realist of our writers.

A.S.: All the same, he isn't a Zola!

J.-C.C.: In some ways I think they are very similar. For example, it's very striking that Proust never speaks of the sacred, there is no spirituality in his work, his preoccupations are entirely earthly, he's a great realist writer, as I said. His long sentences are like some sort of articulated scalpel which penetrates emotions and feelings. It's really not a question of psychology, but a very precise description, almost clinical, of feelings and emotions that human beings experience at a given moment. And since an emotion fluctuates, is changeable, inexhaustible, that sentence must really spread out to penetrate even more deeply. Now that's an instrument which the cinema obviously doesn't have. One must therefore substitute for the scalpel an external eye, a cold eye, the eye of the camera, which will have to be as all-enveloping, indiscreet, precise, so as to see the external manifestations of that passion. (Carrière 1984: 15)

This tortuous passage is structured on a curious syllogism. Swann is a philanderer; Proust analyses emotions; therefore the camera must show the external manifestations of Swann-the-philanderer to approximate Proust-the-analyser. The hidden logic is that realism is not simply the visible, but the sexually visible. Realism is sexual codes (hence the reference to the naturalist writer Zola, who is often caricatured as a writer obsessed with sex). Two marketing codes are at work here: the need to demystify Proust to make him acceptable/visible; the need to mystify commercially viable/visible sex scenes by reference to a reconstructed Proust/Zola.

It would have been perfectly possible for Carrière to defend the brothel scene on the grounds of an essential critique of the hypocritical marginalization of desire, double standards, or male domination. Curiously, he chooses to embroil himself in a tenuous justification which relies on the fidelity norm. Kemp's argument for the brothel scene is based on the notion of social critique (double standards, hypocrisy). But the brothel scene is too much part of a pattern in the film for it to be possible to argue on either of these lines. The pattern is one of the debasement and, more fundamentally, the exclusion of women.

Chlöe, the prostitute, is debased by Swann. All the visual codes suggest this: he is dressed from the waist up, monocle in his eye, cigarette in the mouth, standing over her, rear entry so that she cannot see him while he can see/dominate her. When he leaves, he literally tosses her two banknotes without a word of explanation, and without answering her question. Chlöe is debased because she is a substitute for Odette, as is suggested by visual codes. In the first of the two boudoir scenes, Swann discreetly places two banknotes in Odette's box. In the second boudoir scene, after the visit to the brothel, Odette undresses in front of Swann and presents herself half-naked, breasts bared, just as Chlöe had been. Swann and Odette make love, and although Swann does not stand over Odette, as he had done with Chlöe, since they are both lying in Odette's bed, Swann enters her from the rear, as he had done with Chlöe. The prostitute, then, is a substitute for Odette. But why should Swann want to debase Odette?

A first reason is to reaffirm his masculinity in the face of possible lesbianism. The discreet report of sexual practices in *A la recherche du temps perdu* is here transmuted into a grotesque scene of male dominance, as if the mere fantasized possibility of lesbianism has to be compensated for by the humiliation of Chlöe/Odette. Clearly, though, it is possible to argue that the film deliberately invites this reading. A second reason, linked with the first, is that both Odette and Chlöe hold Swann in their power, Odette because of Swann's infatuation with her, and Chlöe by her assumed knowledge of Odette's past. The notion of Odette's power is clumsily conveyed in the final scene as a 'triumph': Odette walks isolated over the square against the background of a military march-past, and a fanfare is played on the soundtrack as she is framed in the triumphal arch of the Tuileries. But this triumph is undermined by the voice-over dialogue between two men, which occurs more or less in between these two visual codifications of Odette's triumph; one of the two men recollects having bought Odette's services in the past. This pattern of debasement is maintained by the treatment of the two powerful society hostesses, the Duchess and Madame Verdurin, both of whom are ridiculed, the first by the red shoes incident, the second by the locked jaw. Both of these incidents are mentioned in *A la recherche du temps perdu*, but amongst many others associated with the two characters. In the film, however, they are more or less isolated incidents which carry the full significance of the characters' behaviour, and this decontextualization turns the production of character into static caricature.

So far I have showed how the women in the film are debased to neutralize the threat they represent. Odette is also fetishized, in a much more standard way, to achieve the same purpose, the neutralization of the threat of castration, as Mulvey has shown. One cannot fail to notice the monocle in Swann's eye. It is, of course, a favourite Proustian prop, an instrument of distanced observation as well as the signifier of social position. It is, to use Carrière's image, the cold, scalpel-like eye of the camera/male gaze, analogous to the magnifying glass over the picture of Zipporah in Swann's apartment. The magnifying glass, which is not mentioned in the novel, is a fairly transparent symbol of Swann's reductive idealization of Odette. Swann identifies Odette with Botticelli's Zipporah, to the extent that he keeps a reproduction of the painting on his desk. The point of this in the novel is that he refuses to treat

Odette as a person in her own right, freezing her within an idealized image, negating her identity with a palimpsestic icon. But the crucial notion of process in the Proustian text—this is a particular stage of Swann's love for Odette—has been evacuated; and this is as it were compensated for in the film by the curious magnification of the drawing under the glass. The effect of the magnifying glass is to stress all the more the fetishization of the female as object of the male gaze. The image is frozen, freeze-framed one might say, arrested and imprisoned for Swann's static and proprietary consumption. It is an analogue for the (male) spectator's voyeuristic consumption of the female object of desire in the film, underlined by an extensive thematics of gazing and penetration throughout the film, associated with doors and windows. The film opens with the opening of two windows, like eyes, in Swann's apartment; and Swann will constantly be seen to be going through doors or looking through windows, usually in the search for Odette: at the Guermantes soirée; at the Opera; outside the ironically named Café de la Paix; at the Verdurin soirée; outside what he thinks is Odette's apartment. The most dramatic of these is his frantically jealous search of Odette's apartment in the (mistaken) belief that she is hiding her lover. As he throws open all the doors, desire, the gaze, and penetration (of Odette's inner sanctum) are aptly collocated in a thematics of proprietary dominance. In the circumstances, it is no surprise that Odette's 'confession' to Swann earlier in the film should take place by a window opening onto a brightly lit Edenic conservatory, which contrasts with the reverse shot of Swann surrounded claustrophobically by objects and lit in an orange-red light. In the face of the proprietary male gaze, her only escape is the lesbian idyll she wistfully recounts.

MIRRORS

It could be argued, though, that sufficient clues are given to the spectator for a radical deconstruction of this discourse of male dominance. As Baumgarten says, 'Schlöndorff casts Swann as a brutal chauvinist' (Baumgarten: 101). Odette is seen to be imposed upon by a jealous lover, rebels under the proprietary gaze ('But I'm not a museum piece'; *Un amour de Swann*, 58), and triumphs in the end, despite her murky past. Other aspects of the *mise en scène*, however, suggest that the omnipotence of the male and his gaze is maintained despite elements of internal critique. I am referring to the many mirrors in the film. Mirrors are not a Proustian obsession; one might therefore be forgiven for ascribing otherwise undue importance to them in the film. In the opening scene, Swann grooms himself in front of a table-mirror. The mirror is multiple. The mirror fills the frame on one side, as we discover when Swann flips it over to reveal a row of three small circular mirrors on the other side. In fact, only two of these are clearly visible, since Swann's head obscures the mirror furthest to the left. Swann looks at himself more closely first in the middle mirror, and then more closely still in the right mirror, or rather at this face, tightly framed. We realize that each mirror has increasingly magnified his face. This opening scene is echoed in a later scene in Odette's apartment, where Swann twice places a banknote in Odette's box on the mantelpiece. He is both times reflected in the overmantel mirror as he does so. He is a fleeting, distant figure in a side-panel of the mirror the first time. The second time, in a reversal of the opening mirror scene, the mirror fills the frame, as his head and shoulders are reflected in the mirror. The two scenes are too closely paralleled to be fortuitous; but they can be ambiguously interpreted. Swann looks at himself in the mirror in his apartment and then in Odette's as he gives her money, money which is recalled in the scene with Chlöe. We might perhaps infer from this some element of internal critique (Swann as 'brutal chauvinist'); but we could equally well assume that a point is being made about Swann's blindness to the venality of his relationship with Odette (the topos 'love is blind'). A more simple observation would be the fact that the procedure multiplies Swann's image, so confirming the omnipotence of the male gaze.

There is confirmation of this in the magnifying glass over Botticelli's Zipporah, which echoes both the small circular mirrors and Swann's monocle. As we saw, the magnifying glass and what lies under it is the negation of Odette's reality by a palimpsestic icon. Looking at Zipporah, with or without Odette, Swann looks not at Odette, but at his idealization of her, and so ultimately at his reflected image. The monocle/magnifying glass and the mirror all confirm the narcissistic inflation of the male image and the male gaze. Even the structure of character-relationships suggests this effect of Swann as the focal point of the gaze. He is caught in the centre of a kaleidoscope of mirrored and mirroring couples: Chlöe–Odette (connected by Swann); Young writer/Narrator–Charlus; Odette–Charlus ('Have you slept with Odette?' Swann asks Charlus; *Un amour de Swann*, 36); Madame Verdurin–the Duchess (the two classes); Madame Verdurin–Forcheville (both anti-Swann, although for different reasons); the Duchess–Basin (husband and wife). Swann could not be a more perfect 'ideal ego' (see Mulvey 1975: 9–10) for the male spectator: a voyeur, who is at the centre of the film and its actions, in a focal position of control both narratively, and in his relationship with the principal fetishized object of the film, Odette. The narcissism of that ideal ego is stressed by the mirror-play. Even the fact that Jeremy Irons plays Swann is significant here, since much was made of Irons's 'Englishness' when the film was released. The fact that Irons dubbed his own dialogue would be insufficient to counteract the notion of constraint and distance implied by the language difficulty. As Neale says, a reticence with language

Can . . . be linked to narcissism and to the construction of an ideal ego. The acquisition of language is a process profoundly challenging to the narcissism of early childhood. It is productive of what has been called 'symbolic castration'. Language is a process (or set of processes) involving absence and lack, and these are what threaten any image of the self as totally enclosed, self-sufficient, omnipotent. (Neale 1983: 7)

Irons's difficulty with French confirms his omnipotence for the male spectator as much as perfect fluency in the language would have done. Even the nostalgia generated by the film's final scenes functions to underline nostalgia for the male narcissism which Swann embodies through most of the film, until he becomes, almost literally, a ghost of his former self, destroyed by the castrating Odette, who passes by Swann and Charlus, triumphant and ageless, as they reminisce about the good old days, failure, missed opportunities, and death: 'Our life is like a painter's studio, full of abandoned sketches. We sacrifice everything to phantoms which vanish one by one. We are unfaithful to our ambitions, to our dreams', says Charlus, his eyes misty, and his voice heavy with emotion (*Un amour de Swann*, 85).

BUDDIES

I would like to conclude by briefly considering the privileged intimacy of Swann and Charlus's relationship. This more or less frames the film, since the second scene of the film is a discussion between Swann and Charlus about Odette. This is clearly a conscious parallelism by the film-makers; the final scene is nostalgically backward-looking, and counterbalances perfectly the second scene, which is forward-looking as Swann discusses his love for Odette and asks Charlus to convey a message to her. This comes immediately after the opening sequence of the film, in which Swann apparently writes about his love for Odette, while a voice-over, we assume, tells us what he is writing, this being intercut with close-ups of the fragmented and passionately heaving body of Odette.

The two opening sequences clearly and I think knowingly sketch out the major theme of the film, the construction of male desire which focuses on an idealized female fetish. But what the second and final sequences also tell us, I think, is that the film also sketches out the European equivalent of the buddy movie, with a scarcely veiled homosexual framework. It is in the second scene that Swann, consumed with jealousy (we assume), asks Charlus whether he has slept with Odette. This flies in the face of what even a spectator unfamiliar with Proust is likely to have already understood: that Charlus is a homosexual, as will be made considerably more explicit later in the film. If we reflect on Swann's curious question, and put aside the all too obvious codification for jealousy which it suggests, then we are left with a standard situation for a buddy movie: two men whose shared experiences pass through the same woman whom they usually eventually reject or abandon. This effectively places the male spectator in the homosexual position, which is perhaps why one critic, considering the brothel scene, claims that Swann shows sodomitic predilections: 'The obverse of the precious salon life is revealed in the gross brothel scene; and Swann's predilection for sodomy is seen as concomitant to his erotic morbidity' (Robinson 1984: 15). Nowhere in the novel, or even in the film, is it even suggested that Swann is a sodomite. In the film, we see him making love with Chlöe and with Odette from the rear, but it requires a substantial leap of the imagination to go from there to sodomy; unless, of course, the critic is reacting to the spectatorial position I have outlined.

In this chapter, I have tried to show how one of the main nostalgia films of the 1980s places the male spectator in a position of narcissistic homosexual omnipotence, predicated on the debasement and exclusion of women. To the extent that Swann's omnipotence is seen to disintegrate by the end of the film, and that his demise is framed by the sentimental retrospective evaluation of his failure, the male spectator is also placed in a position of nostalgic masochism. I shall investigate the combination of nostalgia and masochism in a later chapter. In the next chapter, I would like to consider how the male spectator might react to the male character, following Rodowick's critique of Mulvey, not just as 'an object of the look', but as 'an erotic object' (Rodowick 1991: 11).

4

Un dimanche à la campagne:
Nostalgia, Painting, and
Depressive Masochism

IN the introduction to this section I explored various ways in which this film is nostalgic: the reference to the *tradition de qualité* implied by the use of a Bost novel, the pre-First World War setting, rurality, and the emphasis on childhood. But at its most basic it is a film about a painter and his relationship with his work, and nostalgia is also, and more importantly, constructed by continual reference to painting. Apart from the discussions concerning Monsieur Ladmiral's career as a painter, many shots are patterned on recognizable paintings in the French Impressionist and Nabi tradition. My concern here is with the implications, both practical and theoretical, of such intertextual references. I shall argue that painting, far from being superstructural decoration, is essential for the construction of nostalgia, and allows us to develop a theory of the nostalgia film which can build upon Higson's ideological analysis of the British heritage film, by introducing the psycho-analytic paradigm which emphasizes the spectator's position in relation to the work of the film.

If I have chosen a film which deals with painting, it is partly because the 1980s saw an interest in the relationship between painting and film. This was exemplified explicitly in films such as Godard's *Passion* (1982), where Godard is not so much recreating famous paintings as 'paintings *in the process of being made*' (Aumont 1989: 224; Aumont's emphasis). And it was also exemplified implicitly in Cavalier's *Thérèse* (1986), in which *mise en scène* is calqued on paintings by Philippe de Champaigne. Further, there was a sustained critical discourse on the relationship between painting and film, centring mainly on the critics of *Cahiers du cinéma*, whose purpose was at least partly to bolster the notion of the auteur in the face of the *cinéma du look* and other 1980s trends, such as the super-productions (Aumont 1989: 252–3;

Darke 1993: 374–5). This interest in film and painting extended into the 1990s with another archetypal auteur from the New Wave, Rivette's *La Belle Noiseuse* (1991). If I have chosen a film by a relatively minor director, rather than Godard, for example, whose project in *Passion* is clearly also nostalgic (Aumont 1989: 227), it is first because *Un dimanche à la campagne* was more popular than either *Passion* or *Thérèse*, and secondly because it exemplifies admirably the mixture of both explicit (in the dialogue) and implicit (in the *mise en scène*) references to painting.

Tavernier said that he 'was very keen to avoid any reference to Impressionism' (Douin 1988: 134), and he approvingly quoted the male lead actor, Louis Ducreux, who said that 'the colors of the film have nothing to do with the colors of [Renoir's] paintings' (Yakir 1984: 22). The choice of real paintings for the film suggests that he was right. Most of them, according to Tavernier, were by Besson, a minor painter from the Lyons School, chosen precisely because they were 'out of step with Impressionism, especially in the choice of subjects' (Douin 1988: 139). Others were a job lot from a local painter's studio (Ravanne, working 1880–1920); the family portraits were specially painted by Jean-Pierre Zingg, and there was even one painting by Ducreux himself (the one Irène pulls out of a trunk in the attic, and which she says she will never sell). Tavernier takes great pains to minimize the impact not just of Impressionism, but also of painting in general, by emphasizing the mobility of the camerawork: 'I didn't want people to be able to say, it's just like a painting, so there's no composition. As soon as it starts to look composed, the camera darts off somewhere else, leaves the characters or goes ahead of them' (Douin 1988: 134). This is particularly the case, for example, in the establishing sequence where the camera travels through the house, tracking across paintings hung in various rooms. Paradoxically, though, the mobile camera has the effect of positioning the spectator as a visitor to a museum, emphasizing rather than neutralizing spectacle.

The film does, however, refer to paintings by Impressionists (mainly Renoir, but also Manet), and, more pervasively, by one of the painters of the Nabi group, Vuillard, usually called an 'intimist' painter because he tended to paint indoor subjects in a bourgeois context: 'Edward Vuillard or the discreet charm of the bourgeoisie. ... Vuillard depicted with a passion the confined family atmosphere', writes one critic (Warnod 1988: 5). And another refers to his work somewhat dismissively as 'the magnification of the banal' (Cogniat 1975: 8), a statement which could equally well function as a description of *Un dimanche à la campagne*. Much of the *mise en scène* of the interiors is strongly reminiscent of well-known paintings by Vuillard. This is particularly the case in the opening shot of the first sequence, with its emphasis on the view from a window, a familiar subject for Vuillard, and one to which the film itself returns on several occasions. But the remainder of the opening sequence, with its long tracking shots of darkly furnished bourgeois interiors, also recalls Vuillard paintings, for example, *Interior with Figure* (1896), or his *Woman before a Window* (1900). Towards the end of the sequence there is a shot of Monsieur Ladmiral shaving, naked from the waist up and framed by the door of the bathroom, which seems patterned on Vuillard's *Self-Portrait* (1925). And later in the film, Gonzague and his wife sink onto the sofa in post-prandial torpor, the *mise en scène* recalling Vuillard's famous portrait of Monsieur and Madame Feydeau (1905).

There are obvious references to Renoir. Tavernier claimed that little girls are a constant motif in his films, constituting 'a poetic way of suggesting the idea of death' (Douin 1988: 140). But their numerous appearances in *Un dimanche à la campagne* remind the spectator of the familiar Renoir motif of two little girls dressed in white, usually in pastoral situations. Even more obvious is the dancing of the waitress and the fisherman in the *guinguette*, or open-air café, which is choreographed and shot in such a way as to be a clear reference to one of Renoir's best-known paintings, *Dance at Bougival* (1882–3). In the circumstances, it is disingenuous of Tavernier to complain that a parallel with Renoir had been mistakenly drawn: 'You put people in a tavern with dance and music and [Renoir's] name comes up' (Yakir 1984: 22). He is more forthcoming about his reference to Manet, his comment on which makes it clear that he is perfectly aware that the spectator will palimpsestically read the *Déjeuner sur l'herbe* (1863) onto the picnic scene: 'You were expecting [Manet's] picnic, I gloss over it, it takes place off-screen and it's on purpose that I don't show it. No déjeuner sur l'herbe!' (Parra 1984: 62).

Painting and nostalgia are inextricably linked in the film. As structuring elements of the *mise en scène*, the painterly references have a dual function. First, they legitimize nostalgia by inscribing it within a heritage discourse, thus firmly positioning the film in social terms as, literally, an art-house product aimed at the middle classes. The references are not just to Auguste Renoir, but also to his son Jean. *Un dimanche à la campagne* refers transparently to Jean Renoir's *Une partie de campagne* (1936), which itself refers to his father's work (indeed, the reference to Manet is also a reference to Jean Renoir's film *Déjeuner sur l'herbe*, 1959). In Renoir's *Une partie de campagne* the Dufour family repair to a *guinguette* in the country, a familiar motif in Auguste Renoir's painting. The earthy exchanges between the innkeeper (played by Renoir himself) and the maid are alluded to in Tavernier's film. *Une partie de campagne* is a vehicle for nostalgia. The brief fling of the daughter, Henriette, with one of the young men, Henri, haunts both of them for the rest of their days; Tavernier's film covers the same topos, the pain of love, in the character of Irène. Such intertextuality highlights the nostalgic function of *Un dimanche à la campagne* by giving the film the authority of a history: it is *like* Renoir's film in many respects, which is *like* Auguste Renoir's painting, which returns us to the legitimization of the film text(s) by high art. Just as the British heritage film has been interpreted as a swan-song for the demise of colonialism and empire, the French nostalgia film represents a profoundly conservative longing for the certainties of past values, prior to industrialization.

Painterly references also have a second function. A gesture towards a painting signals to the spectators that they should be reading nostalgia into the situation. I shall discuss three obvious references, to Vuillard, Renoir, and Manet respectively.

In the first, Irène stands by the same window as the opening shot of the film, looking out onto the garden and the two boys bored at being in the country. The camera becomes very mobile (a sign that Tavernier is worried about the painterly reference taking over), tracking back into the room as Irène turns her head away from the window with a wistfully nostalgic look; the camera tracks past a covered piano, while on the soundtrack we hear a distant piano playing. The camera comes to rest as the figure of the long-dead mother appears reading in an easy chair. She turns to Irène, whose flashback we assume this now is, and utters the same statement as at the beginning of the film: 'When will you stop asking so much of life, Irène?' The camera tracks back and up towards Irène, coming to rest finally on the open window once more. The shot is thus designed to be a polyvalent return: narratively it is a flashback; Irène literally and metaphorically looks backwards; the camera tracks backwards; the mother's words and the *mise en scène* return us to the opening sequence, and are thus a return to one of the major painterly references. These multiple signals for a return are firmly located in the framework of Irène's nostalgic gaze.

The second example occurs during the *guinguette* sequence, and is patterned on Renoir's *Dance at Bougival*. The painting frames the sequence. At the beginning, the fisherman teases the waitress with a fish, and Irène comments to her father that it is that kind of thing which he should have painted. The same two characters reproduce the Renoir painting at the end of the monologue on painting which ensues. The monologue is a disillusioned, world-weary admission of failure:

Ladmiral: I painted the way I was taught. I believed my teachers. I respected tradition, the rules, maybe a bit too much. I saw originality, but in the work of others. Cézanne's major exhibition round about 96 or 97 was interesting, but I said to myself, where can it lead me? Like the first time I saw a Van Gogh. I'd picked him out. I spent a summer in Arles painting. I was with your mother. I'm boring you with my rambling. Perhaps I lacked courage. I could have decided, a few years ago, to change my style. I gave it a lot of thought. But your mother . . . It hurt her to see that I was still searching at my age. I'd just been decorated, our future was assured.

Irène: It hurt her . . .

Ladmiral: If I'd imitated the originality of others, those I understood, Monet, Caillebotte, Renoir, I'd have been even less original, I'd have lost my own special melody. Not that it . . . But after all it was mine. I painted as I felt, with honesty. And if I didn't achieve more, I at least glimpsed what I could have achieved . . . Earlier, when you woke me up in the garden, I was dreaming—you'll laugh—I was dreaming about Moses. I saw him when he was about to die, without regrets, because he had seen, understood, loved what he had loved. You understand Irène? You can die for less.

He and Irène then dance, and it is at this point that the reference to Renoir occurs. In this context it is highly ambiguous; it is both sentimental but also ironic, since it underlines what Ladmiral could have achieved as a painter ('that's the kind of thing you should have painted'), but did not. Nevertheless, the scene is clearly intended to generate the spectator's sympathy. Irène, despite the implied criticism of her father's conservatism when she repeats 'it hurt her', is shown gazing admiringly at her father at two key points: when he says that he painted as he felt, 'with honesty'; and when he draws an analogy between himself and Moses. Like the previous example, this sequence is structured as a return: Ladmiral arrives at the *guinguette* sighing, 'it's been a long time'; the heart-to-heart discussion with his daughter is a raking over the ashes of the past, and past failure; and Moses too was returning to the Promised Land when he died.

The third and final example counterbalances the first. Irène has just left in her car. There is a flashback, which we interpret as Gonzague's, and which refers to the Manet painting. As with Irène's flashback, the mother is present, there is distant music on the soundtrack (a tenor singing), and a complex camera movement, a long crane shot which pans left and up towards the house as the young Gonzague and Irène come out, and then pans right and down back to the picnic. The same elements which structured nostalgia in the first example are found again here, and the sequence, like the other two, is speaking of loss.

Each of these three sequences links a painting with the notion of loss. The spectator is thus encouraged to recognize a painting at the same time as the loss for which that painting acts as a metonym. We recall the past by recognizing the painting, while at the same time realizing that neither the painting nor the past is really recoverable, thus generating the pining for what has been lost. It is not just the intertextual allusion to specific paintings which generates nostalgia, however; it is also the painterly feel of the film as a whole. The film looks like a painting, or sets of paintings, despite the camera mobility. The impression that we are looking at half-recognizable moving paintings creates the same nostalgic effect. Indeed, the more the camera becomes mobile in a desperate attempt to avoid the stasis of a pose, the more we become aware of the temptation of stasis, of death itself, as the most irremediable loss. The approach of death and all that is associated with it, such as failing faculties, is an important theme for the film. Monsieur Ladmiral is, as the title of the novel says, about to die; he complains about the walk to the station; he is the first to fall asleep after the Sunday lunch; he sees things (the two little girls, who, according to Tavernier, represent death), and there is a flashforward (belonging to Gonzague) to Ladmiral's deathbed.

So far I have explored the way in which paintings function to create a sense of nostalgia. This is because they are a crucial part of the way in which this type of nostalgia film works. Andrew Higson points out in his discussion of the British heritage film that 'critical perspective is displaced by decoration and display . . . The past is reproduced as flat, depthless pastiche, where the reference point is not the past itself, but other images, other texts' (Higson 1993: 112). Amongst these other texts are paintings. But this makes it sound as though painting is a merely decorative superstructural detail, whereas in the final part of this chapter I would like to suggest how it can be seen as more fundamental. If the film is successful as a nostalgia film, it is because of the recovery of what has been lost. As Higson says, talking of the way in which heritage films tend to chronicle decline, 'nostalgia is . . . both a narrative of loss, charting an imaginary historical trajectory from stability to instability, and at the same time a narrative of recovery, projecting the subject back into a comfortably closed past' (Higson 1993: 124). *Un dimanche à la campagne* is no different in this respect. The certainties of the past are lost, and the future is as much Irène with her independent high-tech lifestyle (travelling by car, phoning her lover—she is the only one to use the phone in the film), as it is the bourgeois mediocrity of Gonzague. But the recovery mentioned by Higson is more substantial. The film constructs a clearly definable position for the spectator. That position is the psycho-analyst Melanie Klein's depressive position, and it suggests the possibility of elaborating a theory of the nostalgia film which is psychoanalytical rather than ideological.

The three sequences analysed above link paintings with loss. That loss is concretized in each of them as the mother. She appears in the two outer sequences, Irène and Gonzague's flashbacks, and is referred to in Ladmiral's monologue on his career. The place of the mother in the process of mourning is fundamental. For Klein 'persecution [by 'bad' objects] . . . on the one hand, and pining for the loved ['good'] object, on the other, constitute the depressive position' (Klein 1986: 150). Following Freud, who considered that in mourning the subject calls up memories to relive them, before discarding them, Klein has further explained how the process of mourning repeats processes undergone by the child at early stages of development:

While it is true that the characteristic feature of normal mourning is the individual's setting up the lost loved object inside himself, he is not doing so for the first time but, through the work of mourning, is reinstating that object as well as all his loved internal objects which he feels he has lost. He is therefore recovering what he had already attained in childhood. (Klein 1986: 165–6)

The lost object, for the infant, is the mother's breast 'and all that the breast and the milk have come to stand for in the infant's mind: namely love, goodness and security' (Klein 1986: 148). It is the notion of recovery, here stressed by Klein, which is fulfilled by the paintings in the film. The spectator, when confronted by an intertextual reference, whether latent (Vuillard, Manet) or manifest (Renoir), is placed in a position of recall, recognition, and recovery. The spectator recovers what the paintings are metonyms for, the past frozen into significant moments, representations which are, literally, re-presentations, the making present once more of what has been lost.

The role of both parents in this process is important. As Klein points out:

In normal mourning the individual re-introjects and reinstates, as well as the actual lost person, his loved parents—who are felt to be his 'good' inner objects. His inner world, the one which he has built up from his earliest days onwards, in his phantasy was destroyed when the actual loss occurred. The rebuilding of this inner world characterizes the successful work of mourning. (Klein 1986: 166–7)

In *Un dimanche à la campagne*, the mourning structure constituted by the film maps out a recovery of what has been lost. This is not just the past, or more particularly childhood, although the film emphasizes childhood and its private moments through the antics of the two young boys, and the pensive reveries of the young girl. It is also the parents. The spectator, like Irène, recovers the 'good' inner objects: the good mother, in the Vuillard flashback, with her wise question, 'When will you stop asking so much of life, Irène?'; and the good father, in the *guinguette* sequence with the Renoir palimpsest, who may be weak, but has painted with honesty.

Gonzague also, of course, has a flashback, but it is constructed differently, suggesting an important difference between the sexes. Gonzague's intertextual reference, the Manet painting, is only gestured at. It is absent, just as his parents are more absent for him than they are for Irène. In Irène's flashback, she is in the same room as her mother, and in the *guinguette* sequence she takes the place of her mother when she dances with her father, making him young again. Things are different for Gonzague. In the Manet flashback, the children are not seen close to their parents, and his relationship with his father is typically Oedipal, in that he cannot communicate on anything except a mundane level. Indeed, a flashforward to his father's deathbed shows just how different the two relationships are. The depressive position I outlined above is complicated by a mother-fixated masochistic position, where the men are weak, and the women strong.

Mulvey's analysis does not allow for the submission of the male spectator to the object of desire; rather, the object of desire is at one and the same time punished (by plots which prove that she is at fault) and fetishized by the *mise en scène* to neutralize the threat of castration which she represents. Studlar, quoting Deleuze, shows how the masochist submits:

> The masochist does not desire to despoil or destroy the woman, but to idealize her, to submit to her, and to be punished by her so that the father (in himself) may be symbolically punished and denied. The unconscious fantasy underlying this masochistic disavowal of the father is the wish for a re-symbiosis with and fantastical rebirth from the powerful pre-Oedipal mother that will result in the 'new sexless man' who owes nothing to the father and phallic sexuality. Rebirth is equated with castration, which is not an obstacle but rather a 'precondition of its success with the mother'. (Studlar 1990: 233–4)

Un dimanche à la campagne constructs the position outlined here. Gonzague is even more of a failure than his father. Ladmiral, in his long monologue, suggests that his wife had compelled him indirectly not to be what he would have liked to have been, original. Gonzague could also have been a painter. After lunch, he muses on his failed career: 'I should have kept up with my painting. There wasn't time. Well, perhaps not. If I had failed it would have upset papa. I would just have been an imitator following in his shadow. If I had succeeded, I would have become his rival. My first paintings weren't that bad.' The implication here is a refusal of Oedipal conflict, a refusal of phallic sexuality, as Gonzague's excessive deference to his father in the film suggests. As a result, Gonzague is a split man, with a vacillating identity: is he Gonzague (his father's name for him), or Édouard (his wife's name for him)?

But whereas Gonzague is a failure, Irène and her mother are both presented as strong. Indeed, the *mise en scène* stresses this, since both of them are represented within the film by paintings. A painting of Irène is seen in the long opening sequence, significantly at the point where Ladmiral is first shown to be dependent on the other strong woman of the film, Mercédès, as he plaintively complains that he cannot find his shoe-cleaning kit. The same painting of Irène is in shot as what we subsequently interpret as the painting of Ladmiral's wife is scrutinized by Ladmiral, immediately before his flashback to the fireside scene with his wife. Gonzague, on the other hand, is not only not represented by a painting, but after lunch his father jokes about how if he were to paint him, he would paint him with a purple face, commenting that that was perhaps the way he should have painted. Gonzague therefore, unlike the women, is faceless, and his hypothetical face is laughable, as well as associated with his father's failure.

An analysis of the role of painting in this film has shown how nostalgia can be defined for the spectator as an entry into the depressive position which forces the spectator to reconstitute the lost objects. These lost objects are first and foremost the parents, but particularly the mother, as is well exemplified in this film, which constantly recalls childhood for the spectator, dominated by the mother, the ultimate lost object, re-presented in elegiac flashbacks. The depressive position which the film constructs is complicated for the spectator by a mother-fixated masochistic position: the men fail while the women succeed, all of them, not just Irène and her mother, since Mercédès runs the household, and Gonzague's wife has risen socially by marrying him. It is for this reason that I would like to propose that the nostalgia film constructs a position for the spectator which can be defined as depressive masochism, a rejection of phallic sexuality associated with the new, and a submission to the fantasy of childhood dominated by the all-powerful mother, associated with an unproblematic past.

This position is, at least in this film, associated with a regressive formalism in keeping with the apparent aim to resurrect the French *tradition de qualité*. This can be seen in an early sequence in the film, when Ladmiral sets off to meet his family who are arriving by train. The sequence is characterized by an extremely complex set of camera movements, combining repeated tracking, rapid panning, and fast cutting. As the camera follows Ladmiral's departure by panning in the direction in which he is walking, it at the same time tracks in the opposite direction, back towards the house. These are ostensibly point-of-view shots as Ladmiral looks back at the skipping girls, who represent death, according to Tavernier, as we saw above. The problem with this sequence is that the spectator has no sense that the ostentatious camerawork conveys Ladmiral's feeling or mood. It merely draws attention to itself, forcing us to consider its complexity and formal balance. As the *Cahiers du cinéma* critic put it, 'the camera never stops fiddling and pirouetting, just for show, just to fill out and dress up the subject, or perhaps more basically because [Tavernier] cannot stand what the camera sees . . . on the occasions when the scenes might have gained from longer shots with static camera' (Lardeau 1984: 36). The film suffers from the same constraints as those films from the 1950s scripted by Aurenche and Bost, the *tradition de qualité* which Tavernier clearly strove to emulate, and which Truffaut so heavily criticized for its 'scholarly framing, complicated lighting-effects, "polished" photography', complaining that although it aspired to realism, it 'destroys it at the moment of finally grabbing it, so careful is the school to lock these beings in a closed world, barricaded by formulas, plays on words, maxims, instead of letting us see them for ourselves' (Truffaut 1976: 230, 232); in other words, such films failed to produce 'a content which *is* rather than a form which signifies' (Forbes 1991: 94; her emphasis). The obtrusive camerawork, the ironic distance set up by the voice-over, suggest this attachment to form over content, to sentimentalism over emotion. Let me make quite clear that it is not complex camerawork *in itself* which suggests attachment to form over content; after all, such camerawork occurs in the films of Jean Renoir. The point is that where the camerawork of a Renoir is intimately linked to a humanist vision, the tragi-comedy of being human, the sequence I have described in *Un dimanche à la campagne* does not make us feel for Ladmiral as a human being. It is redundant. The sequence, the only one of this kind of complexity in the film, points to a combination of death (the skipping girls) and 'backwards looking', and is, therefore, emblematic of the depressive masochistic position I have outlined: a form of returning backwards which traps us in formal emptiness, nostalgic escapism.

But what is the reason for this escapism, apart from the obvious allure of nostalgia for its own sake? Set in 1912, i.e. just before the cataclysm of the First World War, the film seems to be suggesting that French society is about to suffer, or has already suffered, a similar cataclysm. The only major change in social terms during the 1980s (the rural exodus occurred over a long period during the twentieth century, but most particularly during the 1950–70 period) was the changing status of women in the workplace, associated with the women's movement. Traces of this are in the film, of course, in the shape of Irène, representing change with her car and numerous telephone calls to a lover. Her independence from the family and her dependence on technological change, and the fast pace of city life, are highlighted by comparison with her conservative brother and the tranquillity of the rural setting. In other words, and to put it somewhat bluntly, the film is nostalgic because women have apparently (a word which needs to be stressed) become too strong and men feel that they are failures. This most profound of socio-economic changes of the 1980s is mirrored by a spectatorial position which encourages male spectators to sentimentalize their failure by placing them in a depressive masochistic position.

5
Jean de Florette and
Manon des Sources:
Nostalgia and Hysteria

IN this chapter I shall argue that the popularity of *Jean de Florette* and *Manon des Sources* lies first in their reference to Pagnol's 1930s popular comedies (nostalgia for rural community as well as nostalgia for the golden age of French cinema), and second in the fact that they are melodrama. I shall examine the differences between Berri's films and Pagnol's original film *Manon des Sources* (1952), as well as the novel he based on that original (1962). From this examination I shall draw the conclusion that Berri's films fail to implement the notion of community upon which their success is predicated, and that this failure is bound up with the most striking feature of the films as melodrama: the repression of female characters and the foregrounding of an hysterical sexuality.

A number of strategies could have been used to market *Jean de Florette* and *Manon des Sources*: another Depardieu film, another Montand film (both popular stars), another film by Berri, the maker of the immensely successful *Tchao Pantin* (1983), who not only adapted the novel for the screen, but both produced and directed the diptych. The decision was made, however, to market the film by reference to the source-text by Pagnol (his 1962 novel *L'Eau des collines*): updating Pagnol from his reputation as an out-of-date popular writer/director, and insisting that the film was not a remake of Pagnol's 1952 film *Manon des Sources*. That this strategy worked is clear from the opinion poll commissioned by Berri to monitor the first film's popularity.

When asked what had decided them to see the film, there was an 88 per cent score by respondents for its basis on a novel by Pagnol, an 86 per cent score for the stars, and only a 27 per cent score for Berri as director (compare this with 38 per cent for publicity and 39 per cent for word-of-mouth). Asked what had pleased them most in the film, the respondents gave the following scores: 82 per cent for the setting, 72 per cent for the stars, 53 per cent for the dialogue, 48 per cent for the *mise en scène*, 41 per cent for the music, and 26 per cent for faithfulness to the Pagnol novel (Frodon and Loiseau 1987: 217–18). Even allowing for a carefully orchestrated marketing campaign, I would argue that these figures suggest an underlying trend in the audience for the film: the fact that Pagnol-as-origin and the setting score more highly than the stars suggests a strong attraction to the regional element combined with, indeed indissociable from, the Pagnol factor. In the circumstances, the marketing strategy adopted was shrewd. Its implicit basis is not so much the exoticism which undoubtedly helped Pagnol's films of the 1930s and 1940s, but, I would suggest, nostalgia for the powerful sense of community imparted by Pagnol's *Marius* trilogy (*Marius*, 1931; *Fanny*, 1932; *César*, 1936), as well as for the ruralism of Pagnol's adaptations of novels by Jean Giono, e.g. *Jofroi* (1934) which was 'for the first time in French cinema since the great shock of the advent of sound in 1929, a film which breathed real outdoor air, which smelt of wind and grass' (Jeancolas 1983: 147). The nostalgia for rural community is compounded by a more specifically cinematic nostalgia, since Pagnol's films correspond to the golden age of French cinema, the 1930s and 1940s. Berri's opinion poll suggests that *Jean de Florette* attracted people who did not go frequently to the cinema (Frodon and Loiseau 1987: 217). The diptych thus fulfilled a demand for the recycling of social and cinematic history.

If the films were popular, however, it is also because they are melodramas. In this sense they fail in their attempt to recycle rural community, in spite of the meticulous recreation of Pagnol's Provence. Melodrama is notoriously difficult to define as a genre (see Gledhill 1985: 73–4); in what follows, I shall be referring to work by Nowell-Smith. The eighteenth-century word melodrama, as he reminds us, is formed from drama and music (melos), a meaning which 'survives in the Italian *melodramma*—grand opera' (Nowell-Smith 1977: 112). It is no surprise, then, to find the portentously melodramatic main theme from Verdi's *La forza del destino* used in Berri's films. Typically, melodrama's concern is the family:

The locus of power is the family and individual private property, the two being connected with inheritance ... Patriarchal right is of central importance. The son has to become like his father in order to take over his property and his place within the community (or . . . the father is evil and the son must grow up different from him in order to be able to redistribute the property at the moment of inheritance). (Nowell-Smith 1977: 115)

One can immediately see how the films in question correspond to these themes. The major concern of le Papet and his nephew is property, and its retention within the patriarchal lineage. Le Papet's wish is that Ugolin should find a wife so as to have a son who can inherit the property of the Soubeyran family. The dramatic concentration on the family is achieved in a number of ways which are at variance with Pagnol's 1952 film, and often with Pagnol's 1962 novel, on which the Berri version is based. It is by focusing on the differences between these texts that the specificities of these films as melodrama can be isolated.

First, there is the marked change of tone, centring principally on contrasts between pathos and humour. An example of this in Pagnol's soliloquy when Ugolin is found hanged. He comments: 'That's the Soubeyrans for you, all of them strung up like sausages'; adding to this deflationary comic image by lighting his pipe with one of the candles burning around the coffin. Oscillation between pathos and humour also occurs in the novel, as we shall see below.

Second, there is detheatricalization of the *mise en scène*. Pagnol's film is conceived as a series of tableaux, or theatrical scenes, as one might expect from a writer of plays; indeed, Bazin's main criticism of the film was that it was 'filmed theatre' (Bazin 1983: 93). This is particularly the case in the courtroom scene, where a variety of characters have cameos to play: Polyte, the plaintiff, struck by one of Manon's stones when, as it turns out, trying to rape her; the Brigadier, who plays at being a judge; the teacher, who defends Manon; Ugolin, whose love is revealed when he refuses to prosecute Manon for stealing his melons, since he says he had left them for her. Each of these characters is equally developed within the confines of the scene. By dropping humour and theatricalization of action and dialogue, Berri's film is more 'realistic', of course, and the conventions of realism are, as Nowell-Smith reminds us, 'the basic conventions of melodrama' (Nowell-Smith 1977: 117). By using the crowd scenes as a backdrop to the essential interest of his films, which is the concentration on family relationships (three protagonists from the same family in each film: Jean, Ugolin, le Papet in the first; Manon, Ugolin, le Papet in the second), Berri's films abandon a further characteristic of Pagnol's work, the focus on community values.

The centre of Pagnol's film is the village square with its fountain and its café where stories about the community are told. Moreover, the film is punctuated by important crowd scenes: Manon's 'trial' for assaulting one of the village boys; the Water Festival, when the water stops just as one of the speakers is extolling its virtues; the denunciation of Ugolin; the villagers' attempts to compensate for their complicitous silence by showering Manon with gifts; the procession. Only the denunciation and the procession remain in Berri's *Manon des Sources* (as indeed in Pagnol's novel). The crowd scenes of Pagnol's film are on an equal footing with more intimate scenes. They thus foreground the notion of community by their interplay between Manon's rejection of (and by) the community, followed by reciprocal acceptance. Even though the novel does away with many of the crowd scenes of the film, nevertheless, a sense of community is still prevalent, if only because the historical context of the village is dwelt upon: the age-old enmity between the villagers of Crespin and those of Les Bastides, for example, whereas this is mentioned only in passing in *Jean de Florette*. The café remains a focal point in the novel, as it had done in Pagnol's film, where the villagers exchange stories and views, whereas in Berri's film it serves mainly to advance the action. Moreover, whereas, in Pagnol's film, the café scenes are mostly in middle to long shot so as to incorporate all of the figures sitting around the table, in Berri's diptych there is a constant shuttling between middle-distance shots and close-ups, usually of le Papet and Ugolin, with the effect of extracting them from the community for melodramatic emphasis. The sense of lost community when the various versions are placed side by side is ironically paradoxical given the nostalgic yearning vehicled by Berri's film for the rural paradise of small village communities.

There is a fourth element, which is not tied to the concentration on the family, but rather to the treatment of women in the texts. As befits a theatrical *mise en scène*, Pagnol's film, designed as a showcase for his wife, highlights Manon's role principally through dialogue. Indeed, Bazin speaks approvingly of the film's verbal extravagance, which is not restricted to Manon (Bazin 1983: 93). In the crowd scenes mentioned earlier, both main and secondary characters speak constantly. This is particularly the case in the courtroom scene, where Manon dominates the proceedings, tying the plaintiffs into knots. Her eloquence is evident throughout the film, in striking contrast to Berri's Manon, who speaks rarely, and then through clenched teeth, her asociality emphasized by her often-repeated goat-call. The silencing of the contemporary Manon is all the more peculiar, given that melodrama usually 'allow(s) more space for its women characters and for the representations of passion undergone' (Nowell-Smith 1977: 116), and also given that eventually it is Manon who will survive the drama, regaining her rightful property. Here again, we can see major changes from source-texts which signal this silencing.

In Pagnol's novel, it is not just Manon and Baptistine who live together, as in Berri's film, but Manon's mother as well. The three women live in a matriarchal paradise: vegetables and animals multiply profusely, thanks in part to the 'inexhaustible spring' (Pagnol 1988: 231). Men only occasionally visit the cave where the women live, and these men are foreigners to the area anyway, tree-fellers (friends of Baptistine's dead husband), whose work takes them far away (see Pagnol 1988: 231–2). The matriarchal paradise is combined with a feeling for the power of women. This is particularly the case with Baptistine, whose role is much stronger in both Pagnol's film and the novel, where she is a powerful witch-like figure who casts an evil eye on the village, and is persuaded to lift the spell at a later date (Pagnol 1988: 327, 337). In Berri's film, although she does teach Manon how to trap birds, thus retaining the educative function she has in Pagnol's versions, she is portrayed as a frightened wild creature, who speaks a hybrid French-Piedmontese (a sign of 'strangeness' and asociality). Manon is similarly portrayed in Berri's film; she scampers up trees at the approach of strangers, speaks little, mostly uttering her goat-call. This is broadly consonant with the novel's treatment of Manon, with the significant difference that, as was the case with Baptistine, the elements of magic and myth associated with Manon are ruthlessly eradicated. In the novel, Manon is a witch/fairy endowed with magical powers. When Ugolin first sees her dancing naked (with one of her goats; she dances alone in Berri's film) she becomes for him the 'divinity of the hills' (Pagnol 1988: 262). His later observations of her develop the notion of her power over nature in her relationship with her 'familiars'. She talks to her dog: 'they certainly were secrets, and perhaps worse, because black dogs, especially those with eyes covered with hair, have never had a good reputation' (Pagnol 1988: 280). Her harmonica playing attracts a lizard: 'Ugolin, uneasy and charmed, looked at the long glistening beast listening to the luminous girl, and thought: "The old people weren't very wrong when they said she was a witch!" But one day he murmured, smiling with pleasure: "When a witch is pretty, well then she's called a fairy!" ' (Pagnol 1988: 280). The demythification and silencing of Manon which operates within Berri's film is accompanied by a visual treatment which turns her into a standard 1980s icon, 'about as much like a goatherd as Catherine Deneuve in a promo for Chanel perfumes' (Canby 1987: 25). Manon's silence does, of course, fit with a psychological motivation. We assume that she went 'wild' after the trauma when she happened on le Papet and Ugolin unblocking the hidden spring which her father had killed himself trying to find. She will only speak again when her Prince Charming kisses her, and re-educates her into speech (he is a teacher) and morality (it is he who persuades her to unblock the spring feeding the village fountain).

The treatment of female characters is predictable, first because it conforms to prevailing gender stereotypes, but second, and more importantly, because the silencing of the women is a necessary precondition for the focus on the male triangle in the first film, which comprises the Father, the 'bad' Son (Ugolin, le Papet's nephew), and the 'good' real Son (le Papet's illegitimate son), locked in Oedipal struggle. The treatment of the men is typical of melodrama in the 'impairment of . . . "masculinity" ' (Nowell-Smith 1977: 113). Nowell-Smith suggests that the male in melodrama is often 'passive or impotent', and that these are 'forms of a failure to be male', if one assumes the usual dichotomy of male/active versus female/passive (Nowell-Smith 1977: 115–16; there are of course immense problems with this view; see Gledhill 1985: 76). Recalling that the function of melodrama is to work out the problems of patriarchal normalization, Nowell-Smith points out that this acceptance of castration by the otherwise rebellious son can only be achieved at the expense of repression, and that repression always resurfaces in melodrama as hysterical excess (in the Freudian sense) in relation to its attempt to conform to the patterns of realism:

The laying out of the problems 'realistically' always allows for the generating of an excess which cannot be accommodated . . . The undischarged emotion which cannot be accommodated within the action, subordinated as it is to the demands of family/lineage/inheritance, is traditionally expressed in the music and, in the case of film, in certain elements of the mise en scène. That is to say, music and mise en scène do not just heighten the emotionality of an element of the action: to some extent they substitute for it . . . It is not just that the characters are often prone to hysteria, but that the film itself somatises its own unaccommodated excess, which thus appears displaced . . . Often, the 'hysterical' moment of the text can be identified as the point at which the realist representative convention breaks down. (Nowell-Smith 1977: 117)

Although the teacher in Berri's *Manon des Sources*, Manon's eventual husband, is conventionally treated (but then he is hardly developed as a character), the three major male characters, Jean, Ugolin, and to a lesser extent le Papet, show signs of 'impairment', or impotence, characterized by excessive *mise en scène*, as is particularly obvious when the film is compared to the avowed source-text, Pagnol's novel.

   The first of these chronologically is the visit by Jean and family to the village. They are shot in extreme long shot, and pass from the light through the narrow opening between the houses into the shadow of the buildings. The shot adopts the point of view of the men in the café whom we only see in the next shot. Apart from the fact that motivation for the shot confusingly follows the shot itself, the camera is placed at Manon's height, not at the height of the men whose point of view the shot apparently espouses. This, as well as the melodramatic use of light and shade (repeated as they leave the village), is already excessive as well as disorienting. Point of view becomes even more disorienting subsequently. As Jean and family approach, the point of view shifts from the men in the café to le Papet, who exchanges looks with Jean as Jean passes by in medium shot, at which point there is a cut to the next shot of le Papet's face in close-up. Since the end of the previous shot showed Jean looking at le Papet, we assume that the new shot is Jean's point of view, only to discover that the camera lingers on le Papet's face, as Montand becomes pensive, suggesting a return to le Papet's point of view (an implicit 'inner monologue' shot), or, possibly, a third party point of view. On Jean's return from the baker's, a player throws his ball apparently on purpose to splash the family with mud. This is a significant change from the novel, where Jean is further from the players, is struck on the back unintentionally, and throws the ball back, not looking at the players. In the film, Jean runs forward and makes as if to throw the ball, but refrains from doing so as he and le Papet stare at each other, le Papet key-lit, and framed in Jean's uplifted and quivering arm. This is pure melodrama: anger scarcely contained, but contained nevertheless, and the encounter staged as Oedipal struggle, as the anger is directed, by virtue of lighting and camera, not at the villagers, but specifically at le Papet. The oscillating and disorienting point of view (men, le Papet, Jean/Papet/third party) clearly helps to signify excessive emotion.

A similar problem with point of view occurs in a later sequence, where the rainclouds fail to unleash the expected rain, and Jean rails at the heavens. Excess occurs in camera movement and position; the camera swoops down in a long lateral travelling crane shot as it follows, and in fact precedes, Jean, adopting the kneeling height that Depardieu sinks into at the end of the travelling. As Jean realizes that the rain will not fall, and rises to his feet, the camera sweeps vertiginously upwards in a dizzying high angle, as Jean rather comically addresses God. Although the scene is faithful to the novel's dialogue, the camera position is problematic. Whose point of view is this, if not God's? In the novel, the comical effect of Jean's imprecations is emphasized by his statement that he had 'just been a little ridiculous' (Pagnol 1988: 165); there is no such deflationary strategy in the film, which completes the sequence melodramatically with a shot of the distant hills echoing with Jean's imprecations.

The next knock of fate is the immediately following sirocco sequence, equally excessive with its all too obvious yellow filter, Jean's feverish departure (in the novel he goes off munching a sandwich), and the exhausted admission of failure (not in the novel): 'Now I know why God gave me this hump' (in the novel he walks 'muttering insults under his breath to Fate, Providence, and the Sahara'; Pagnol 1988: 169). As so often, he rallies, and tries to dig and then blow his way down to the water in a sequence which recalls the invocation sequence by its high angle, squashing him into the cavity, where he drinks greedily from an uplifted wine-bottle, suggesting an obsession completely out of control. Both Jean's action (the greedy drinking) and the camera angle (an almost vertical high-angle, followed by an almost vertical low-angle reverse shot as Ugolin looks pityingly down at Jean) combine to foreground excess, all the more obvious when compared with the source-text: in the novel Jean drinks only once he is out of the hole he has so laboriously dug. The high-angle shot in the film recalls not only the invocation to God, but also an earlier sequence in the film where le Papet spies on Jean through a telescope from an escarpment (the spying is in the novel, but not the telescope). Here, too, Jean is shot from a high angle, and imprisoned in le Papet's telescope lens, as he tries his hand at breeding rabbits. The pattern is melodramatic in the sense that the Oedipal drama is carried by excessive *mise en scène*. The three instances of dizzying high-angle shots suggest forcefully Jean's imprisonment within the gaze of the patriarch/God, while he is involved in reproduction, sinking hutches into what is unambiguously called 'Mother Earth' in the novel (Pagnol 1988: 184), or digging his way down into what the novel suggests is a womb (Pagnol 1988: 195) to find the spring which will allow his vegetables and animals to flourish. He will unintentionally kill himself trying to return to this Mother, aided and abetted by the machinations of the Father who tries to protect his property.

Excess of a different and more disturbing kind occurs with Ugolin. In the novel the high point of Ugolin's obsession is 'a magical ceremony' (Pagnol 1988: 309) which entails a pseudo-religious ritual:

Having written Manon's name on a piece of paper, he placed it in the middle of the table and surrounded it with his relics—the little scrap of green ribbon, the ball of hair, a mother-of-pearl button, three olive pips. Then he dug up his gold louis, as if to imprison Manon with his riches. Then, in order to reinforce this charm, he joined his hands and invoked the Holy Virgin, who was no doubt surprised by these incongruous appeals . . . He took the ribbon, looked at it, caressed it, kissed it, then suddenly got up to open the drawer of the little cupboard. There he found some thread and a needle, which he did not find easy to thread. He took off his shirt, sat with his chest bare on a chair near the lamp, and started to sew the green ribbon onto his left breast. The needle was thick and the blood spurted out in drops. He clenched his teeth and pulled on the rough double thread, tearing his flesh. Four times he pushed the needle in and drew the thread tight. The fifth time he pierced only the ribbon and tied a dressmaker's knot. Finally, his face pale and drenched with sweat and tears, he took the piece of mirror from the wall and gazed at the blood-spattered green ribbon hanging from the soft red hair on his chest.

'That way', he said, 'it will always be over my heart.'

Then he drank a large glass of wine and stretched himself out on the bed, with a hand clasped to his burning breast.

That is to say, poor Ugolin of the Soubeyrans was going mad, and visibly wasting away. (Pagnol 1988: 309–10)

The sewing of the ribbon is, as can be seen, incorporated in a fastidiously performed ritual which to some extent neutralizes its impact. Moreover, the description is factual, almost clinical, which encourages distantiation. The final statement also encourages distantiation; as so often in the novel, a humorous tone deflates the self-mutilation. We see Ugolin as if from the outside; he is, by the criterion of common sense, quite mad, and this can seen by his refusal to feed himself. In the same scene in the film, the ritualistic element is eliminated. There are harrowing close-ups of Ugolin's grimacing face, covered with sweat. The elimination of ritual has two effects. It does not allow spectators to distance themselves from Ugolin; on the contrary, the close-ups encourage identification. And the failure to provide a ritualistic context does not allow spectators to rationalize Ugolin's mutilation within the framework of a magical discourse. Spectators are forced to experience an extreme form of violence, no longer as an initiation, but more immediately as hysterical castration, all the more since the activity (sewing), the object sewn (Manon's ribbon), and, arguably, the part of the body sewn into, the nipple, suggest femininity. Empirical observation suggests that the penetration of the nipple by the needle affects female spectators as much as, and perhaps more than, male spectators; Ugolin's body becomes not so much genderless as transgendered, available as a sado-masochistic fantasy for both male and female spectators.

The same sado-masochistic voyeurism occurs with le Papet in the final scene of the film. In the novel, his death is followed by the birth of Manon's son and the reading of his letter to Manon *en famille*, interspersed with ribald and incredulous comments (Pagnol 1988: 439–40). In the film, the letter is read in voice-over as he prepares for death. In the novel, a sense of community prevails as the old is followed by the new, and dark deeds are atoned for. In the film, the prominence given to le Papet's death—it is the final sequence, over which the credits eventually roll—elevates him to the status of tragic hero. Le Papet's downfall is caused by his obsession with property and lineage. It is the narcissistic apotheosis of the Father who kills the thing he most loves (not the Son, but the capacity of the Son to transmit property), whereas in the novel his death is eclipsed by the happy ending. His death resolves the Oedipal scenario. As le Papet writes in his letter, in heaven he will see his son in a non-conflictual situation: 'instead of attacking me he will defend me' (Pagnol 1988: 440). Where Ugolin had merely pierced his body in symbolic castration and admission of failure of that same body to attract the object of his desire, le Papet's death is more or less a suicide, the ultimate form of mutilation.

The melodramatic finale is underlined by an excessive *mise en scène*. In the third shot from the end, he prepares for death; excess occurs in its length (it is 2 minutes 35 seconds long), its lighting (much of it is in an obscure half-light, occasionally lapsing into almost complete darkness), in the camera movement (a complex choreography combining tilts, pans, and lateral travelling), and, finally, a confusing syntax in the use of close-up, as the camera tracks in close-up over a variety of objects while le Papet reads his letter. As he begins reading, the camera focuses on the envelope addressed to Manon, juxtaposed with his glasses and a pen. This is an 'illustrative' visual code which supports the dialogue ('reading a letter'). The camera tilts towards a family photograph illuminated by an oil-lamp as the letter announces the *coup de théâtre*, that Jean was le Papet's son, the oil-lamp figuring 'revelation', and rather comically also illustrating the statement that le Papet 'had let him die a lingering death' (in French 'mourir à petit feu'). The remainder of the first half of the shot is problematic, however, since the illustrative function of the images gradually breaks down. The camera focuses on le Papet's ornate cane as he muses on what might have been a happy family; then it focuses on a banal picture of a camel at sunset as he talks of his shame, on the carved head of an African woman as he says that Delphine will be able to support what he is saying; then, finally and rapidly, on the clock, comb, and ring, as he says that it was 'all the fault of Africa' (Pagnol 1988: 440). In other words, the camera travels over objects *before* they are alluded to in the soundtrack; the camel and the carved head would have been more appropriate for the statement that it was 'all the fault of Africa', and we might have expected such patterning from the simplistic coding earlier in the shot. And whereas in the novel he dies clutching a rosary (signifying repentance), the film's long final shot (3 minutes 30 seconds) over which the credits roll is a close-up on le Papet's hand in which, as well as a rosary, Florette's comb is cradled, one of his few mementoes of her. During this final shot, Verdi's music is reprised for the last time, heavily underlining the notion of Destiny and, more particularly, the sense of failure.

To conclude, Berri's film attempts to articulate the sense of community prevalent in Pagnol's texts by providing a regressive context (the rural other, the golden age of French cinema) which is bound to create nostalgia in French spectators. The films fail to create the sense of community which partly made Pagnol's films popular, however, because that community is a thing of the past. Berri's films require a different popular medium, melodrama. This is because melodrama's excess functions as a metaphorical symptom of social change. Berri's films, by their nostalgic celebration of a mythical rurality, figure the most important social change in France this century, the conversion from a rural to an industrial economy. They also point to disturbing features in the crisis in masculinity. I have tried to show how melodrama writes excess into the *mise en scène*. Excess is articulated by the principal male characters, and this excess is intimately bound up with what Nowell-Smith calls 'impairment', i.e. failure and impotence, vehicled by sado-masochistic devices, whose common feature is castration and feminization, whether it be Jean's attempt to recover the lost 'source' (French for spring), or Ugolin's painful writing of femininity into the fabric of his body, or le Papet's resolution of Oedipal crisis by the ultimate form of mutilation, suicide.

Thus a profoundly conservative hankering for the certainty of an hierarchical rural social order is coupled, unsurprisingly, with an Oedipal configuration of a return to the origin. As I have tried to show by tracing the various stages from the source-texts, these two configurations of melodrama, nostalgia and hysteria, are predicated on a silencing of women characters. Myth and magic are repressed by the realism upon which melodrama traces its hysterical symptoms. The repressed always returns, however, and excessively so, here in the form of a hysterical male sexuality, masochistically inscribing its loss of the mother on the body, piercing nipples and excavating surrogate wombs, which only Manon des Sources can find with the help of her familiars.

6

Coup de foudre:
Nostalgia and Lesbianism

Coup de foudre (1983) is usually seen as an example of mainstream lesbian film, and has often been bracketed with similar Hollywood films from the 1980s, such as *Lianna* (1983) and *Desert Hearts* (1986) (see Holmlund 1991; Merck 1986; Straayer 1990). This might on the face of it seem surprising, given that lesbianism in *Coup de foudre* is closeted behind gestures and dialogue which are more likely to lead to the conclusion that it is a film about female bonding. *Coup de foudre* is also a nostalgic film, and it is the uneasy marriage between female bonding/covert lesbianism and nostalgia which I shall explore in this chapter. I shall be arguing that this marriage is important because it allows the spectator more easily to construct a female perspective, predicated on the rejection of patriarchal law. In this respect, lesbianism is tangential to the film's concerns, although this is not to deny the validity of lesbian counter-readings. By linking nostalgia and lesbianism, however, the film creates ambivalence, since its nostalgia is clearly predicated, as indeed one might expect from the Kleinian analysis outlined in the chapter on *Un dimanche à la campagne*, on nostalgia for both father and mother. Far from suggesting that this ambivalence is contradictory, as if lesbianism excluded nostalgia for the father, I shall show how it is a crucial part of the function of nostalgia.

NOSTALGIA

Nostalgia is created by a triple historical time-scale: the 1940s with the parallel histories of the two women; the 1950s with their meeting and subsequent common history; and the autobiographical present, as the film's ending makes clear that the histories referred to are seen through the eyes of the director-as-child. Within the first two periods mentioned, all the hallmarks of the nostalgia film occur. There is meticulous period reconstruction in décor, costume ('Isabelle depends a lot on costume to act, and Guy Marchand chose his braces himself, the same as his father's'; Kurys 1983*a*: 26), and music; in the latter case, the Glenn Miller of the liberation and the ironically used Perry Como song 'I wonder who's kissing her now' of the mid-1950s.

There is loss, a crucial component of nostalgia. The film opens with various aspects of separation caused by war: the Jewish internees are separated from their families; Léna tells her new-found friend that her mother has died two months ago; her friend can only communicate with her husband from a distance; Léna can only communicate with her eventual husband by means of notes and gestures; Madeleine loses her husband in a gun-battle between Pétainist militia and Resistance fighters.

There is also reference to the experience and points of view of children. As Kurys herself pointed out, the film 'is seen through the eyes of children, it's me who is telling the story and it's my memory' (Kurys 1983*b*: 122). The two women meet for the first time thanks to their children acting in the school play; there is an intrusive sequence structured around Léna's children's view of adult sexuality as they spy on the maid and her boyfriend kissing through an open door; and the final sequence, crucially, as I shall discuss, forces the spectator retrospectively to view preceding events from a child's point of view.

Audiences may well have seen it as mainly a nostalgic film, which to some extent accounts for its popularity (the twelfth most popular French film in 1983, with more spectators than *Superman 3*), but a clear audience segment both in the USA and in France saw the film principally as a mainstream lesbian film.

LESBIAN READINGS

Diane Kurys was keen to downplay the lesbian subtext, claiming that she did not want spectators to be able to reduce the story to a story 'about lesbians', which would have been an oversimplification of biographical truth, as well as pandering to male fantasy: 'Several of the backers wanted an explicit lesbian scene—it's one of their main fantasies' (quoted in Pally 1984: 16). If it was nevertheless seen as a lesbian film, one of the main reasons is the general lack of gay films with positive images of gays, and the even greater lack of specifically lesbian films, particularly in France, where there is less of a tradition of cultural lesbianism than in the USA. This no doubt accounts for the flurry of critical excitement over *Coup de foudre* in the gay press of the USA. The film was called 'the best gay film of 1984' by Steve Beery of the *Advocate* (quoted in Holmlund 1991: 176), and 'the most sensitive gay film [she had] seen in years' by a contributor to *Womanews* (ibid.).

The review of the film in the only well-known French lesbian journal of the period, *Lesbia*, suggests that lesbian audiences might have read the film in the same way as in the USA:

I'm impressed. I had expected comfortable commonplaces on friendship between two women stuck between their husbands and their kids. I was led up the garden path by all the film critics; they had kept quiet that *Coup de foudre* is one of the most beautiful films about homosexual love between women. Diane Kurys herself has steered clear of alluding to it; nothing is insinuated, there is only the blinding truth in each image, each word, each look. They meet and already they can't leave each other! From complicity to confidences, their intimacy increases, they confess their attraction amidst laughter: 'I miss you', 'Why am I so good with you?' They touch each other with looks, words, gestures. Miou-Miou is remarkable in these half-tone sequences where her burgeoning desire brushes against a shyly trembling, sensual Isabelle Huppert. Oh, of course, nothing is said, except by the husband, mad with rage: 'You know what it's called: dykes'. Without batting an eyelid, his little wife tells him that she can't live without her friend. It's as simple as that. Although you had to let yourself see it . . . My friend complains in her seat: 'All those prigs (*beaufs*) who didn't realise it!' 'Elementary my dear: I'm impressed . . .' (Jouve 1983: 28)

The male gay reviewer of the leading gay periodical in France placed the film historically, pointing out that the discretion shown by the film is consonant with a period when the gay movement, which eventually came out of the various protest movements in the wake of May 1968, did not exist. As he points out, 'a relationship of this type, plausible in 1952, would no longer be so today, precisely because [gays] have struggled to impose a recognition of homosexuality' (Sanzio 1983: 125).

It is precisely the fact that a gay community exists which can lead to gay readings of otherwise ambivalent texts. This is clear from comments made by Holmlund, who states that 'reception and context are key . . . We should not continue to insist that authorial intent and/or textual structures in and of themselves define what is a "woman" or when a "lesbian" is a lesbian' (Holmlund 1991: 148). Holmlund, trying to legitimize the massive enthusiasm of lesbian audiences for the film, suggests, somewhat lamely, that in a scene such as the swimming-pool scene where the two women admire each other's bodies, 'it is easy to imagine them as lovers, and their constant exchange of clothes and fashion tips legitimizes lesbian readings of them as femmes, not just friends, for lesbians know how much femmes like to dress up and step out' (Holmlund 1991: 158–59). Straayer points to the exchange of glances which, she suggests, are eroticized by the women's 'physical proximity and subtle body contact', combined with the fact that they are more often than not both together in the frame, viewed as a couple (Straayer 1990: 53). Such shots tend to be contrasted with shots of 'lone males', thus 'depicting female bonding as the exclusion of men' (Straayer 1990: 54). Men in the film act as 'intermediaries' between the two women. Thus, in the nightclub scene, 'two male onlookers become intermediaries by diverting the women's glances and easing the tension created by their physical embrace' (Straayer 1990: 55); or again, the experience Léna has on the train with the soldier is a means of being initiated by Madeleine, who informs her that it was an orgasm; or, finally, it is Léna's husband who calls the women dykes, 'not only reveal[ing] the fears of a jealous husband but confirm[ing] the audience's perceptions' (Straayer 1990: 55). Ultimately, then, the only difference between a lesbian reading and a female bonding reading is one of degree, and degree of perception. As Straayer herself points out, *Coup de foudre* challenges mainstream cinema because it deals with female bonding, leading to ambivalence:

The focus on two women together threatens to establish both asexuality and homosexuality, both of which are outside the heterosexual desire which drives mainstream film and narrative. Therefore, simultaneous actions take place in the text to eroticize the women's interactions and to abort the resulting homoerotics. These very contradictions and opposing intentions cause the gaps and ambiguous figurations that allow lesbian readings. (Straayer 1990: 56)

It might have been possible at a greater level of abstraction to claim that the implicitness of the lesbian context reflects a specific strategy, close to Irigaray's contention that the only possible disruption of phallocratic law is not its attempted replacement, but a disruption and modification, 'starting from an "outside" that is exempt, in part, from phallocratic law' (Irigaray 1985: 86). It is clear, however, that *Coup de foudre* does not construct a space outside the law, since there are obvious constraints on a lesbian reading, as indeed the same critics sympathetic to lesbian readings have pointed out.

CONSTRAINTS ON LESBIAN READINGS

The most striking of these constraints is the consistent use of the 'vous' form between the two women throughout the film, suggesting respectful distance. Kurys sees it as a phenomenon of its time; the 'strait-jacket side of the 1950s', she calls it, saying that the two women 'are intimate while keeping a kind of distance' (Kurys 1983*b*: 119). The presence of children, and of a child's viewpoint, also acts as a constraint for a lesbian reading, as Merck has explained, suggesting that

The sexual curiosity incited by [the film] is rendered innocent by [its] use of children as . . . fascinated onlookers. Léna's husband—who experiences the film's one, very displaced, primal scene when he interrupts Madeleine and her art teacher dressing after sex—may 'wonder who's kissing her now', the soldiers may spy on Léna's seduction on the train, but then so do the little girls when they watch the maid kissing her boyfriend. (Merck 1986: 172–3).

The only sex acts which are narrativized are heterosexual acts; sex between the two women is always displaced, for example in the ironically used song 'I wonder who's kissing her now', or in the relative lack of nudity, displaced onto the naked women Madeleine sculpts at home. It is true that there are moments of intimacy, such as the bedroom scene where Léna brushes against Madeleine's arm as they lie in bed, or the swimming-pool scene. In this scene, the two women look at themselves in the mirror; Léna says that she thinks her breasts are too small, to which Madeleine replies, 'they're adorable'; after a brief hesitation she says, 'why do I feel so good with you?' It is the women's intimacy which is stressed here, however, rather than their desire for each other. It is important, however, that their exchange is preceded by a man showing off his body to Léna by the side of the pool, the point being that sexual spectacle is contrasted with non-competitive female bonding. Indeed, this also seems to be the point of the scene in the nightclub, where the two women decide not to follow up a possible encounter with two men who have been watching them dance. The two women leave arm in arm, Léna saying that she did not feel like it because 'he had a skinny bottom'. Again, the possibility of heterosexual exchange is contrasted with non-sexual female intimacy. Even less equivocal are the two heterosexual encounters, Madeleine caught by Léna's husband after sex with her art teacher, and Léna herself, who has an orgasm after non-penetrative sex with a soldier on the train to Paris.

If I have spent some time reviewing the lesbian problematic raised by this film, it is partly to emphasize what we do not see, which as a result causes ambivalence on the two levels of cinematic identification. On the level of secondary identification, i.e. identification with the characters on screen, we might well ask ourselves whether the two women really did have an explicitly sexual relationship, but we cannot know. On the level of primary identification, i.e. Metz's notion of the 'pure act of perception', the 'transcendental subject' (Metz 1975: 49), there is an undermining of the 'untroubled centrality and unity of the subject' (Doane 1980: 28), insofar as this subject is constituted by gender. What might then become important for a lesbian reading is less the hypothetical lesbian content than textual operations which work to establish a woman-centred viewpoint, both narratively and in *mise en scène/* cinematography. The debate on whether the film constructs a lesbian viewpoint forces spectators to confront the woman-centredness of the film not just as a monolithic phenomenon, but as shifting, variable, and above all multiple. As soon as we start asking to what extent the film is lesbian, we are asking ourselves how the film constructs *different and various* female positions for the spectators (both male and female), not a single position, in opposition to the normative male position.

In the remainder of this chapter, I shall analyse two sequences of the film in detail, to show how the normative male position is undermined by the elaboration of a female-centred perspective. These two sequences act as keys to trace the move from male-dominated space where women are spectacles of the male gaze, to the literal breaking of the mould by the self-mutilating violence of the male, i.e. castration of the male and the introduction of a female-oriented gaze, whose function is to reject the male-centred position. The analysis of a third sequence, the final sequence of the film, with its problematic reuniting of male and female perspectives in the wistful gaze of the child, will force us to confront ambivalence head on.

THE CONSTRUCTION OF A FEMALE-CENTRED PERSPECTIVE

The first sequence is the reunion between Léna and Madeleine; the second occurs shortly afterwards when Michel ransacks his wife's clothes shop. Léna and Madeleine's reunion is mainly filmed from Léna's point of view. It shows Léna's resolve and impatience through her abrupt and purposeful dialogue, and through extremely mobile camerawork. This signals a change in the relationship between the two women, since Madeleine had up to this point been constructed as the more forceful and independent character. Madeleine's mother, shot against a backdrop of window-rails, appears threatening, in a *mise en scène* suggesting imprisonment. The beginning of the sequence therefore constructs a scenario of initiation as Léna retrieves her now passive, melancholic lover from the negatively construed family. The remainder of the sequence functions as a transition from family space, which has obtained throughout the film at various points, mainly at mealtimes, to a female space. Straayer has pointed out how point of view neatly introduces the spectator into that female space:

The camera temporarily identifies with the look of Léna/Huppert approaching Madeleine/Miou-Miou through a subjective tracking shot, and then holds steady while Léna enters the frame. The viewer is carried into the women's space via an identification with Léna's look, then observes their embrace from an invited vantage point. (Straayer 1990: 53–4)

A female perspective is constructed as a combination of passion in the form of the light wind (machine) ruffling the women's hair, and innocence, in the form of the cultivated garden, signifying the innocence of Eden, or at the very least a refuge, in contrast to the next shot of Madeleine's father and son in long shot framed by thick, and more obviously 'wild', foliage. As Straayer points out, however, this shot is important for the limits it imposes on the Edenic female space: 'These two males foreground the generation missing between them—Madeleine's husband. Hence their look both acknowledges and checks the dimensions of the women's visual exchange' (Straayer 1990: 54). The next stage in the construction of a female perspective will call into question male authority and the violence which upholds it.

Not long after their reunion, Michel ransacks his wife's shop, driven wild when he sees Madeleine, whom he thought his wife had agreed never to see again in return for the buying of the shop. The sequence is characterized by fast cutting; from the shot in which Michel hurls the plant he has brought his wife down onto the glass table, there are seventeen shots in forty-seven seconds (see Fig. 1; the numbers refer to shots, and are placed where the spectator might imagine the camera to be in each case). A peculiarity of the sequence is the oscillating point of view. Only two shots can be

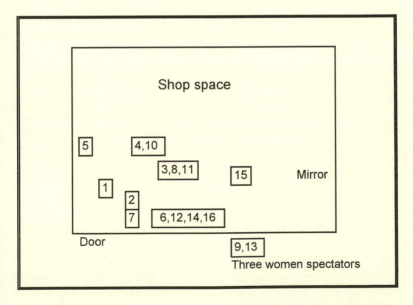

Fig. 1. *Coup de foudre*: Michel ransacks the shop; camera position in relation to shots.

construed as 'belonging' to the principal actors in this sequence: 4, when the spectator sees the two women huddled together as if from Michel's point of view; and 5, when the spectator sees Michel from a position matched onto 4 (the assumption being that it is Madeleine and Léna's point of view). The remainder are either shots containing all three characters (1, 2, and 13), or, more usually, shots containing Michel alone, but not from the two women's point of view. The point of view to which these shots 'belong' is suggested only in shot 7, when there is a cut to three women onlookers peering through the shop window. In shot 9, Michel picks up a large bronze container and hurls it at the camera, shattering the glass of the shop window, thus suggesting that the majority of the shots in the sequence up to that point were from outside the shop, and from the women onlookers' point of view. Although only shots 9 and 13 are clearly from the 'outside', since Michel is seen behind the broken glass of the window, given the position of the camera in shots 6, 12, 14, and 16, the spectator is likely to assume that the point of view is that posited by shot 7, that of the women onlookers.

The fact that Michel hurls an object at the camera and breaks the glass of the window suggests that the look of women has been 'let in' to rejoin that of the two women protagonists, thus creating a women's gaze, whose function is to critique Michel's stereotypical display of male violence. There is more than a critique in fact, since the only extreme close-up in the sequence is of Michel's bloodied hands, held over his genital area. The violence of the male has well and truly been castrated by the female gaze constructed by the cinematography. Indeed, there is a small detail during the sequence which a first viewing does not show, but which is nevertheless clear. In shot 12, as Michel rages in front of two mirrors on the wall to his left, two women can be seen in the mirror closest to the camera. These women are not Madeleine and Léna, but members of the film crew, who also watch Michel attentively, but rapidly move out of shot as Michel jumps across the field of vision. Michel is thus surrounded by women gazing at him attentively, as he rampages in the shop.

A female perspective is therefore established by the ransacking of the shop. It is emphasized by the sequence which follows. Michel visits Costa, just as Léna had earlier in the film, to find out where the women have gone to. The sequence emphasizes male solitude in contrast to female solidarity. It is a mirror scene, but unlike the mirrors in the shop, where Madeleine and Léna looked at themselves together, Michel has his back to the mirror and grunts in response to Costa's question, suggesting by comparison with female bonding scenes that there is very little empathy between the two men. The fall of the male is highlighted by the play in which Costa is acting, *Ruy Blas*, by Victor Hugo. The dialogue we overhear is from Act I, Scene iii; Costa plays a Falstaffian nobleman who has seen better times, and who is about to be abducted and sold to pirates. The undermining of Costa is of course constant throughout the film, whether it be his attempts to sell questionable items, such as the stolen Modigliani, the untrainable dog Tito which turns out to be a bitch, or the consignment of US Army shirts with one sleeve only, or whether it be the way in which he is ridiculed by the two women for his attempts as a mime artist.

To recap, the film is less lesbian than woman-centred. It is woman-centred by virtue of its ridiculing and rejection of the men in the film. In this respect, the combination of lesbianism and nostalgia has a crucial part to play, since both help to emphasize that rejection. Lesbianism, however implicit, clearly suggests exclusion of the men. Nostalgia provides a historical frame which emphasizes lesbianism in the sense that social structures in the 1950s clearly made lesbianism more problematic than in the more liberated 1980s. Audience awareness of social constraints turns even implicit lesbianism into a heroic struggle for affirmation, at the same time as it legitimizes that implicitness by suggesting that two women in this position could not have been open about their relationship. The woman-centredness of the film is brought into question, however, by the final sequence, which reunites male and female perspectives in the wistful gaze of the child, despite the fact that narratively the sequence reiterates and emphasizes the exclusion of the male.

NOSTALGIA, RETROSPECTION, AND AMBIVALENCE

The final sequence of the film is ambiguous in its presentation of a woman-centred perspective, since the strong feeling of nostalgia which it conjures up is nostalgia for both father and mother. There is no reason why a woman-centred perspective should exclude the possibility of nostalgia for the father, were it not for the fact that that perspective has been predicated on the exclusion of the father and the patriarchal law he represents. I shall first discuss how the final sequence, which begins with Léna and Michel's discussion at twilight overlooking the beach, constructs nostalgia for both father and mother, before turning to some final theoretical considerations.

There is a series of shot-reverse-shots of Michel and Léna broken by a medium long shot which introduces one of their daughters. This shot establishes the father as the object of the daughter's gaze, reintroducing the male as object of affection for the daughter, and therefore, at least potentially, as object of identification for the spectators. And yet three shots in particular reaffirm the female perspective. In the first, the camera pans right to frame the mother looking at her daughter. In the second, the daughter stares out to sea, just like her mother in the preceding shots. And in the third, Léna stares directly at the camera, which we assume to be in the daughter's position given that it is framed by shots of the daughter. These shots, then, are maintaining the female perspective, mapping daughter onto mother onto film-maker. On the other hand, ambiguity is is reintroduced in the two following shots, which echo the earlier close-ups of Michel and Léna, suggesting the mapping of daughter onto mother; but at the same time the position of the camera suggests that the daughter might just as well be looking longingly at her father as at the sea.

The final shot of the film carries an epigraph which tends to emphasize the father at the mother's expense. It reads: 'My father left at dawn. He never saw my mother again.' The epigraph could have read 'I/my mother never saw my father again.' The epigraph carries on: 'It is now two years since Madeleine died. To the three of them I dedicate this film', which merely confirms, by its final sentence, the attachment to the father at the same moment as it unequivocally establishes the nostalgic retrospection of the child's view.

It has to be said, of course, that in attempting to prove my point about the establishment of a woman-centred perspective, I omitted evidence which prepares the spectator psychologically for the return to the father. In spite of ridicule, Costa is ultimately presented as an endearing fool. As Madeleine says early on in the film, if she and Costa got married, it was because he made her laugh, as he also does the spectator in the bungled mime sequence. Equally, and more persuasively, given that the exclusion of the male centres principally upon him, Michel is not just presented negatively in his violence and possessiveness, but as a caring father to his children. This is in contrast to both Madeleine, whom we see more often than not berating her son, and even to Léna during the picnic sequence, where she complains when Michel and the girls play ball while she reads. We can add to this the section of the film where the two women forget one of Léna's children in the street due to their excitement over their common project of the shop. A wistful return to the father is then psychologically motivated for the spectator.

Nostalgia, and more particularly nostalgia for the father, and lesbianism are therefore far from being mutually exclusive. On the contrary, they are interdependent, functioning to emphasize the rejection of the male perspective, lesbianism by its exclusiveness, and nostalgia by its historical valorization of that exclusiveness. The fact that nostalgia in the film includes the male perspective as much as it apparently excludes it suggests ambivalence, in the Kleinian sense of the word. Ambivalence for Klein goes hand in hand with splitting mechanisms in the depressive position, which, as we saw in the chapter on *Un dimanche à la campagne*, is crucial to nostalgia. Klein defines the depressive position as 'processes of introjection and projection [which], since they are dominated by aggression and anxieties which reinforce each other, lead to fears of persecution by terrifying objects. To such fears are added those of losing . . . loved objects' (Klein 1986: 150). She explains how, the closer the good and bad objects come together in the adaptation to reality, the more they are split into further good and bad objects as a means of defence. As the ego gradually adapts to reality, and this mechanism applies not just to the infant, but also, as Klein reminds us, to the general process of mourning at any stage of life, the less defined the splitting becomes:

The unification of external and internal, loved and hated, real and imaginary objects is carried out in such a way that each step in the unification leads again to a renewed splitting of the imagos. But as the adaptation to the external world increases, this splitting is carried out on planes which gradually become increasingly nearer and nearer to reality. This goes on until love for the real and the internalized objects and trust in them are well established. Then ambivalence, which is partly a safeguard against one's own hate and against the hated and terrifying objects, will in normal development again diminish in varying degrees. (Klein 1986: 143–4)

The ambivalence I have indicated in the film, the interdependent rejection and inclusion of the male perspective, is thus understandable as a function of nostalgia, insofar as nostalgia is constructed like mourning. It is both a protection against and a reparation of the lost object.

In plainer, but oversimplified terms, the film criticizes the father (this constitutes the protective function), while at the same time longing for his imagined return (the mourning for and imagined reparation of the lost object). Nostalgia, by its very constitution as a process, requires the kind of splitting procedure exemplified by this conjunction of rejection and inclusion of the father. The spectator is placed in a position of mourning which attempts to reintegrate what has been lost: the good objects, the parents before the separation, as the opening sequences also suggest with their emphasis on loss (Léna's mother, her friend's husband, Madeleine's husband) and separation (the difficulties Léna and Michel have in making contact). *Coup de foudre* may have been read as lesbian by some spectators, *faute de mieux*. Ultimately, however, lesbianism is displaced not just by lack of explicitness, but also by the work of the camera and editing, which establishes nostalgia for the lost father as a major part of the film's concerns. The crisis of masculinity dominates even films which might have been thought to escape the mould.

7

The *Polar*

THE *polar*, or police thriller, is one of the staple genres of French cinema. In 1980, for example, 24 of the 160 French or majority French co-productions were *polars* (15 per cent). Their popularity can be gauged by the fact that of the 159 films (including US films) in the period 1980–87 to have more than 500,000 spectators in Paris, 16 were *polars* (10 per cent). It is a genre which has often been seen as a rite of passage for young film-makers, because a *polar* is assured of a reasonable success. A number of young film-makers began their careers at the beginning of the decade with *polars*, and went on to become well established: Arcady with *Le Grand Pardon* (1982), Beineix with *Diva* (1980), Béhat with *Urgence* (1985), Missiaen with *Tir groupé* (1982).

THE *POLAR* AND IDEOLOGY

French commentators considered that the *polar* was in a period of renewal in the 1980s, due in part to the decline of a readily identifiable auteur cinema, and in part to the eclipse of 1970s oppositional cinema. As one critic put it, 'the wave of French *polars* is due to the chronic absence of subjects in the traditional fictions, as if the *polar* had inherited from the bereavement of left-wing fiction' (Tesson 1985: 117). That it could do so is because it is uniquely placed by its subject-matter to articulate socio-political concerns, as the major French writer on the genre points out:

Like any film, the *film policier* reflects the society of its time. But by revealing what happens behind the façade, by evoking taboos, by chronicling changes in the law, in the nature of crime and its repression, it no doubt reflects that society more faithfully than any other genre. (Guérif 1981: 31)

It is also, by virtue of its complex history, uniquely placed to articulate questions of national identity in relation to the USA, or, more precisely, American culture.

Historically, the *polar* is a complex interweaving of literary and filmic strands which intersect with French and American literary and film genres. On the French side, Gothic and realist novels in the French tradition (Balzac and Hugo) lead to the *romans policiers* of the early twentieth century, which translate filmically into the early Fantômas films by Feuillade (1913–14), and the later Maigret films (1930s–1940s). On the American side, there is equally a combination of the literary (the hard-boiled novels of Hammett and Chandler) and the filmic (Hollywood gangster films of the 1930s, and films noirs of the 1940s and 1950s). The two sets come together in the translation of novels by Hammett and Chandler in Gallimard's *série noire* from 1947 onwards, leading to many film adaptations in France (see Guérif 1981: 17–31). Given this complex history, it is understandable that the shock of post-war Americanization should be reflected in the *polar*, since, as Forbes points out:

The thriller . . . provides an excellent vehicle for describing, criticizing and coming to terms with modernization. As is well known, the emergence of the detective story as a genre is linked with industrialization, the growth of cities, the crimes associated with urbanization and the mechanisms of policing developed to cope with them. (Forbes 1992: 74)

During the 1980s, a further factor played an important role in defining the strategic importance of the *polar*. French cinema in the 1980s, Hayward suggests, is all 'style, be it retro-nostalgic or hi-tech . . . At the interface between nostalgia and hi-tech, because they will be astride the two categories, come the *polars*' (Hayward 1993a: 284). Nostalgia for a vanishing way of life combined with American-inspired high-tech: the *polar* faces Janus-like in two directions, as we shall see in some of the chapters which follow. This can be seen not just in terms of general style, but also in terms of the *polar*'s subject-matter, which changed from the 1970s to the 1980s.

The defining characteristics of the political thriller of the 1970s were disillusion and paranoia. This could be seen both in the honest cop, obliged to obey orders from above, who became a prisoner of his situation, and 'in the absence of the heroism from which the lawgivers, inspired by the American tradition, derived their charm, as well as the lack of a moral ending that was so common in the 1950s' (Forbes 1992: 61). In the 1980s, the old-style French cop became a US-style cop, increasingly indistinguishable from the criminals, exemplified, as Guérif and Mérigeau point out, by the actor Alain Delon: 'Delon is thus the link between the American tradition of the private detective, fighting both crime and institutionalized police, and a contemporary trend which has seen the cop become like the dropouts he is pursuing' (Guérif and Mérigeau 1982: 71–2), as can be seen, for example, in the Mangin/Depardieu of Pialat's *Police* (1985). More caustically, Tesson considers that the new type of *polar* 'has turned the crime squad into a band of trendy young private detectives, both outside the police by their "look" and inside by their functions' (Tesson 1985: 118), as is clear in the immensely successful *La Balance* (1982), awarded a César for best film in 1983, and the eighth most popular French film of 1982. Indeed, *La Balance* is a good example of what Hayward, amongst others, calls the ultra-codification of the genre:

The genre drops the 1970s tradition of referring to contemporary reality such as the political scene, police malaise and error, including fighting each other at cross-purposes. In general, the French *polar* has now fallen under the influence of the American and Italian thrillers to the extent that it has become ultra-codified so that it cannot breathe. The film might well be redolent with ambiguity and cynicism as it starts off, but it is unable to sustain the clichés/codes and so, not knowing where to go, often ends in a blood bath or with some unrealistic compromise. (Hayward 1993*a*: 290)

These comments, it should be said, apply more to mainstream *polars*, such as *La Balance*, and less to the *polars* produced by younger directors such as Beineix and Besson. The work of these directors to some extent remythologized a flagging genre, as Tesson points out, but at a cost:

When Melville filmed *Bob le flambeur*, he needed a very precise district (Pigalle), and its décor (bars, striptease joints). Sign of the times, the districts have been replaced by new clichés: car-parks and lofts . . . Although the *polar* has managed to remythologize via the décor, which is immediately fetishized (*Diva*) . . . it suffers on the other hand from poor screenplay . . . The scriptwriters of the *polar* manifestly no longer know how to write dialogue which *constructs a story*. It's either the punchy sloganeering of advertising or knowing commentary where the writers distance themselves from the story, above the genre and the characters, and wink collusively at the spectator. (Tesson 1985: 117–18; his emphasis)

The effect referred to by Tesson might well be called the pastiche effect which is so much part of postmodern culture, and which can be seen in several of the films which I shall explore in later chapters, whether it be the affectionate pastiche of *série noire* as well as of his own earlier films by Truffaut in *Vivement dimanche!* (1983), or the complex intertextual collages of the *cinéma du look*, as exemplified in the work of Beineix, Besson, and Carax. In such work, to recall Jameson's definition of the postmodern text, 'depth is replaced by surface, or multiple surfaces (what is often called intertextuality is in that sense no longer a matter of depth)' (Jameson 1993: 70), and 'pastiche eclipses parody' (Jameson 1993: 73). Since the difference between the two is not necessarily clear-cut, it is worth quoting Jameson's attempt to differentiate between them:

Pastiche is, like parody, the imitation of a peculiar mask, speech in a dead language: but it is a neutral practice of such mimicry, without any of parody's ulterior motives, amputated of the satiric impulse, devoid of laughter and of any conviction that alongside the abnormal tongue you have momentarily borrowed, some healthy linguistic normality still exists. (Jameson 1993: 74)

The difference between *Vivement dimanche!* and the films of the *cinéma du look* is precisely one of film language. The *cinéma du look* articulates a change in film language, which focuses in particular on the status of the film image, inscribing it within the trajectory of postmodern culture, as defined by writers such as Jameson and Baudrillard: the image as simulacrum, the image without origin, endlessly reproduced and recognized as already present in the culture, and therefore always already a pastiche, steeped in the irony of the loss of origins. As this comment suggests, the films of the *cinéma du look* are predicated on nostalgia, their narratives and the films they gesture to suggesting retrospection, as we shall see. But the key word is 'irony', because such films inscribe images or narratives from previous films in ways which are playfully ironic. The question to bear in mind for the films of the *cinéma du look* is whether the nostalgia generated by retrospection is an uncritical reinscription of the past and past values, an empty gesture, or a more critical reworking and rethinking of the past. It is tempting to suggest that old New Wave directors such as Truffaut and Godard use intertextual references more critically than directors such as Besson and Beineix. However, when Truffaut in

Vivement dimanche! includes affectionate references to his previous films, or Godard in *Détective* includes equally affectionate references to Hollywood B-movies, his own films, and other New Wave films, I am not convinced that this is anything other than postmodern gesture, as empty as references to *Citizen Kane* in Beineix's *Diva*. Without wanting to appear merely iconoclastic, I would like to suggest that some films of the *cinéma du look* use intertextuality more productively than might have seemed to be the case for disaffected French critics in the 1980s. My essays on *Subway* and *Mauvais Sang* (1986) will attempt to show how intertextuality serves as a structuring device rather than as the sentimental retrospection of Truffaut's *Vivement dimanche*! This generates a nostalgia which is more critical than, say, Tavernier's pitch for the French *tradition de qualité* in *Un dimanche à la campagne*. My reappraisal of the *cinéma du look*, however, needs to be placed in the context of what 1980s commentators did not like about it, and that will be the subject of the next part of this introduction, where I shall explore the debate concerning the film image, and its ideological implications.

THE CRISIS OF THE FILM IMAGE

In the early 1980s, French cinema was doing well commercially. Between 1981 and 1982 the number of people going to see films in France had increased by 6.84 per cent; some 200 million spectators for 1982 was the best score since 1968. Nor was this increase purely for American films, since French films had attracted 49.6 per cent of the public in 1981 and this had increased to 53.3 per cent in 1982 (this was to change by the mid-1980s). This success was, however, at the expense of art-house and auteur films. If French films did well, it was usually because of carefully orchestrated publicity and the newish marketing manœuvre of saturating cinema theatres with a film for a very short period of time. In 1972, for example, only five films were showing in twenty theatres in the Paris region, whereas in 1982, *L'As des as* (a Belmondo vehicle) was showing in 52 in the Paris region, and 300 nationally (Carrère 1983: 6). The complaint made by critics was the old chestnut of quality versus quantity, coupled with a suspicion of advertising not just in the promotion of films, but in the way that it seemed to be infiltrating the world of film, first institutionally, by the increasing number of directors involved in the making of commercials, and second, by the use of advertising images in the films of younger directors such as Beineix.

It should be said, however, that the increasing involvement of film directors with the advertising world was certainly not confined to the younger generation of directors, who, apart from Beineix (commercial spots: Scotch, Valentine paints, Stéfanel; public service commercials: an AIDS commercial; Sécurité Routière; Médecins du Monde), include Gainsbourg (Lux, Brandt, Woolite, Gini, Lee Cooper, Maggi, etc.) or Jean-Pierre Rappeneau (Vie Active). Chabrol made spots for Winston cigarettes, the Renault 5, and others (Schifres 1983: 42). Indeed, one of the leading directors of the 1980s, Chatiliez, was the leading director of advertising shorts prior to his first feature film, *La Vie est un long fleuve tranquille*. The French reaction to the impact of advertising is perhaps all the more strong since advertising on television only became possible from 1968 onwards, whereas in the UK it had started in 1955, and had attracted many British directors. In the eyes of many critics, however, the involvement of younger directors such as Beineix in advertising was what had led to the deterioration of the film image. Since *Diva* has been called the first French postmodern film (by Fredric Jameson), and it inaugurated the *cinéma du look*, it is appropriate to focus on reactions to it to gauge the change it seemed to bring, before exploring the debate on the image which followed in the mid-1980s.

Critical reactions to *Diva* were either cautious or overtly hostile. The photography and décor were generally praised, but it was pointed out that the film was quite obviously mannered and excessive in its iconography: 'Mannered, recherché, emphatic . . . resplendent gratuitousness of the image . . . fascination for good-looking compositions . . . exaggerated taste for the unusual' (Bosséno 1981: 30). At best, it was said, this was at the expense of a message: '[The] preeminence of the image . . . is at the expense of meaning, of the "message" which is expected from more or less every film nowadays' (Ramasse 1981: 68). At worst, the *Cinématographe* reviewer tartly wrote, 'you think you are watching a film; you are just window-shopping', a charge levelled by several other reviewers (Cuel 1981: 76). The *Cahiers du cinéma* reviewer astutely pointed to a paradox: one of the film's strengths might be its quality of strangeness, but in this it was disappointing because it was less troubling (the hallmark of strangeness) than familiar (Sainderichain 1981: 66). It is this familiarity, the feeling that the images of *Diva* are already seen, that was at the core of the discussion in the pages of *Cahiers du cinéma* during the remainder of the 1980s.

This was sparked off by confrontations between Beineix and film critics during the 1983 Cannes Film Festival, where Beineix had entered his second film, *La Lune dans le caniveau* (1983). By the time the film was shown, Beineix had attracted the reputation of a difficult director who had problems with his actors and his producers. When the principal actor of *La Lune dans le caniveau*, Depardieu, expressed reservations about the film, and a disobliging private comment by the director of Gaumont films, which was producing the film, was made public, the uneasiness which some reviewers and critics had felt for *Diva* became outright hostility (cf. Parent 1989: 192–6). *La Lune dans le caniveau*, was roundly booed at Cannes, and this as much as anything caused its subsequent commercial failure. In the fracas at Cannes, Beineix made stubbornly provocative comments in the defence of his film, which rejected the concerns of traditional French cinema as outdated, and appealed to apparently amoral concerns connected with an attraction to what appeared to be the concern of advertising, the image. These were seized upon by writers associated with *Cahiers du cinéma* who inaugurated a serious discussion about the changes occurring in French cinema. Beineix's comments were reported in an article of 1983 by Alain Bergala:

> When Beineix declared to whoever was prepared to listen that he 'couldn't give a shit about truth' and that he wanted to create a cinema of the Image, which would at last correspond to 'the exploding of morality and dogma', he couldn't have made it clearer that he wants to put an end, once and for all, to the old modern cinema—which he wants nothing to do with—and wants to announce the new cinema of his dreams, the cinema of advertising commercials and videoclips, an art of the Image as seduction and magic, all surface. (Bergala 1983: 5)

It is worth pausing for a moment to consider what might lie behind the acerbic tone of these comments.

Traditionally, French cinema's concern, both theoretical, whether addressed by Bazin in the 1950s or Godard in the 1970s and 1980s, and practical, whether this was achieved through Bazinian realism or Godardian avant-gardism, was the revelation of some kind of Truth, either with the help of the image (Bazin and realism), or through the image, seen as a ruse, as make-believe (e.g. Bresson, or Godard). Beineix's position seemed to imply an acceptance of surface, an interest in the image for its own sake, a pleasure not in the discovery of Truth, but in the play and circulation of images from a variety of sources, whether from videoclips, or from advertising images. The image in the *cinéma du look* became crystal clear, the objects within it isolated, a mannerism transferred from advertising's need to highlight its product (one thinks of the objects in Gorodish's flat, for example), and placed in startling juxtaposition with other objects, in line with advertising practice which uses such juxtapositions to renew the product it is promoting, to give it the strangeness of novelty which it may lack in its own right (e.g. the obtrusive bottle of Martini placed on a clumsy metal drill in Jules's flat as he and Alba listen to the recording of the diva). Film narrative changed as well, becoming more like videoclips, with elliptical and rapid montage (e.g. the establishing shots of the lighthouse in *Diva*), and with a penchant for references to older film styles and periods, in particular the 1940s and 1950s, as with the use of film noir, with Bogart and Bacall look-alikes, to sell Winston cigarettes, or hi-fi; in *Diva*, for example, the period is alluded to in the décor of Jules's flat, in particular by the limousine mural in Jules's loft. As another critic with a penchant for the window-shopping metaphor put it:

Nobody is taken in, you know that these are images, and you take pleasure in them. You do not look anymore, you simply recognize, as if you were leafing through a catalogue . . . What this shopwindow effect leads to in the end is the impression of a morbid museum catalogue effect; everything that is shown instantly becomes a museum piece. (Chévrie 1987: 28–9)

The result is an all-knowing loss of innocence even as the innocence of youth is striven for. The films of the *cinéma du look* are fundamentally films for the young: neo-Romantic heroes stricken by *amour fou* in a fairy-tale world of stereotypical gangsters and heroines, who are just sufficiently strange to give piquancy to the stereotypes they incarnate. Peculiarly, even the innocence which these films strive for is undermined by a weary cynicism. In *Diva*, for example, Gorodish says to Jules, 'there are no innocent pleasures' (*Diva*, 35). This is coupled with self-irony. For example, when Jules asks Alba what manner of place Gorodish has taken them to after Jules has been shot, Alba answers, as she pretends that the two apples she is playing with are breasts, 'the castle of the witch who makes poisoned red apples for the toothpaste commercial for filmstars' (*Diva*, 74). The characters of these films are derisive, as Beineix himself was fond of saying. Talking about *37°, 2 le matin* (1986), for example, although the comments apply equally to all of his films, he said that 'the action is perhaps a conventional comic action, but it goes off the rails and you suddenly find yourself deep in derision, in total absurdity' (Beineix 1985: 59), characterizing the tone of the film as 'a romanticism in which you no longer believe' (Beineix 1987: 43). Beineix's characters, Prédal suggests, although this could be said of the *cinéma du look* generally, 'manage at one and the same time to take themselves terribly seriously and to look at themselves from the outside, turning their integration into their environment into a merely relative one' (Prédal 1991: 468). The ideological function of the *cinéma du look* thus becomes clearer: it is a vehicle for the expression of a marginal and anomic consciousness by the younger generation. As Hayward points out, this attitude was due to the loss of credibility of the Socialist government, elected in 1981 on a platform of social reforms, but soon becoming indistinguishable from the right-wing government which preceded it. The result was that the political cinema of the 1970s was replaced by 'an apolitical cinema that was designer- and consumer-led' (Hayward 1993*a*: 233).

The essays in this section will attempt to shift the discussion of the 1980s polar away from this socio-political perspective, however, towards an investigation of what film noir and police thriller have traditionally been seen to mediate: a crisis in masculinity.

8

Vivement dimanche! Or How to Take Away with One Hand What you Give with the Other

CRITICS saluted Truffaut's *Vivement dimanche!* as a lightweight but fitting conclusion to his career: lightweight because it is a pastiche of film noir, fitting because it pays homage not only to film noir, but also, by its many references, to Truffaut's mentor Hitchcock, as well as to Truffaut's own films. To dwell principally on the film as a patchwork of references, however, obscures one of the main problems raised by it, namely that the film is riven apart not so much by a multiplicity of intertextual references as by a substantial fracture (of which intertextuality forms only a part), not untypical of film noir: that between the dominant male narrative style of the genre and the attempt to place the Fanny Ardant/ Barbara character into the dominant narrative position. Curiously, though, the fracturing is ambivalent. The dominance given to Fanny Ardant/Barbara is undermined by a variety of narrative and stylistic devices which reimpose a patriarchal framework, thus denying or minimizing her dominance.

INTERTEXTUALITY

Truffaut published a book of interviews with Hitchcock (Truffaut 1968). This, combined with the general admiration of the New Wave directors for Hitchcock, explains the urge of many reviewers to see references to Hitchcock in *Vivement dimanche!*, *Vertigo* (1958) and *Saboteur* (1942), for example (Trémois 1983: 13, who confuses *Saboteur* with *Sabotage* (1936)). In the case of *Vertigo*, the central character is confined to a wheelchair and tended by two women, a nurse and his fiancée, and observes what he considers to be the murder by a neighbour of the neighbour's wife. The film revolves around his attempt to persuade others that what he thinks he has seen is the truth. In the case of *Saboteur*, a young munitions worker is accused of sabotage; he escapes from the police and meets a girl who at first wants to turn him in, but then decides to help him. Roddick sees similarities with *The Trouble with Harry* (1954) (Roddick 1983–4: 61). There are references to other films of course: the shooting sequence could be a reference to Renoir's *La Règle du jeu* (1939) (Lardeau 1983: 56), the watch ticking on the wrist of Julien's murdered wife a reference to Franju's *Thomas l'imposteur* (1964) (Adair 1983: 313). There are also strong parallels with Robert Siodmak's *Phantom Lady* (1944). A business-man is accused of his wife's murder; only his secretary believes him to be innocent. She dresses as a floozie, wearing a dress remarkably similar to Barbara's in *Vivement dimanche!*, so as to get information from a musician who takes her to a sleazy jam session (which is echoed by *Vivement dimanche!*'s nightclub). She eventually discovers that the murderer is the businessman's best friend.

It is to Truffaut's own films that commentators have pointed most systematically. Barbara Becker's typewriter is a carbon copy of the typewriter stolen by Antoine Doinel in *Les 400 coups* (1959); the hotel room in *La Peau douce* (1964) is also number 813 (Trémois 1983: 13); the detective agency plays an important part in *Baisers volés* (1968) (Le Guay 1983: 37). Barbara's theatrical stand-in recalls *Le Dernier Métro* (1980), as indeed does the general situation of a main male character (the theatre director in *Le Dernier Métro*) forced into hiding and powerless while his female companion takes charge (Le Guay 1983: 38). The solicitor's telephone confession recalls *L'Homme qui aimait les femmes* (1977) (Le Guay 1983: 38), as do the shots of women's legs (Trémois 1983: 13). And, finally, there are the names: Massoulier, the murdered man, is a name mentioned at the beginning of *Le Dernier Métro*; Julien is the Christian name of the main character in *La Chambre verte* (1978) (Allen 1986: 213), and Becker, Barbara's surname, is the name of the schoolteacher that Julie Kohler impersonates in *La Mariée était en noir* (1967), as well as being the name of the director of one of the great post-war *polars*, Becker's *Touchez pas au grisbi* (1954).

The film is then a good example of the pastiche inherent in postmodern culture. As I mentioned above, however, the dis-locations which intertextuality may lead to pale in comparison with the major, and intended, fracture in film genres. Truffaut said that *Vivement dimanche!* mixed two genres, film noir and screwball comedy, characterizing it in one interview as 'a nocturnal rain-soaked film, with the atmosphere of the *série noire* and American comedy' (Guérif 1987: 5), and in another as 'thriller and comedy of the sexes' (Rabourdin 1985: 191). I shall use this polarity as my guiding thread in the following discussion which will focus on the two apparently incompatible texts whose interplay structures the film: Charles Williams's novel and the Victor Hugo play in which Barbara has a part.

Truffaut said he chose Williams's novel because it 'tells a criminal story from the heroine's point of view' (Rabourdin 1985: 9). This is manifestly not the case. The novel is a first-person narrative told by the hero, Duke Warren. A typical film noir would have had a (male) voice-over to approximate the narrative voice, which is not the case in *Vivement dimanche!* It is, however, true that *Vivement dimanche!* is more obviously narrated from the heroine's point of view than the novel. The opening shots are of Barbara on the sunlit streets of a southern French town, for example. And the second sequence, that of the shooting by the lakeside, leaves the spectator in the same sort of doubt as Barbara will be seen to have as to whether Julien is guilty or not. But it is not just the narrative voice which operates in Barbara's favour. All of the major changes to the novel have one thing in common: they minimize or ridicule minor characters, and devolve most of the action to Barbara.

For example, the police in the story are represented by the clichéd pair of the world-weary sheriff who is older and wiser and has seen it all before, and his young brutish deputy (Mulholland) whom Duke Warren detests partly because Mulholland had acted in an amateur production of *Detective Story* with Warren's wife. In *Vivement dimanche!* only one policeman, Santelli, plays a significant role. Mulholland's role as the presumed lover of Warren's wife disappears, but the amateur theatrics are retained in the form of Barbara and her ex-husband who are rehearsing a play by Victor Hugo.

A second example is the role of Doris, ex-lover of the murdered man, Dan Roberts, who works at the Crown (movie) Theatre. In the novel Doris holds the missing piece of the jigsaw, the identity of the murderer. Her confession to the police, one of the set pieces of the novel, disappears in the film. The result is that Barbara is no longer mostly a bystander or collaborator in the solution to the mystery since in the film she figures the jigsaw out completely by herself.

Barbara's dominant role is stressed by the fact that she takes over the detection at an early stage of the film, whereas in the novel she does so only at the end of the tenth chapter (out of a total of twelve chapters), provoking the comment from Warren that for the first time in his life he 'depended totally on others' (Williams 1963: 156; the novel is not currently available in the original English-language text).

Barbara's dominant role is the main reason, it would seem, for the introduction of the play rehearsal. The play, *Le Roi s'amuse*, was written by Victor Hugo in 1832 and banned after one performance, although many spectators would know the story as the basis for Verdi's opera *Rigoletto*. It is the story of the jester of François I, king of France, detested by the courtiers for his gibes and for his procurement of their wives as lovers for the King. The jester, Triboulet, who is played by Barbara's ex-husband in the rehearsal, has a daughter, Blanche, who is played by Barbara. Triboulet's love for his daughter is extreme, indeed almost incestuous, hence the producer's comment to Barbara when she complains that her ex-husband is pawing her that Hugo 'didn't have anything against incest' (*Vivement dimanche!*, 92). He keeps Blanche hidden away for fear that she might be corrupted. The King discovers her and rapes her. She nevertheless loves him, and Triboulet's plan to wreak revenge on the King backfires when Blanche overhears the murder plot and takes the King's place. She does so dressed as a man. The situation thus parallels that of the film narrative. The function of the play within the film is to underline Barbara's assumption of a male role (that of the detective) and the rejection of father-husband tutelage, at the same time as it underlines her allegiance to a new male, Julien.

This allegiance is ironically emphasized by the first rehearsal scene. We have just seen Julien insulted by an anonymous phone-caller; we are in some doubt as to whether he is innocent or not of Massoulier's murder. A shot of his worried face cuts to Barbara declaiming a speech which is a hyperbolic declaration of love to the King, of whose presence she is unaware. Since she has had an argument with Julien as a result of his wife's phone-call, there is no reason why we should think that this declaration is directed to Julien, were it not for the fact that the pairing of Ardant/ Trintignant in what is at least partly a 'light' film suggests the boy-meets-girl topos. Our suspicions will be confirmed subsequently, when we see her worry at the news that Julien is the prime suspect. Our task as spectators runs parallel to the detective story narrative in that we are asked to detect the solution, or rather resolution, of the argument which separated Julien and Barbara.

The second rehearsal scene emphasizes the point of the first, Barbara's bid for freedom from her ex-husband. It is taken from an earlier point of the same act from the play when Triboulet is drooling over his daughter. Barbara's ex-husband takes the opportunity to fondle her, and she complains about it. Julien is waiting in the wings, however, and takes her away from the theatre. The scene in the film thus parallels that of the play: rejection of Father (her ex-husband), abduction by King-Lover (Julien). The emphasis given to incest in the film during this scene is instructive. As with many films noirs, the heroine marginalizes herself from the constraints of her family to vie with the hero for dominance of the narrative. It is thus logical that as Barbara and Julien discuss the best way of dealing with the situation as they stand in the wings, Triboulet's speech, taken from Act III of the play, is a lament at the loss of his daughter. It is also in the logic of the film that Barbara should be dressed in a page's outfit, since she is taking on a male role. It is, however, not in keeping with the logic of the play, since Blanche only dresses as a man in the final act, whereas the scene rehearsed in the film is the first scene of the play to introduce the extremely virginal Blanche (in Act II). Barbara's costume is therefore introduced to emphasize her assumption of a male role, as will be clear when she becomes a private detective. She will take on a double male role: she is acting a female role impersonating a king, and she will also be dressed like a film noir private detective. The sartorial cross between musketeer and private detective is of course intentionally humorous, and fulfils Truffaut's wish to combine what he saw as the seriousness of film noir with the lightheartedness of screwball comedy.

The third rehearsal scene is even more telling in terms of Barbara's assumption of a male role. She returns to the theatre to find that her role has been taken over by a substitute. The producer hides behind his newspaper so as to avoid looking at her.

Meanwhile she sits on the chair where her ex-husband has left his jacket, becoming the watcher rather than the watched. The thrust of this scene is that Barbara has at last freed herself not only from her husband (who plays her father in the play) but also from the father-figure represented by the producer. Barbara thus becomes the central character of the narrative, and Julien is relegated to a passive role. He is the damsel in distress, the sleeping beauty (incongruously, given his nerve-racking situation, he falls asleep, thus allowing Barbara to take over his role) to Barbara's errant knight. His passivity is emphasized of course by his imprisonment in his office, but this is taken further by a *mise en scène* which suggests a return to childhood: he is seen against the models of houses (he runs an estate agency), suggesting children's games (doll's houses), and he throws childish tantrums. Even the other male characters seem to diminish themselves in one way or another. The police chief has an inferiority complex ('It's not because I am younger than you that I shall let myself be intimidated', he says to Julien); Louison, the pimp, is assumed to be a woman by Barbara. Christine Gledhill's description of the classic film noir as an expression of the crisis of male desire is perhaps the most apt conclusion to what I have said so far:

[The] unstable and fractured characterization of women contribute[s] to the instability and uncertainty of the hero's world; to the ever deceiving flux of appearance and reality. In this sense [such characterizations] express a male existential anguish at the failure of masculine desire. (Gledhill 1980: 18)

PROSTITUTION

The final major change to the novel which I would like to discuss is the introduction of corruption in the form of prostitution, of which there is no mention in the novel. Why was it felt to be necessary? It is, we could argue, a logical necessity of the narrative, in that the construction of the hero by the narrative requires a ritualized passage through symbolic hell, where the hero's identity is called into question. The underworld populated by prostitutes and pimps functions as a rite of passage; Barbara must sacrifice her normal identity to uncover the truth which will unlock the passive male hero's desire. The development of their kissing is instructive in this respect. To his surprise, she kisses Julien in a doorway so that a passing police car will not recognize him. In the following scene on the hilltop he kisses her to her surprise; the rapid dialogue is that of the comedy of the sexes:

Barbara: Why did you kiss me? there are no policemen around.
Julien [*walking back to the car*]: Who knows?
Barbara [*walking back to the car*]: Another mystery (*énigme*). (*Vivement dimanche!*, 144)

The reference to a mystery follows Julien's philosophical musings on death, death due to a crime being 'abstract, as though the solution of the mystery were the first priority'. As Gledhill writes, 'the enquiries of the police or private detective [in film noir] come eventually to concentrate on the state of the hero's, and more frequently, the heroine's heart' (Gledhill 1980: 15). Subtextually, then, the 'mystery' mentioned in this scene is the disappearance of the hero's desire. His desire is not in fact 'another mystery'; it is the fundamental enigma which determines the narrative. In both these scenes, the kissing is a game in which the desire of the players is equal. It is only after Barbara has returned from the underworld that they kiss each other passionately, in what is clearly no longer a game, with Julien laying Barbara down beneath him on the office table, his desire clear and dominant, her desire equally clear and compliant (even though it is she who seems to pull him down on top of her), as is stressed by her position.

A second, perhaps more compelling reason for the introduction of the underworld is the necessity of the genre. Film noir could not function without an emphasis on a combination of criminality and sexuality. Barbara's gradual absorption into that world is carefully prepared. Her arrival late at night in the hotel in Nice without any luggage causes eyebrows to be raised. She subsequently becomes aware, after being stared at by the (male) late-night reveller, that her costume, hidden underneath her mac, could suggest that she was a prostitute dressed up for the enactment of a presumably male fantasy. On her return, as she is trying to think of a way to enter the nightclub, she is accosted by a man who mistakes her for a prostitute. This gives her the idea of penetrating the nightclub by playing just such a role.

Prostitution is introduced when she has assumed the function of the normally male detective, and is investigating the hotel. It is as if the narrative is trying to compensate for Barbara's dominance. After all, film noir does not usually suggest a descent into the underworld for the male hero which involves him becoming a pimp. He may have to assume the same standards as the criminals with whom he is dealing, and appear immoral for the benefit of the truth, but this does not normally question his sexual mores in the way we see here for Barbara. The film is thus fractured. It proposes a strong female character who has assumed all the characteristics of the film noir hero (except his anxiety about the opposite sex), and whose dynamism relegates all the male characters to impotence (she rejects men who accost her, she acts for Julien, she browbeats the policeman, defends herself more than successfully against the detective intruder, and so on). But the film constantly struggles against her hegemony on several different levels.

On the narrative level, she is unquestionably the constant victim of male violence. Julien shouts at her, puts his hand over her mouth to stop her screaming; she is accosted twice in the course of the film; her room is broken into by the detective. The *mise en scène* of the beginning of the scene is important: the shot of the handle turning, accompanied by threatening music and followed by a shot of her worried eyes, encodes the cliché of the helpless woman about to be sadistically attacked. The fact that the detective turns out to be a frightened mouse, thus undermining the cliché, does not necessarily invalidate the point I am making: that the break-in forms part of a consistent pattern of male aggression. Perhaps the best example of this is the scene with Louison where Barbara is slapped and hurled to the ground for questioning Louison's gender (the worst possible insult according to him). This echoes an earlier scene in the film where Julien slaps Barbara as punishment for her assumption of his role which has made him immobile and therefore impotent. The point I am making is curiously, and graphically, illustrated by an English review of the film in which one-quarter of the review dwells on the face-slapping:

Miss Ardant enjoyed her latest Truffaut outing in which she co-starred with Jean-Louis Trintignant but revealed that when she had to have her face slapped for a crucial scene M. Trintignant was not man enough for it. She said: 'He would not do it so Truffaut said he must do it himself. In the film you see the hand of Truffaut slap my face. In the shooting seven times he had to do it. Yes, it became a little painful'. (Owen 1983: 27)

We find the same pattern as the one I have traced in the narrative of the film: a female hero who makes the males pale, and who must therefore be disciplined.

On the level of the *mise en scène*, Barbara is constantly being framed, most particularly through doors. The best example of framing is at the theatre when a door-prop is shifted (by two men), while her ex-husband walks through it (a similar gag was used by Godard in *Le Mépris* (1963)). They place the door in such a way that Barbara is perfectly framed in her page-boy outfit, the emphasis being on her legs. The scene encapsulates her fractured characterization. She may well be a proto-male with her equivocal costume, but she is above all the typical film noir fatale, her sexuality signalled by her long legs. At the same time as she is framed by the door as an object of male consumption, the point is emphasized that she cannot escape through the door, whereas her ex-husband can. A second, although problematic, example of framing is the shot of Barbara's face through the window of the nightclub. It is no ordinary window, however, since what she looks through is the image of a naked woman. This visual conceit is problematic because Barbara is in the position of the normally male detective voyeur, gazing through the object of voyeuristic fantasy, the body of a woman. The implication would seem to be that she is escaping the framing device. But in fact, one can argue that the device equates her eyes with what we cannot see of the rest of her body (and which is represented by the naked woman through which she gazes). The framing device contains her 'male' voyeurism, reminding the spectator that she also represents a fantasized female body.

COMEDY

The disruption of the film's discourse by humorous elements and intertextuality equally prevents the possibility of Barbara's strong character being taken seriously. Film noir discourse is not normally disrupted by comical elements (at least not intentionally), nor by constant references to other films. The effect of intertextuality in *Vivement dimanche!*, the fact that the film is constantly saying 'I am not only what I appear to be, but also a patchwork of other films', disrupts the very discourse which seems to be constituting

Barbara as an untypically strong female hero. The same could be said of the comical elements.

There are first disruptive narrative cameos, notably the Albanian refugee in the police station and the one-fingered typist who applies for Barbara's job. Truffaut's own comments on the first scene stress the need for improbable disruptive elements so as to privilege pleasure over maintenance of an otherwise tedious realist narrative:

When you make a film you must have a feeling for the times when realism must be stressed, and those when the spectators' attention must be distracted. Stories are always improbable, but that isn't important as long as pleasure remains dominant. Pleasure must be stronger than analysis . . . The two police-station scenes worried me. Interrogation scenes are so conventional. I tried to follow them with unusual things. In the first scene, there's an Albanian refugee asking for political asylum . . . Such things are a great help to me. They provoke laughter and a sort of relief. But above all, they help to make believable what comes just before and just after them. (Rabourdin 1985: 193–4)

One might accept Truffaut's point here, were it not for the fact that such interventions in the narrative are systematic, and are clearly predicated on his desire to mix two different genres, thriller and comedy. His comments also beg the question of whose pleasure is involved, a question I shall return to in my conclusion.

A second type is slapstick. The second example which Truffaut gives in the above passage is the gushing water-tap, which, apart from being a recall of cinema's origins through Lumière's early film *L'Arroseur arrosé* (1895), is a clear slapstick gag which undermines the sense of seriousness engendered by the protagonists' predicament as well as undermining the police chief's position of authority. Another example of this type is the solicitor lighting a cigarette while the first is still in his mouth, a hyperbolic sign of confusion. The novel simply states: 'I saw George take a cigarette. He noticed that he already had one smoking in the ashtray, and he put the other one back' (Williams 1963: 175).

A third type is a rather self-conscious self-reflexivity. Barbara kisses Julien in a doorway to prevent the police seeing him, and comments, 'I've seen it done in films' (*Vivement dimanche!*, 143). Another example is Julien and Barbara's scene on the hill overlooking the town. In the novel, Duke Warren gets out of the car and surveys the lights below; but he cannot help thinking of the corpses, and climbs back in to take the food and drink offered by

Barbara. In the film, such material concerns vanish as the windswept hero stares into the distance and muses philosophically on death: 'Death is strange isn't it? When people die of an illness, it's unfair, but it's really death. When it's a crime, a murder, an assassination, death becomes abstract, as if solving the mystery becomes the most important thing; as if one were in a thriller' (*Vivement dimanche!*, 144).

The three types of hyperbolic disruption point to the fracture which I have emphasized is at work in the film, a fracture apparently explained by the conjunction of genres, but which I have tried to reinterpret as a symptom of the struggle for dominance of the narrative. Barbara's attempt at dominance is doomed to fail since the film's purpose is to reveal the male protagonist's desire and thus to reinstall him in the dominant narrative position, as would be expected in film noir discourse. This explains the wedding scene, the penultimate scene of the film, which is incongruous for film noir, but clearly acceptable as a resolution for a screwball comedy. Barbara becomes Hugo's virginal heroine Blanche, dressed, as her name implies, in white. She resolves the fracture by giving up her freedom to roam and by accepting the subservient role assigned to her by patriarchal law, a law she had herself helped to re-establish by the tracking down of its crooked representative, the solicitor. She has uncovered the truth of the bad femme fatale (the Hitchcockian blonde wife) who had literally perverted the Law (by becoming the solicitor's lover).

The two opening sequences and the two closing sequences are paradigmatic in this respect. The film opens with Barbara walking down a sunlit street and is set to jaunty music; this is followed by the lake sequence with its mysterious *mise en scène* and soundtrack (from comedy to thriller). At the end of the film, Julien and Barbara are united in a wedding scene framed by a shot of a children's choir before it and a shot of children's feet playing with a lens hood after it. Barbara's role in the film has thus been to divert the male fascination for danger (shooting ducks, and hunting human quarry) into the establishment of a family (the sentimental shot of the children's choir immediately after the deviant solicitor has shot himself; this reverses the opening sequence: from thriller to comedy). The closure established by the wedding thus turns the film away from film noir, whose function is more to question patriarchal values than to support them:

The ideological significance of lovers living happily ever after lies in the unspoken, and usually invisible, metamorphosis that is implied to take place at the end of every happy ending. By means of this metamorphosis lovers are transformed into fathers and mothers, into families. The magic circle of transformation is broken in *film noir* which, in presenting family relations as broken, perverted, peripheral or impossible founds itself upon the absence of the family. (Gledhill 1980: 25).

Vivement dimanche! is a vehicle for the arousing and channelling of male desire into hegemonic patriarchal formations. The pleasure which Truffaut saw as indispensable for the spectators' uncritical acceptance of an improbable narrative is a strictly gendered pleasure, that of male arousal.

9

A Fistful of *Polars*:
Chronicles of Discomfiture

TRUFFAUT'S final film was a *polar*, an affectionate retrospective and regressive gesture to a popular genre refracted through an auteurist lens. In 1985, two other auteurs also made *polars*. Godard's *Détective* opened in May 1985, with the curious combination of Nathalie Baye and the pop singer Johnny Hallyday. A few months later, Pialat, whose 1983 film *A nos amours* (1983) is considered one of the key films of the 1980s, released the starkly titled *Police* (September 1985), starring Depardieu and the then teen idol Sophie Marceau. I shall also be considering in this chapter a more commercial and, to use Hayward's term, ultra-codified *polar* by Bob Swaim, whose brashly American and immensely popular *La Balance* (1982) also starred a miscast Nathalie Baye as a prostitute and Philippe Léotard.

Before engaging with the focus of this chapter, I need to return to comments made in the introduction to this section, so as to justify my focus. There, it was suggested that the wave of *polars* by auteurs and others in the 1980s was due in large part to the demise of 1970s left-wing fiction, the *polar* filling the socio-critical gap by its interest in the notion of the law. While this may be true of Chabrol's *polars* which dissect bourgeois hypocrisy, such as the diptych *Poulet au vinaigre* (1985) and *Inspecteur Lavardin* (1986) starring Jean Poiret, and his much underestimated *Masques* (1987), or of Corneau's key *polars Série noire* (1979) and *Choix des armes* (1981), it is not so true of *Police* and *La Balance*, and still less of *Vivement dimanche!* and *Détective*. *Police* and *La Balance* give the spectator a critical view of the state of French society in the mid-1980s mainly by default, in that their apparent interest is realism.

The opening credits of *La Balance* suggest that the film will be anchored in a contemporary reality:

Faced with an increase in crimes of escalating violence the Criminal Investigation Department created special undercover squads known as 'Brigades Territoriales', the only squads infiltrating the underworld. Each squad relies on their own network of informers without whom they cannot function. The informer is called a 'balance' by the underworld.

Swaim claimed that he had spent six months investigating the 'Brigades Territoriales', saying that his film was 'the French police as it is today. Everything you see on screen is authentic, first and foremost the character of the informer who accounts for 90 per cent of successful police cases in France' (Tchernia 1989: 13).

Like Swaim, Pialat stayed for some time (three months) with the Brigades Territoriales (Pialat 1985*a*: 15), and his film is even more realist by its documentary feel. This is created by the use of non-professional actors, unostentatious camerawork, no non-diegetic music (with one exception to which I shall return), and the omission of the kind of spectacular violence or sexuality associated with the new 1980s *polar* as exemplified by *La Balance*. Whereas in *La Balance*, for example, the hero and heroine's last love-making scene uses non-diegetic rock music, crude back-lighting, close-ups, and slow motion, the scene in the police station in *Police* is allusive; as Pialat pointed out, 'it could have been done in a more trivial manner, with her clothes around her knees or ankles' (ibid. 17). Instead, the camera travels away from the fully clothed couple as they begin to make love. Perhaps most importantly, the documentary feel of *Police* is created by the rejection of classical narrative techniques. The narrative may be more obviously chronological than usual for Pialat, but it is broken up by temporal gaps, the most obvious one being the jump from the night Maxime is stabbed to a hospital scene several months later.

The main interest of *Police* is Depardieu's role, as Pialat himself acknowledged in interviews: 'for me, the character Mangin is certainly what is best about the film' (Pialat 1985*b*: 70). Indeed, Sophie Marceau's role was originally intended to dominate the film, but during filming Depardieu's 'became the main role' (Pialat 1985*c*: 10), and he won a prize for it at the Venice Film Festival of 1985. The relationship is the narrative centre of the film, but the shift of attention to Mangin/Depardieu focuses the film on the male view of the relationship, Noria/Marceau remaining stereotypically enigmatic. Pialat points out that his relationship with Marceau was non-existent (Pialat 1985*a*: 17), and that he, like Depardieu, found her 'intimidating' (ibid.), an epithet repeated in the film's dialogue; life, typically for a Pialat film, shading into art (see Vincendeau 1990).

Similarly, *La Balance* may well be a typical example of the ultra-codified *polar* where 'the corruption of the police is merely a pretext for scenes which flatter the basest instincts of the spectator', where 'everything is geared to effectiveness, to car chases, ambushes or plumbing the depths of convention' (Prédal 1991: 406); but it is also of some interest for the same reason as *Police*: Léotard's role as Dédé. Although the film was panned by the critics, it won the best film award in the 1983 Césars. The two lead actors, Baye and Léotard, also won best actor awards, and Léotard was singled out as the most interesting aspect of the film, the film's few moments of emotion, according to one critic, being due to him (Mérigeau 1982: 38). It is not then by their apparent realism, but by their focus on the male, that I would like to link these films.

Likewise, the two films by the New Wave directors show typically auteurist and similar preoccupations which have very little to do with social critique. *Vivement dimanche!* is a self-referential, self-indulgent exercise in looking back, as Barbara's costume indicates; it is the only *polar* of the period, claims Tesson, with that crucial sartorial signifier, the trenchcoat (Tesson 1985: 117).

Détective's focus is precisely the lack of a subject, an issue debated by Pialat and Godard the previous year in *Le Monde* (reprinted in a volume devoted to Pialat; see Devarrieux 1992). As Godard explained in an interview to the *Cahiers du cinéma* following the release of the film, 'There is no subject and it became transformed into a quest to discover why there was no subject' (Godard 1985: 623). In this respect, the film is not much different from several other films by Godard during the 1980s, such as *Prénom: Carmen* (1984), *Je vous salue Marie* (1985), or *King Lear* (1987), which all take a recognizable 'subject' and dislocate it violently so that the film paradoxically gestures incoherently and as if parabolically at what is posited as a possible coherence, a coherence which in the end is always abrogated (although *Détective*, based only on a genre, rather than a specific text, seems to be little more than the sum of its fragmentary parts). But just as the chapter on *Vivement dimanche!* will have shown how the interest of the film is less its self-referential intertextuality than its engagement with gender issues, so too the interest of *Détective* is the crucifixion of an idol, the pop singer Johnny Hallyday, caught in the fatal intersections of several competing narrative lines.

The purpose of this chapter then is to show how, despite their very different styles, from the archly hyper-realist *Police*, to the equally archly anti-realist *Détective*, to the commercial shock tactics of *La Balance*, there is a common pattern: the discomfiture of the male. I take the term from a *Cahiers du cinéma* interview with Godard following the release of *Détective*. The interviewers suggested that the film was similar to many shown at Cannes in that year, in that 'men are discomfited (*défaits*; literally 'undone', or defeated), men seem to be weak (*il y a une défaillance du mâle*)' (Godard 1985: 620), to which Godard replied, with apparent irrelevance:

It's true that men hardly know how to make films any more. Thankfully part of me is a producer and not just a director. People live in extremely closed universes. It would seem that the women are no longer present in the cinema, that actresses no longer bring what they used to bring with them into the universe of the producers. Women producers neither, incidentally. Men are discomfited, yes, and I have always filmed in the situation in which I find myself. *Détective* is a discomfited screenplay (*un scénario défait*). And I have always started by undoing things (*par défaire*). (ibid.)

All three films are narratives of loss. In *Police*, Mangin loses his lover Noria. In *Détective*, Jim/Hallyday is harried for money from two sides, the pilot and his wife on the one hand, and some gangsters on the other. The man upon whom he is relying, the boxer whom he is promoting and whose fight will allow Jim to raise the required money, leaves him, causing Jim to be killed. In *La Balance*, Dédé is taken into custody for his own protection because he has killed a gangland leader, so losing his cherished freedom. This is presumably what Godard's interviewers might have had in mind when they asked him about 'discomfited males'.

The least subtle example of this is, as might be expected, the least subtle film, the commercially articulated and commercially successful *La Balance*. The César Léotard won was 'the summit of his career' (Brisset 1990: 58). He had begun his career in the early 1970s in small roles with well-known directors: Truffaut's *Deux Anglaises et le continent* (1971), and Miller's *Camille ou la comédie catastrophique* (1971). He carried on with small and eventually second roles at the rate of two or three films a year until his first leads in Pialat's *La Gueule ouverte* (1973), in which he starred with Nathalie Baye, and then in Daniel Duval's *L'Ombre des châteaux* (1976), as an under-privileged delinquent, followed a year later by the lead as a divorced father in François Leterrier's *Va voir Maman, Papa travaille*. In 1979 he led with Nathalie Baye in Eduardo de Gregorio's political drama *La Mémoire courte*, playing a small part with Baye again in Tavernier's *Une semaine de vacances* (1980). After *La Balance*, he once again returned to second roles.

The spectator's fascination for Dédé rests on the fact that he is a complex object of erotic contemplation for the spectator. He is complex because he is coded as the archetypal macho male of the *polar* with his rugged face and rolling gait, his reticence with language, and his bouts of frustrated anger directed towards his lover or objects such as rubbish bins. But he is also coded as the feminized lover. We first see him twenty minutes into the film, introduced in the previous scene by Palouzi's comment that Dédé is 'a good-looking bloke'. In the following scene, Dédé strides towards the camera in a mid-distance low-angle shot, the effect of which is to emphasize the authority of rugged male beauty. He chooses a rose from a stall, introducing the feminized lover, just as Palouzi is saying in voice-over that 'you can't work with a man who's in love'.

The flower may be a banal signifier of love, but it is also a crucial element of the *mise en scène* because it refers the spectator back to the scene where Massina, the gangland boss, is introduced as he arranges flowers in his restaurant. The implication of this *mise en scène* is to draw a parallel between the two men, who had been rivals for Nicole's affections. It is not the only parallel, since both men have an abiding interest in food. We will shortly find out that it is Dédé who does the couple's food shopping and prepares cordon bleu meals with ingredients which Nicole is unable to understand, let alone prepare. Similarly, in the scene where Dédé visits Massina in his restaurant, Massina is authoritatively tasting the food. Why the constant paralleling of these two men?

Both are feminized, but Dédé positively in relation to Massina's negative feminization. For Dédé's feminization to coexist with his machismo, it must be seen to be somehow 'good', particularly since he is at least theoretically a pimp. Only a character coded as more 'bad' can achieve this. Massina's feminization is connoted as 'bad' in two ways. The first is that where the *mise en scène* associated with Dédé is stereotypical and stereotypically 'good'—the red rose—that associated with Massina is connoted as 'bad': the flower is seen in close-up as Massina takes the scissors to it; he then points the scissors menacingly towards his henchman as he places the flower in the henchman's suit pocket, the implication being not love, but death—the henchman's funeral if he does not recover the lost drug money. The second more general way in which Massina's feminization is connoted as 'bad' is in the couples we see. Dédé is frequently seen with Nicole, whereas Massina, although clearly heterosexual in that we know early on that he has slept with Nicole, is never seen in the company of women, but always with his violent second-in-command Petrovic. On the one hand, then, there is the heterosexual couple, stereotypically 'in love'; on the other the all-male criminally more deviant couple (by their aggressivity) of Massina and Petrovic, a couple which highlights the 'goodness' of Dédé and Nicole.

Dédé is complex not just because his stereotypical masculinity is tempered by feminization. A second element, which to some extent works against the feminization, but which emphasizes the erotic display of the male body displaced into violence, is masochistic disfigurement. When first picked up by the police, Dédé has his face rammed into a glass display case. In an early interrogation scene, Dédé repeatedly bangs his head on the desk (so that the policemen could be accused of beating him up), his disfigured face shown in close-up. When later pursued by the police who are unhappy about the time he is taking to give them information which will incriminate Massina, he escapes in the middle of shaving, 'heroically' knocking out several policemen, only to be caught by a rookie, and ridiculed for his facial appearance. He later entertains two of the policemen in a restaurant; they drag him outside, rough him up, and pour seafood over his white suit as a punishment for his delaying tactics. A final example occurs when the young policeman gets badly beaten up by Petrovic. Dédé is blamed for it, and beaten up in turn; he ends up venting his frustration on rubbish bins in the street, and lying in the gutter in the same position as Paulo, the murdered informer of the opening scene. All of these scenes have forms of disfigurement in common, and they bear out Neale's point that ' "male" genres and films constantly involve sado-masochistic themes, scenes, and phantasies', and that the hero in such films is 'marked as the object of an erotic gaze' (Neale 1983: 8).

Dédé fights verbally against the degradation these sado-masochistic scenes encode, but it is aspects of the *mise en scène* which interest me here. In one of the interrogation scenes, Palouzi tries to put a cigarette in the almost naked and handcuffed Dédé's mouth. Dédé reaffirms his autonomy by grabbing the cigarette. The fight scene between Dédé and Massina reaffirms both feminization (Dédé is eating after the heist that went wrong, and 'eating' by this point in the film is clearly associated with a feminized domesticity) and reaction against that feminization, since Dédé will kill Massina by forcing the gun into Massina's mouth. The subtext of the struggle for phallic control is only too evident in the close-ups of the two sweating males locked in an erotic combat whose *mise en scène* echoes Dédé and Françoise's love-making scene. The struggle, moreover, occurs in the outside toilet, connoted as feminine by the washing-lines heavy with drying clothes.

Dédé the feminized lover has fought back to reclaim his lost male authority, only to be turned over to the police for his own safety by Nicole, effectively losing both Nicole and his freedom. Feminization, as well as women, are therefore both established as a potential threat, ready to disfigure the ruggedness of a 'real man'. The most peculiar scene in this respect is the café scene where Dédé shouts at Nicole. Dédé's aggressive outburst initially seems to be part of a twist in the plot. The intuitive reading of this scene is that he is making public a break between himself and Nicole so as to throw the police off the scent. In fact, it is an excessive display of aggressive frustration at being caught in a trap of his own making, because he loves Nicole. As he says in that scene, reducing Nicole to tears, he should never have fallen for a prostitute (the French is infinitely more vulgar: 'bander pour une pute'), the point being that it doubly undermines his male pride. He is vulnerable, and he is also classed as a pimp, as we are reminded several times during the course of the film.

In *Police*, we see loss from the other side of the Law/Not Law divide, in the form of Mangin/Depardieu as a policeman. Much the same pattern occurs as in *La Balance*. The dialogue of the long opening interrogation much admired by critics sets the tone for Depardieu's version of male aggression: 'I'll crack if I have to worm [the information] out of you, and when I crack I get mean, and rough.' He, like Dédé, does not hesitate in striking the woman he will eventually love, Noria. His attitude is almost grotesquely sexist; for example, he calls one of his short women colleagues LSD, an acronym which he explains to her stands for 'she sucks standing up' ('elle suce debout'). In the same night he will woo the female owner of the restaurant, peeping into her blouse and commenting that 'there's still some high society in there', try to pick up his student commissioner colleague Marie Védret, and, finally, declare his passionate love to Noria.

Like Dédé, however, his aggresivity is tempered by his love for Noria, this being consonant with Depardieu's 'feminized' star persona. His declaration of love is curiously stereotypical in this respect, the dialogue and its implications suggesting a simplistic psychology. When Noria comments on his attitude to women, he says, 'my mother didn't love me, so I'm taking my revenge on all women', to which she replies that he likes 'having an excuse to be macho'. A few exchanges later, he is confessing to Noria that she intimidates him, sketching out a banal woman-as-enigma stereotype, and he later confesses that he had never loved anyone before. The only elements which palliate these banalities are the suggestion that he feels like a youngster again ('We've talked all night, unaware of the time. I haven't done that since I was 15 or 16'), and, more pertinently, the combination of this statement with Depardieu's 'authenticity', coupled with particularly claustrophobic camerawork. The camera never seems to leave the confines of the car they are in, keeping both Noria and Mangin in static medium close-up or straight close-up almost throughout, in contrast with the *cinéma-vérité* technique of hand-held and extremely mobile camera in more public places such as the police station and restaurant. *Mise en scène* imprisons Mangin, echoing his psychological imprisonment in the inadequacies which his tyrannical and agitated bluster usually hides.

For, much like Dédé, Mangin's liaison with Noria undermines the aggressive and apparently self-confident identity established at the beginning of the film. Narratively, he becomes what he had accused Lambert the lawyer of becoming, a crook. Now it is true that elements of corruption had been signalled in the scene where Mangin entertains Lydie the prostitute in his flat, which, he keeps on repeating to her, had cost him a fortune, all on the black market. But it is only towards the end of the film, with his literal going over to the other side, when he returns the money Noria stole from the traffickers to them, that the dialogue underscores the reversal as René says that 'it's the world turned upside down'. Mangin will then have a drink with the petty thief he beat up at the beginning of the film, and will subsequently in the car trot out the cliché, acknowledged as such, that 'cops and crooks are all alike'.

Where Dédé as petty thief was given moral stature by the narrative, Mangin's authority as representative of the law is gradually undermined, so that they both end up somewhere in the middle ground. Mangin's final discomfiture is more pronounced than Dédé's, however. When Noria announces that she is leaving him, Mangin pleads with her. But he does not say that he loves her. He says, twice, staring into the distance, that he only wants her to love him, underscoring the self-centredness of his feeling of loss. He gets out of the car, and the two final sequences are disruptively tragic in tone. The disruption is partly due to the introduction of non-diegetic music (Gorecki's Symphony No. 3, some five years before it became famous), conspicuously absent until that point, combined with strikingly abstract décor, a backdrop of blue-grey criss-crossed steel girders, as though the frequently seen mesh of the police station had melodramatically hypertrophied, sketching out an excessive and excessively obvious mytheme of the catcher caught. It is also partly due to the final shot of Mangin undressing and freeze-framed with a lost look in his eyes. The shot is disruptive not just because of the freeze-frame, but more because it is impossible for the spectator to locate it temporally or geographically from clues in the décor. In fact, ironically, it is the only surviving shot from a sequence which was jettisoned, and which had an additional character, Mangin's housekeeper. The film's editor, Yann Dedet, explained in an interview that the shot occurred in Mangin's flat the morning after one of his daughters had told him that she no longer wanted to live with him. Dedet's explanation of the scene perfectly encapsulates the feeling of loss which the film generally creates, and its connection with sexuality:

He was asleep on his sofa fully dressed, his housekeeper arrived, he sobbed in her arms, yes he sobbed, he talked about the death of his wife (he is a widower), he started to kiss her, you knew that they were going to make love, she walked out of shot, Gérard turned round, took off his jacket, and had that lost look. (Dedet 1985: 23)

Unbeknownst to the spectator, but no less potent for it, the shot combines the loss of wife, daughter, and lover in a moment of male discomfiture frozen for the male spectator's literally melodramatic and self-dramatizing *delectatio morosa*, which only loveless physical sex can relieve.

The third man of this chapter is the rock star Johnny Hallyday, an obvious intertextual reference to another singer-actor, Charles Aznavour, in Truffaut's quirky homage to film noir, *Tirez sur le pianiste* (1960), one of the singer's early roles (he began his long acting career—some forty films to date—in 1959), but perhaps his best known. Hallyday began his film-acting career in the early 1960s, playing either himself (*Cherchez l'idole*, 1964, in which Aznavour also plays; Lelouch's *L'Aventure c'est l'aventure*, 1972) or a variety of gangster parts in films by little-known directors (e.g. *A tout casser*, 1968). His only major lead in the eight feature films before *Détective* was as Hud Dixon in *Le Spécialiste* (Corbucci, 1969), who sets out to clear his brother's name in the wake of a bank robbery. Despite his associations with the gangster genre, the French public would have seen him more as the leading French rock star of the 1960s and 1970s, and at the time of *Détective*, his liaison with Nathalie Baye was much talked of in the popular press.

The character he plays in *Détective*, Jim Fox Warner, a boxing promoter, is constantly harried by the two parties to whom he owes money. Unsurprisingly, one of the major themes of his dialogue is fatigue; 'I'm tired', he says, twice, early in the film, a theme which is ironized through excess towards the end when Jim orders Eugène to ask the computer the following question: 'how many times since I was born have I said that I am tired?', to which Eugène responds, '25,300 times'. 'And women?', Jim pursues. 'How many have I held in my arms?' '632', is the answer. Jim becomes increasingly interested, and bends down to look over Eugène's shoulder. 'And on my hands?' '39', says Eugène. Jim asks a final question: 'On my back?', to which the answer is 'three'.

Jim is not just tired, but preoccupied with failure, as one of the many puns in the dialogue suggests: 'échéance, ça rime avec déchéance', he says, 'debt rhymes with degeneration/decline' (and not necessarily 'death', as the subtitles have it, although it might be understood from the context). Jim is frequently seen holding Conrad's *Lord Jim*, a novel which focuses on failure, as Lord Jim atones for his cowardice during a shipwreck. Jim-in-the-film explains to Émile what the significance of the novel is: 'She said if I opened this book at random at any turning-point in my life, I'd find something of value to me. She gave it to me 30 years ago, and whenever I open it someone always turns up, so I've never read a word of it.' When Jim is shot, at the end of the film, he asks Françoise to read from it. What she reads is, as one might expect from Godard, a recycling apparently composed of elements from several chapters (11, 33, and 35), and which changes the implications of the text. The 'something of value' revealed to Jim (and to the spectator) as he dies is a kind of tragic stoicism, quite at odds with the novel, despite the inclusion of the well-known reference to Lord Jim's romantic self-ideal:

And the testimony to that faithfulness which made him in his own eyes the equal of the impeccable men who never fell out of the ranks. Stein's words, 'Romantic! Romantic!' seem to ring over those distances. 'Oh nonsense, my dear fellow!' I began. He had a movement of impatience. 'You don't seem to understand', he said incisively. Then he looked at me without a wink. 'I may have jumped, but I don't run away'. 'Better men than you have found it an expedient to run, at times', I said. He coloured, while in my confusion I half-choked myself with my own tongue. 'Perhaps so', he said at last. 'I'm not good enough; I can't afford it. I am bound to fight this thing down. I am fighting it _now_.'

Within the overall framework of failure which the reference to the novel emphasizes, the implication of the quotation is that Jim-in-the-film is heroic, a plucky fighter, because he did not run away from those pursuing him for money. But Jim-in-the-novel is harshly judged on the final page, because 'he goes away from a living woman to celebrate his pitiless wedding with a shadowy ideal of conduct' (Conrad 1968: 253). A further complication in this network of misquotations and misleading connotations is that Jim-in-the-film _does_ choose the woman rather than the ideal, because he tries to escape with Françoise, but is gunned down before he can do so.

Lest we lose sight of the wood for its dissembling intertextual trees, the point to hold on to is that the novel connotes failure and that Jim-in-the-film has failed on several counts. He fails to return the money he owes. He fails to return Françoise's love unequivocally; he tells her that the reason he wanted to see her despite an early refusal was because 'I've so little money right now that I can't even afford hookers', and only decides to go with her when abandoned by his boxer. And, of course, he fails to escape, in a scene where the more unsavoury character Émile is also shot, but given a much more grandiose cinematic treatment in comparison to Jim's relatively anonymous and undramatic tumble down the lobby stairs, a Brueghelian backdrop Icarus upstaged by the pedestrian Émile.

Détective is a narrative of tiredness and failure. It is also, as might be expected, a narrative redolent with melancholic nostalgia. The nostalgia is generated partly by affectionate intertextual references to Hollywood B-movies (the film is dedicated to Edgar G. Ulmer, amongst others) and New Wave (by the presence of Léaud, for example, or the reference to Godard's own *La Chinoise* (1967) in the resolution of the murder mystery). Nostalgia is also generated by the dialogue. When Jim and Émile are waiting for Françoise, they reminisce. Jim, his face creased in his only smile of the film, recalls his youth: 'I wanted to see the world, and it was a winter night in Dijon when I left. The last train for Paris. It came from Vienna or Trieste in those days.' When Françoise arrives, she asks them what they have been talking about: 'Men's talk', says Émile, only to be corrected by Jim: 'melancholy talk'.

Nor is *Détective* so different from the other two films discussed in this chapter in relation to its focus on the male body. But because it is Godard, the fascination for the male body located essentially in Léotard's physique in *La Balance*, and in claustrophobic *mise en scène* in *Police*, is in *Détective* mediated through the dialogue. Jim says, ironically from the spectator's point of view given the spindly and pasty white punk appearance of Tiger Jones, that 'the male body is beautiful'. 'A male body', muses Françoise as the camera focuses on her face, and remains on it during the ludic and apparently ludicrous punning dialogue which follows:

Jim: You have to learn how to break (*rompre*), kid, not interrupt (*interrompre*), that's the secret, break, not interrupt.
Françoise: Break, corrupt (*corrompre*).
Tiger Jones: Don't worry, Mister Jim. I'll K.O. Tiger Jones.
Françoise: Isn't he Tiger Jones?
Jim: Yes, but a champion's fight is always against himself.

Jim too should have learnt how to 'break', i.e. retreat from his adversary, his adversary being himself, the melancholic, nostalgic failure, the discomfited male, who dies defeated in a fragmented 'undone' (as Godard put it) metadiscourse ('un scénario défait'). It is a discourse which parodies not only the *polar* genre, but itself as parodic metadiscourse. More crucially, it also seems, by its frequent excess (e.g. Jim saying he is tired 25,300 times in his life), to parody what has been the theme of this chapter, the discomfited male, central to the *polar* genre, as the disparate *La Balance* and *Police* have shown, and indeed central to the image of the male in the 1980s. If Godard did not answer the *Cahiers du cinéma* interviewers straightforwardly, it is perhaps because he felt he should retreat in ironic irrelevance ('rompre') to a melancholic metadiscursive solipsism: 'a champion's fight is always against himself', an auteur in search of a lost auteurism.

10

Diva's Deluxe Disasters

DIVA was one of the most popular films of the 1980s, both inside and outside France. It seemed to mark a break in French cinema where the film image was concerned. Fredric Jameson, in an essay first published in 1982, called *Diva* the first French postmodernist film, dissecting its combination of the old and the new (Jameson 1990). This chapter will be concerned with that combination. After reviewing Jameson's argument, I shall explore what makes *Diva* 'new' beyond the new type of film image it promotes, which I discussed in the introduction to this section: the pastiche of the *polar* and an apparently contemporary concern with the status of women. I shall then discuss what makes the film 'old': the status of women, and the neo-Romantic quest. My aim is to develop Jameson's argument and to sketch out an answer to the question at the end of his essay: is *Diva* 'regressive or conservative recuperation' or 'a historically original "imaginary solution of real contradiction", which may be explored for Utopian elements and possibilities, including some whole new aesthetic in emergence' (Jameson 1990: 62; he is quoting Lévi-Strauss)?

Jameson's essay usefully delineates various simple binary oppositions: Gorodish is active, whereas Jules is passive; Gorodish is at ease in a certain type of postmodern urban space (his loft dotted with isolated fetish objects, the disused hangar), whereas Jules seems overwhelmed by it (his cluttered loft, the metro, the arcade); Gorodish is 'a new kind of character' (Jameson 1990: 55), the counter-cultural businessman, whereas Jules is a very traditional *naïf*. And since *Diva* appeared in the same year as the Mitterrand government, Jameson links all this to an ideological opposition between a post-1960s multinational modernity represented by Gorodish, and a discredited French left populism represented by Jules. Although Jameson does not mention it, the opposition between internationalism and parochialism is clear even in the names of the characters: Gorodish sounds vaguely middle European, whereas Jules, as the diva says to him, 'sounds old-fashioned for a young man' (*Diva*, 33). What also makes *Diva* a mixture of old and new for Jameson, distinguishing it from an American postmodern film such as de Palma's *Blow Out*, is that the celebration of the technological does not occur at a surface or formal level, but is integrated within the narrative:

The new-technological content of post-modernism has been recontained, and driven back into the narrative raw material of the work, where it becomes a simple abstract theme: the Diva's horror of technological reproduction, along with the incriminating posthumous testimony on the other tape—these have become 'meanings' inside the work, where analogous material in *Blow Out* is scarcely meaningful or thematic anymore at all, generating on the contrary a whole celebration and 'acting out' of the reproductive process as form and as the production of sounds and images. (Jameson 1990: 62)

This chapter will to some extent take issue with that last comment, as well as amplifying aspects of the oppositions established by Jameson.

PASTICHE OF THE POLAR

The most obvious characteristic of the 'serious' as opposed to comic *polar* is its gritty realism. As a genre, it is fundamentally conservative and rooted in ' "facts" and "truth" rather than fiction and phantasy' (Neale 1980: 37). In that context, the film stands out. As one reviewer put it: 'Flashy, outré, derisive, modern in every way in which the modern is excessive . . . [Beineix] does not simply catalogue, with enthusiastic candour, the most contemporary and transient mythologies: he shows that he is not duped by them' (Carcassonne 1981: 76). One aspect of excess is that the *polar* does not normally have anything to do with opera, for example. *Diva* also explodes the traditional *polar* by its play with stereotypes. There is, for example, its atypical hero, who is not the disillusioned, hard-bitten 30-year-old with principles, but an amoral opera-loving youth on, of all derisive things, a moped, whose obsession is not the truth of Law, of Order, the traditional concerns of the *polar*, but the pursuit of pleasure and perfection, part of youth culture with its modish lifestyle of lofts and its conspicuous consumerism. As Beineix comments, 'in the classic *cinéma policier*, there is a certain orthodoxy, and the reason that *Diva* shocked quite a lot of people is that we were playing with familiar archetypes ... [We] hijack them to reintegrate them into modernity' (Beineix 1989: 50).

It is the emphatic, indeed overemphatic use of stereotypes which distinguishes the film from other *polars*. Gorodish, for example, is unambiguously connoted as the knight errant on his white stallion, in the form of a Citroën *traction avant*, itself a mythical stereotype, as Gorodish, again unambiguously, tells Saporta: 'the *traction avant* was a car used both by the police and by gangsters' (*Diva*, 76). Jules is spirited away by Gorodish to what Alba describes as a fairy-tale castle; the manner in which Gorodish deals with the vicious Le Curé who is about to kill Jules is fairy-tale-like: a simple squirt of chemical. In the novel, Jules is shot by the pursuing gangsters, but loses them, phones Gorodish, and takes refuge in the toilets of a chemist's, where Gorodish comes to collect him. The difference between the novel and the film is instructive. Beineix and his co-writer, Jean Van Hamme, went for maximum dramatic potential (the arcade as a vision of the inferno), and defused the dramatic almost magically by the use of the chemical gas gag, which turns Gorodish into a derisive and ironic mixture of silent comedian and knight in shining armour, both roles made forcefully and unambiguously clear to the spectator.

Unambiguous references of this kind shift the tone of the film into pastiche and irony. There are many ways in which this functions, one of which is intertextuality. The use of the white Citroën is a clear reference to the early Feuillade Fantômas series. The meeting between L'Antillais and Gorodish underneath the pavement is preceded by a direct reference to *The Seven-Year Itch* (1955) as a woman's dress is lifted by the upflow of hot air. In the informer's death scene, the woman in the old couple is called Garance, recalling Carné's *Les Enfants du paradis*. The solving of a huge jigsaw puzzle in an echoing room is a direct reference to Welles's *Citizen Kane*. The point of such intertextual references is not playfully to explore the filmicity of the film, but rather to engage in sophisticated pastiche and irony, another example of which is the use of *polar* conventions.

The police in the film not only have a relatively passive, almost comical role to play, in the sense that they mostly react to events instigated by Saporta or Gorodish, they are also constantly undermined by a complex irony. Zatopeck, the young male detective, is several times ridiculed by Saporta for believing in a stereotypical drugs trafficking ring. The point here is that the ring exists in the narrative, and Saporta is the head of it, but at the same time it is true that it is one of the staple situations of the genre. The police dialogue is conventional, and occasionally comical in its conventionality, as when Zatopeck, in Jules's loft in a traditional, and therefore banal, stake-out scene, remarks, 'c'est pas banal ici' (*Diva*, 31).

The criminals are also parodied. Le Curé's hallmark is that his dialogue is almost always a statement preceded by 'j'aime pas', more often than not heavily underscored visually (the crane-grab crushing the car after he expresses his dislike for cars; the bust of Beethoven smashed in a puddle after he expresses his dislike of Beethoven). When he and L'Antillais rough Jules up, they make comments on the desirability of order, comments which spectators cannot help but perceive as anything other than ironic, and doubly so, since order/disorder is precisely the structure on which the *polar* is predicated; but it is normally the order of bourgeois law which is re-established, whereas, in the scene mentioned, it is the criminals complaining about the disorder introduced into their world by Jules and the audio-cassette. And at the same time as they claim the need for order, they are paradoxically causing further disorder in the already ransacked flat.

Irony, pastiche, derision, fantasy, the privileging of stereotype over narrative cohesion: these are all ways in which *Diva* might be said to break the mould of the *polar*. It also seems to suggest a relative freedom from the traditional female stereotyping, and thus to vehicle an awareness of the changing political and social conditions for women.

WOMEN IN *DIVA*

Women have many and various roles in the film, and the principal role, that of the diva herself, shows not simply a strong, independent woman, but one who is black and whose role is non-racial; with the exception of an implausible sequence where she is called 'the queen of Africa' by the black street-seller (*Diva*, 38), the film, as Kelly points out, 'makes no special point of her race' (Kelly 1984: 39). Moreover, her ethnicity is paralleled by the woman in the other major couple, Alba, Gorodish's Vietnamese companion, also in appearance independent, with no particular emphasis on her race. Paula, the policewoman, is made to look particularly intelligent by juxtaposition with her self-obsessed and sexist partner. Nadia, and indeed the diva, have pivotal roles in that their voices are on the two tapes which cause the world of high art and the underworld to meet.

The men, for their part, are 'new men'. Gorodish, most obviously, is a 'homemaker' (Kelly 1984: 39), and his lethal disposal of the gangsters—squirting a spray into the face of one, tricking the other into stepping into the lift-shaft—is feminine in so far as it suggests 'tactics conventionally associated with a woman's defenses, not a man's offensive' (Kelly 1984: 40). Jules is typified as a 'weak' man, swooning and sensitive. The utopia of multi-culturalism coupled with feminism and the much-hyped 'new man', so apt for the socialist 1980s building on the feminist 1970s, is only an appearance, however. The status of women within the film forms part of a very familiar and regressive ideology, that of women as male fantasies.

In the parallel couples, Gorodish–Alba/Jules–diva, the two women never meet, and their isolation in the face of the remarkable and almost implausible empathy established between the two men is all the more emphasized. The only female solidarity within the film, between prostitutes, also emphasizes that isolation as well as undermining it. The women's isolation serves to highlight their iconicity. This is particularly the case for the diva, given that she is an opera singer. She is frequently in frame alone, even when with Jules, e.g. in the sequence when he returns her dress. A very revealing sequence in this respect is the walk in Paris, where there is a shot of a statue, with a matching shot on the diva, as impenetrable as the sculpture, while Jules studies her admiringly. The walk is the only occasion she is in the world outside her profession, since at all other times she is isolated in her hotel or on the stage, and yet even here the *mise en scène* stages the diva by framing her in the Arc de Triomphe, and replacing the noisy bustle of the city by mood music. The diva is therefore an object to be admired, a stereotype of the passive female, since she has things done to her rather than doing anything herself (apart from singing). This is equally true of the other women in the film, who are, like the diva, at the mercy of men: Jules steals the diva's voice as well as her dress; Gorodish threatens to send Alba back to Vietnam; Saporta has Nadia murdered. The two women who are not killed, Alba and the diva, are both non-white, suggesting very strongly a typical male fantasy of the compliant Eastern woman: Alba gives what she steals to 'her men'; the diva does not seem to mind that Jules has stolen her voice and her dress.

Alba, too, emphasizes her status as object by pinning photos of herself in Gorodish's flat. She too is frequently framed in windows or, for example in Gorodish's flat and in the castle, in mirrors. She corresponds to the male fantasy of the Lolita figure, or the child prostitute, a paradox neatly encapsulated in the sequence when she plays hopscotch on the painting of the naked woman on Jules's floor. Indeed, the parallel couples have age differences in common, so that together they suggest an atomized family: Gorodish as (God) the Father, all-knowing and all-powerful, with Alba as his daughter (the exact nature of their relationship is never clarified) on the one hand, with the diva as a mother-figure, the Black Virgin by her insistence on the purity of voice, and Jules as her adoring son (again, there is ambiguity as to whether they make love, although it is clear that Jules has sexual feelings for the diva, since he asks the prostitute to wear the diva's dress when they make love).

The film is far too sophisticated not to show some awareness of these undertones, clearly inscribing within its images a critique of the male gaze. The diva is seen reflected in the Taiwanese businessmen's sunglasses in the opening scene at the Opera, an all too obvious comment on the proprietary gaze of the male; and Alba, in the record-shop sequence, is obliged to show photographs of herself naked, ironically commenting 'can I get dressed now?' to the cashier who has accused her of stealing (*Diva*, 17). Nevertheless, the women are not themselves for men: they are goals, and this is suggested by the play on costume. Alba's skirt in the record-shop sequence has a picture of the Opera on it, and the diva's dress is pure white. What these aspects of costume suggest is that Alba 'is' the city, and the diva 'is' purity, both of which the two men wish to control and/or acquire.

THE NEO-ROMANTIC QUEST

The second aspect of the 'old' is connected with the status of women in the film, more specifically with the notion of purity just

1. (*left*) Édouard Vuillard, *Window* (1914); cf. the opening shot of *Un dimanche à la campagne*

2. (*above*) Édouard Vuillard, *Self-Portrait* (1925); cf. M. Ladmiral's morning wash in *Un dimanche à la campagne*

(Both reproduced by courtesy of Artificial Eye)

3. Édouard Vuillard, *Monsieur et Madame Feydeau Sitting on a Sofa* (1905); cf. Édouard/Gonzague's post-prandial admission of failure in *Un dimanche à la campagne*
(Reproduced by courtesy of Artificial Eye)

4. Pierre-Auguste Renoir, *Dance at Bougival* (1882–3); cf. the shot of the waitress and the fisherman just before Irène and M. Ladmiral dance at the *guinguette* in *Un dimanche à la campagne*
(Reproduced by courtesy of Artificial Eye)

5. Irène and M. Ladmiral dance at the *guinguette* in *Un dimanche à la campagne*
(Reproduced by courtesy of Artificial Eye)

6. Jean returns to Mother Earth in *Jean de Florette*
(Reproduced by courtesy of Polygram Filmed Entertainment/Pictorial Press Ltd.)

7. The elegance of closeted lesbianism in *Coup de foudre*
(Reproduced by courtesy of Gala Film Distributors)

8. Framing the woman who wants to do and know too much in *Vivement dimanche!*
(Reproduced by courtesy of Artificial Eye)

9. Dédé's self-inflicted disfigurement in *La Balance*
(Reproduced by courtesy of Revcom/Arrow Film Distributors)

10. Françoise comforts Jim in his tiredness (*Détective*)
(Reproduced by courtesy of Artificial Eye)

11. The detectives in *Diva* overwhelmed by postmodern disaster
(Reproduced by courtesy of Electric Pictures)

12. Fred with 'le gros Bill' and 'le roller' in *Subway*
(Reproduced by courtesy of Artificial Eye)

13. The flight of the predatory *femme fatale* in *Mauvais Sang*
(Reproduced by courtesy of Artificial Eye)

14. The 'pregnant' new man who resurfaces in Jacques's drunken
confession in *Trois hommes et un couffin*
(Reproduced by courtesy of Loeb et Associés)

15. The Le Quesnoys in *La Vie est un long fleuve tranquille*
(Reproduced by courtesy of Electric Pictures)

16. Depardieu and Blanc camp it up in *Tenue de soirée*
(Every effort has been made to obtain permission to reproduce this print. Any omissions will be rectified in future editions)

mentioned. The film articulates very traditional and conservative concerns with Beauty in its most abstract aesthetic sense. *Diva*'s postmodernism incorporates a reaction against the modern. The choice of an iconic décor such as the loft, or of images which can be identified as advertising clichés, is, in this argument, explained by the need to use a contemporary image to vehicle the real concern of the film which is the revaluation of art, as is illustrated by Jules's mania for one of its supposedly higher forms, classical music. Beineix talks of his aim as 'cinéma poétique total' (Parent 1989: 256), of retrieving what a previous film style had evacuated, the notion of the beautiful and colour:

Advertising has never invented anything except what artists have invented. On the other hand, it has been able to capture, inflect, parody, imitate. It appropriated the Beautiful which the cinema of the New Wave had rejected, which makes certain ignorant critics say that beautiful equals advertising. It kidnapped colour, which the cinema no longer violated, so preoccupied was it with being true to life, which makes certain cretinous critics say that colour equals advertising. It dispensed with stories, which the narrative cinema was unable to do without, so some stupid critics are saying that a film without a story equals advertising. Finally . . . it generally captivated young people, whose aspirations the ageing cinema no longer translated, so that some old critics who are only interested in what's dead and gone, or those who are dead and gone are saying that youth cinema equals advertising. (Parent 1989: 263–64)

The yearning for a transcendent truth, a pure art, is clearly part of *Diva*'s discourse, as Beineix himself points out. When talking about his adaptation of the novel, he pronounced himself pleased with the dialogue, saying that 'there is a discourse on art, on commerce and on the commerce of art of which retrospectively I am quite proud' (Parent 1989: 266). Given that the only statement of any import concerning this issue in the film is the diva's short outburst at her press conference, 'it is up to commerce to adapt itself to art, and not up to art to adapt itself to commerce' (*Diva*, 33), Beineix's statement is more significant for what it aspires to rather than what he has achieved.

To the notion of transcendent Beauty we can add the notion of excess. Beineix comments on modern cinema's abandonment of 'reality', a reality which is 'more and more transcended by colour, the excess of the décor, and by a certain type of playfulness (which is not that of truth). The author does not speak the truth any more, he speaks differently' (Parent 1989: 241). Transcendence and excess are combined in the self-imposed discipline of the film's colour scheme. Beineix stated that 'The basic concept was to make a "blue" film', and that although this in itself was not new, 'our originality lay in our persistence' (Beineix 1981: 25) in the face of all kinds of technical problems. Beineix is striving for transcendence through excess, a neo-Romantic project made more interesting than this definition might suggest by the obsessive repetition of opposites and doubles, which establish the familiar, and very traditional, pattern of the labyrinth through which the hero must travel to reach his goal, which is, in traditional narrative, his identity.

THE LABYRINTH OF DOUBLES AS QUEST METAPHOR

The film promotes a double neo-Romantic hero. Jules describes himself as 'un lyrique', and the description is applied to Gorodish by Alba in the following scene (*Diva*, 19), creating the double hero, both immature/mature, innocent/all-knowing, the first of many doublings. The aim of both men is the use of sensation to achieve purity. This is perhaps less clear in Jules's case, although his fascination with a perfect reproduction of the diva's voice, and his paranoid fixation on his hi-fi and its reproductive abilities, suggest it. It is clearer in the case of Gorodish. He is absolutely marginal. Unlike the novel, we know nothing about his past; any connections he may have had with the underworld are implicit, rather than explicit as they are in the novel. Moreover, he is described by Alba as 'un métèque, un rasta' (*Diva*, 18), both references to other races to which he does not belong visually. He is not only absolutely marginal, he is supremely elevated above the fracas of the real world, 'in his cool period' as Alba puts it, 'dreaming of stopping the waves' (*Diva*, 18). We later discover that this statement is at least partly true in that Gorodish is trying to solve a puzzle of a large wave with a small bird at its centre. The bird signifies escape, as do Susan's jigsaws in *Citizen Kane*. The shot of the bird taken out of its central position in the jigsaw by the Taiwanese and placed in the centre of a wad of notes suggests the temptation of commercialism and the paradox of an unattainable but threatened purity. This theme is treated more humorously, even ironically, as if the spectator is being told that it is a mirage, in the Zen art of buttering bread sequence.

The point of this sequence is to stress transcendence from banal reality. With a snorkel mask on his face to protect his eyes from onions, Gorodish says:

Some people get high on airplane glue, washing powder, complicated things! Me, my satori, is this!! zen and the art of buttering bread!!! . . . There's no more knife, there's no more bread . . . there's no more butter . . . there's only a gesture which is repeated . . . a movement . . . space . . . emptiness!! (*Diva*, 34; (even the over-frequent and unjustified use of exclamation marks in the film script, although presumably unsupervised by Beineix himself, but all the more significant for that, suggests the promotion of excess as an integral part of the film's discourse)

Gorodish's disquisition could be a motto for the whole film, which takes ordinary everyday objects, and throws them together in an attempt to get them to cancel each other out so that purity, defined as the non-object, or more precisely the non-product, objects untainted by their value as objects of exchange, may transpire. This is why the diva's recorded voice is so precious, and, an even more compelling sign of purity; it has not been used in commercial exchange. Like the jigsaw bird, it is threatened by commerce, by exchange; indeed, the point is explicitly made by the position of the bird on the wad of notes which is the down payment by the Taiwanese for the recording. If sound is ultimately the greatest purity, it is because images have been circulated and thus soiled.

Diva is a film about loss and about being lost. The loss is of innocence, an original purity, associated with sound. Hence the thefts which occur in the film, many of them associated with sound (cassettes, records), principal among which is the original theft (which the diva calls both theft and rape, 'vol/viol') by the son of his mother's voice at the beginning of the film (in the novel, this does not occur until we have been introduced to Alba) in an effort to rediscover what has been lost, the sound cast out to an audience into a performance space. The sound is rediscovered at the end of the film as Jules gives the diva her purity back again in an empty Opera house, the pure space of performance without the exchange implied by an audience. Given the central notion of loss, the film is understandably then also about being lost in a motherless world.

The final scene between Jules and the diva at the end of the film (is it sexual or not?), with its ambiguous fusion (mother/lover), suggests precisely that the centre of the labyrinth is the return to the mother. The pure sound of the diva/mother-goddess is what comes before language, non-differentiation and symbiosis with the mother.

Diva is a traditional narrative of initiation, a rite of passage through a variety of labyrinths, as Beineix himself suggested: 'It's a film which is a labyrinth, a film which echoes itself, a film of correspondences and displaced connotations; it's like a puzzle' (Beineix 1982: 6). The labyrinth is signalled here by the obsessive repetition of confusing double-talk and double-image. Two narratives intertwine, and within those two narratives, images and characters repeat themselves: two lofts, one cluttered, one empty; two Taiwanese (there was only one Japanese in the novel) and two gangsters (Le Curé and L'Antillais); two cassettes which contrast two worlds, that of high art, of the Virgin, and that of the underworld, of the whore; two white Citroëns. These doublings have been discussed by Hagen who points out the insistence on reflections: puddles, chrome headlights, windows, mirrors, glasses, and so on. Whereas he infers from such semiotic structures 'a visual and aural equivalent for losing oneself in music' (Hagen 1988: 157), in other words a coincidence of form and content, I am suggesting that beneath the modern trappings lies an old and recognizable story: the quest for the holy grail, for the hidden casket/cassette. It is an allegory of transcendence which rejects precisely those elements which it uses to construct itself: the objects taken from the material world, images of products. The material world is a confusing labyrinth of theft and commerce.

The aim of this essay has been to attempt an answer to Jameson's question: is *Diva* 'regressive or conservative recuperation' or 'a historically original "imaginary solution of real contradiction", which may be explored for Utopian elements and possibilities, including some whole new aesthetic in emergence' (Jameson 1990: 62). Jameson's own answer is equivocal:

Fortunately the film does not conclude either: the final frightened handclasp, the Diva's surrender to technological reproduction, her consent to Jules's virtually sexless worship of her . . .—all this, freeze-framed for a last instant on the great state [*sic*], in theatrical space, then rapidly recedes from us, suspended, into a distance which leaves the future wide open. (ibid.)

In terms of the advertising debate of the 1980s, which Jameson's essay, written in 1982, could not have taken into account (although the reprint of the essay in 1990 could have), *Diva* inaugurates a new film style, which is not so dissimilar to American postmodern films such as *Blow Out* after all, in that it too, particularly when one thinks of the obsessive blueness of the film, generates 'a whole celebration and "acting out" of the reproductive process as form and as the production of sounds and images' (ibid.). Then there is also the film's playful irony, which spills over into the disabused self-irony typical of postmodernism. As Beineix has said, 'humour and derision . . . are typical of our age. What can we believe in today?' (Beineix 1989: 50), adding elsewhere that, in *Diva*, 'modernity is treated derisively' (Beineix 1982: 6). The combination of obsession with form and derisive self-irony does suggest that we are dealing with a 'historically original' film, which includes 'some whole new aesthetic in emergence'.

On the other hand, the status of women in the film, the film's conservative neo-Romanticism, and its suggestion of a return to the origins suggest 'regressive or conservative recuperation'. Is this not what Jameson is saying, that it is impossible to decide between recuperation and Utopia? that the film in this respect 'leaves the future wide open'?

My analysis suggests not. The two terms of Jameson's opposition are not mutually incompatible. Indeed, the film is postmodern precisely, one could argue, because such contradictions inhabit and structure it. The film's contradictions cannot be resolved, since they are its deepest structure. The film demonstrates the postmodern principle of culture as jumble, as bric-a-brac, and art as both *bricolage* and collage/collision; art in other words which in relation to its material is, like *bricolage*, too close (enthusiastic self-display, 'I did this all myself'), but also, like collage, too far (despairing self-irony). Indeed, the best description of the film is Jules's description of his loft, which, with ostentatious apocalypticism, celebrates collision: 'a deluxe disaster' (*Diva*, 23).

Unlike Jameson, then, I do not see the ambiguous ending of *Diva* leaving 'the future wide open'. Everything about the ending suggests paranoid closure: it is, literally, a return to the past. The film ends where it began, in the Opera; at the beginning of the film,

Jules stole the diva's voice; here he returns it to her, giving her back
what she always had anyway. The closure is, moreover, a fantasy of
purity: the voice is untainted by commerce and doubly so, since
Jules, by returning the only recording to her, has saved the voice
from being commercially reproduced, and the empty stalls mean
that the voice is not even tainted by the commerce implied in
performance, as was the case at the beginning. The fact that the
only listener is the diva herself, who exclaims 'I never heard myself
sing' (*Diva*, 85), merely emphasizes the closure. Jules, meanwhile,
has chosen the oblivion of self-effacement, since what defined his
importance during the film was his possession of the voice, which
he has now returned. Far from suggesting a wide-open future, the
film, with its labyrinth of doubles and repetitions, turns in on itself
like a completely spherical mirror, in a kind of enthusiastic sterility,
as Jules sinks wanly into his Mother-Goddess's arms.

11

Subway: Identity and Inarticulacy

I SHALL begin my analysis of *Subway* with what one could call the orthodox view of the *cinéma du look*, as vacuous hyper-realist surface. A recent expression of this view can be found in Buss's history of the French *polar*, or police thriller. He is here referring to a much-remarked sequence of *Subway*, where Héléna/Adjani, bored with the society dinner she is attending with her husband, tells the assembled company to 'fuck off' ('je vous emmerde'):

One of the central scenes shows Adjani rebelling against the stuffiness of a typical bourgeois dinner, before opting to join Lambert. Otherwise, there is very little plot, the message being in the excitement and the display of alternative lifestyles ... *Subway* ... is not about character, but about violence, energy, dynamism and, most of all, about cinematic style ... From the opening frames, Besson is concerned with creating a visual style, mainly through the use of colour, in order to direct and concentrate the audience's attention, much as the maker of a pop video tries to find a visual language that will not only translate the emotions of the music, but also correspond to the singer or group's significance for its fans ... From *Diva* and *Subway* to *Nikita*, the post-modern thriller was sharpening the surface image for its own sake, like a hyper-realist painting, without much concern with what was represented or belief in its 'meaning'. (Buss 1994: 131–3)

Buss is here repeating the view of critics such as the *Cahiers du cinéma*, forcefully expressed during the 1980s. My problem with this view is that it takes little account of the ideology of the *cinéma du look*, and even less the theoretical positions in which it places the spectator. I shall therefore briefly review two commonplaces concerning the ideological function of the *polar*, namely that it is uniquely placed to comment on society, and that the genre vehicles a complex and shifting debate in terms of national identity, particularly in relation to the USA. I shall then return to *Subway* to show how the film's 'meaning' is not just valueless, simplistic, superficial rejection, but a more complex interference of intertextual objects which generates a specific ideological position, one of utopian reintegration into the community. This reintegration is in fact undermined by a third commonplace of the polar, the masochism of the noir hero, whose marginalization no utopia can satisfactorily resolve.

FROM PASTICHE TO MUSIC AS MYTH

The pastiche and irony of intertextuality have a centrifugal force. Whereas in a film such as *Vivement dimanche!* that force is to some extent neutralized by a strong narrative line, in the postmodern *polar*, such as *Subway*, it threatens to overwhelm narrative pleasure by its dislocative strength, partly because the narrative verges on the improbable and the ironic. Fred blows up the safe at a party simply for fun, loses important papers, is pursued into the underground both by Héléna whom he loves, and who will gradually fall in love with him, and by her husband's men who want to retrieve the papers. He takes refuge amongst a society of outcasts, and steals money which allows him to fulfil his ambition of forming a band who will give him the singing voice he lost as a child. The intertexts include 'punk subculture and television designer-violence', as Hayward somewhat dismissively puts it (Hayward 1993a: 233), as well as the myth of Orpheus and its film version by Cocteau (1950). It is on this intertext, and the other important intertext mentioned by Hayward, Godard's *A bout de souffle* (1959) that I would like to concentrate. The centrifugal force of pastiche is, however, counterbalanced by what I would like to term the centripetal reconstruction of a precarious national identity through the intertextual references, in which music plays an important part.

   In the final sequence of *Subway*, Fred is enjoying the performance given by his band, as parallel shots show Héléna running in slow motion to meet him. He is shot and lies on the ground while the song lyrics say 'this poor world is such a mess'. Héléna weeps over him in a series of shot-reverse-shot close-ups. The music fades as the hero utters his dying words: 'Can I ask you a question? Do you love me just a little bit? [*Héléna kisses him.*] I'll call you later.' [*Fred dies.*] The music fades back in with a repeated line, 'guns don't kill people, people kill people', as a struggle ensues between Héléna and her husband's right-hand man. We see them shouting but do not hear the words. There is a cut from the struggle to Fred who turns his head, and begins singing along to the music.

The final sequence is a direct reference to the closing sequence of Godard's *A bout de souffle*, where Michel runs down the street, pursued in parallel shots by Patricia to the sound of strident big-band jazz, over which only his shuffling footsteps can just be heard. This is followed by a similar structure of shot-reverse-shot close-ups (two shot-reverse-shots to *Subway*'s three), the difference being that Patricia does not weep, nor does she kiss Michel. A similar attitude is conveyed as in *Subway*, however. To the rather naive song which says 'this poor world is such a mess' corresponds Michel's statement, 'c'est vraiment dégueulasse' ('life's a shit'), doubly misunderstood, first by one of the spectators in the film who thinks he said 'you are a real shit' to Patricia, and by Patricia herself who asks what the word means. The intertextual reference to *A bout de souffle* is revealing, since it establishes a complex dialogue, not just with French film culture, but more interestingly with American film culture, with which Godard was already engaging in *A bout de souffle*, usually seen as an homage to film noir.

Indeed, like *A bout de souffle*, *Subway* is American in cinemato-graphic style, and intentionally so, as the following interview with Besson clear:

Interviewer: People say that your technical know-how is American, even Spielbergian! What do you think of that?

Besson: . . . Everything depends on what you put into it. Take a car chase in France. It will be filmed over two to three days, with cameras close to the ground, fast pans, and bits from the same shot edited together. Routine, basically. The Americans take two to three weeks, cover all the angles, and end up with explosions. The difference is in the time we take. Our car chase at the beginning of the film was filmed over twelve days, and takes three minutes of screen time. We did it carefully, with lots of shots, never using the same one twice, etc. It obviously makes the sequence punchy (*ça donne du punch*). (Cognard 1985: 61)

The 'punchy' style is what makes it attractive to younger spectators, of course, precisely because it is what they are more used to; it should not be forgotten that *Subway* appeared in the year before viewing figures for American films overtook viewing figures for French films in France.

However, *A bout de souffle*, as a recent commentator has shown, can be seen less as an imitation of film noir than as a critique of that imitation:

Michel is condemned ... not principally for any social or sexual transgression—the staple fare of noir—but for attempting to assume a role quite unsuited to him ... Condemned ... to a Frenchness he never truly escapes ... he thus comes to represent the essential limitation of ... an imitative French version of Hollywood. (Smith 1993: 73)

Similarly, although I would not wish to suggest that *Subway* sketches out a critique of American film style or American cinema in the same way as *A bout de souffle*, it does nevertheless show a similar ideological fracture by its other strong intertexts with a uniquely French flavour. The film is French in décor, not just because it is set in the Paris métro, but more particularly because the set was reconstituted by Alexandre Trauner, best known for his sets of Carné's films in the 1930s. If I mention what might seem like a relatively trivial point, it is that the set quite obviously plays a considerable part in the attraction of the film's postmodern images. Trauner himself saw his brief as the creation of 'something amazing for the décor so as to seduce the spectator's imagination' (Cognard 1985: 67), and Besson relates how the set threatened to take over the narrative:

[The first of the eleven scripts of *Subway*] was different in that we were much more taken by the décor than by the story. The difficulty we had was that the métro had taken over. We couldn't find a storyline strong enough to take the décor's place ... The décor [of the final version] is not as you might have thought a privileged space which supports specific relationships between characters. It's an excessive décor (*poussé à fond*) which is equivalent to a character (*prend la valeur*). (Cognard 1985: 60–1)

More substantially, however, *Subway* is a reworking of Cocteau's *Orphée*, the descent into the underworld of the hero who would be a poet. It is true that Orphée is an established poet, whereas Fred wants to be one, and it is true that there is a modish role reversal in the sense that Orphée follows his wife into the underworld, whereas Fred is followed by Héléna. These differences, like the differences between the concluding sequences of *Subway* and *A bout de souffle*, are telling, and I shall return to them. Nevertheless, it is the similarities which concern me here, and they are clear if not conclusive. At the general narrative level, both Death in *Orphée* and Héléna in *Subway* are cold women who will gradually fall in

love with Orphée and Fred, and both Orphée and Fred will find
their lost voices. More circumstantially, the interrogation scene of
Orphée where Death is asked to account for herself in having fallen
in love with a mortal parallels the dinner party where Héléna causes
a scandal because she has fallen in love with Fred and rejects the
upper world. There are also clear parallels between the two
underworlds where *mise en scène* is concerned: ruins parallel what
lies behind the glistening surface of the Paris métro; motion is
magical, whether floating motion in *Orphée* or roller-skates in
Subway; there is a gallery of odd characters in both films.

Between these two poles of French and American film culture,
somewhat artificially separated for the purpose of analysis, lies
what makes the film interesting ideologically: its music, or rather
what that music tries to express, as is made evident in the final
sequence. It is, to quote Jameson (quoting Lévi-Strauss) on *Diva*,
'an imaginary solution of a real contradiction' (Jameson 1990: 62).
Besson's aim was to create a film whose music was somewhere
between America and Europe: 'For *Subway* [Eric Serra] has
composed something between the Stones and Police. [For the lead
role] we thought of Sting. For us he was exactly right for the role'
(Cognard 1985: 58, 60). The final sequence is a magical resolution
of difference, not just at the level of the music itself, a kind of
transatlantic rock, which gets young and old, classical music lovers
and punks, happily clapping hands and dancing together in a
mythical resolution of class, age, and even ethnic differences (the
band is carefully multi-ethnic). The *mise en scène* interestingly,
given that the music itself effaces any trace of Frenchness, still
manages to suggest a resolution in the very traditional figure of the
accordion-player (*Diva* also felt the need for an accordion player
. . .) sitting next to one of the speakers and singing along to the
music. The conclusion to the film has the magic of myth-making,
since the traditional *polar* ending (the death of the marginalized
cynical hero) is circumvented: Fred is killed only to resurrect
singing, having found the voice he lost. His singing ('ba, ba, ba',
etc.) establishes a tongue-in-cheek closure for the film, whose
second shot in the opening credit sequence is an epigraph: 'To be is
to do (Socrates). To do is to be (Sartre). Do be do be do (Sinatra).'
Values, the questioning of values, and proposed simplistic solutions
are thus vehicled through music. Through music the film constructs
a rejection of existing heterogeneous social formations; the creation

of the band is both a marginal, counter-cultural activity, as well as a very personal project for Fred. The final sequence substitutes simple and magical solutions for the complexity of urban existence.

This simplicity is paralleled by characterization. As Revie explains, referring to 'le roller' and 'le gros Bill', the more oddball minor characters in the film are

Representative of one particular activity, as is emphasized by the specialization of the musicians ... In allowing one form of activity to dominate and shape their existences, they represent the revolt against the need to pay attention to the multiple facets of an increasingly complex urban existence and their near monomania is seen as a form of heroism. (Revie 1994: 35)

The characters have the simplicity of cartoon characters, as the film itself acknowledges in the characters of the traditional police pair, who are called Batman and Robin; like *Diva*, a certain derision functions in this film. But it is precisely the simplicity of these cartoon creations which gives them their ideological force, and which, moreover, allows us to explore more clearly than Jules in *Diva*, for example, the theoretical positions in which they place the spectator.

DISPOSSESSION AND INARTICULACY

Subway is a film which rejects mainstream social formations by its emphasis on marginal characters and the magical resolution of difference. It also rejects the normal *polar* style of gritty realism, partly by its American-influenced brashness, partly by its emphasis on monomaniacal ciphers rather than 'rounded' characters. This double rejection of the Law, both as a social structure within the thriller narrative (what the criminals try to circumvent), and as the regulatory mechanism of the genre (the rules of the *polar*), is enacted within the film.

There are two father-figures, both of whom represent the Law (in its first sense): Héléna's husband, the socially respectable business-man, and the Inspector. Both are types from the traditional *polar*, both have the power of the word, imparted to them by the Law, the Inspector excessively so by his precise and often pedantic use of words, the husband by an opposite tendency to use words sparingly but tellingly. Both are treated humorously; they are figures of fun to be thwarted.

The husband is thwarted by his wife who rejects her role as her husband's property in an extraordinary sequence which more than any other seems to disarticulate the film. Héléna meets her husband in a café in the métro after spending the night underground. She explains how she invited Fred to the party, how he blew open the safe, and then returned the money, but lost the papers. Her husband shows her a roughly written note, apparently written by Fred, which suggests that he is a vulgar blackmailer. Héléna begins her monologue:

Héléna: Happy now? I'm just a nobody you picked up, Mr Moneybags (*Monsieur Gros plein de fric*). You're suffocating me, Mr Moneybags, you're crushing me. I need air. I didn't even cheat on you last night. I didn't even feel like it. I spent most of the night watching fireworks. It felt good. Because I'm sick of your way of life, your schemes, your smiles, and even your money.
Husband: Well why don't you divorce me then? [*Calls his man over.*] Jean, take care of that young man, and fast.

The sequence disarticulates the film not so much by its obvious banality, but because of the contrast between that banality and the melodramatically excessive acting of Adjani, who cries through most of the sequence, her porcelain-white doll-like face racked by pain, as the camera lingers on her in close-up, contrasted with the inexpressive swarthy face of her husband. This is so excessive in relation to the dialogue that it is as if the film is trying to meld two different discourses—the banality of the *polar* situation and the banality of a true love story—with a melodramatic amalgam. The sequence ends on an extreme close-up in profile of the husband, as though to re-establish both his authority and the authority of the *polar* framework; but both have been undermined by the melodrama.

The other character who has the Law, and more obviously so by his position and by his articulacy, is the Inspector. He is thwarted by the ubiquitous skater as the representative of the underground counter-culture, who knows everybody, all the passages, and moves with ease around the labyrinth. As befits the representative of the Law, he is more able than the husband to uphold it. He catches the roller-skater, doing so by assuming the traditional film noir role of the private detective, travelling alone underground, whereas his henchmen and the husband and his men tend to travel in packs. Nevertheless, Fred eludes him; the Law of the Father(s) is rejected, circumvented, to be replaced by a more urgent quest.

As the film progresses it becomes clear that it is not structured on an escape from the Law above ground, as the opening sequence might have led one to think, so much as a quest below ground. The film constructs the search for the lost voice, the 'singing voice' Fred has lost. He lost his voice at 5 years old in a car accident which occurred, significantly, after his father bet he could drive his car underneath a lorry. In other words, his father stole his voice (castrated him), and Fred's search can be seen as the search for the pre-Oedipal mother, for the time before accession to the Lacanian Symbolic and patriarchal Law. The penultimate shot of the film is crucial in this respect. Fred's vocalizations (predictably, there is no exact way to describe his baby-like 'ba, ba, ba . . .', since this is neither humming nor crooning; Fred's vocalizations are outside the Symbolic) not only reject the Law by their irreverent reworking of the existentialist ethic (see the epigraph at the beginning of the film), but also by signalling his magical rebirth in the face of the law of the *polar* where the marginal hero must die. It is significant in this respect that while the spectator has to wait for Fred's rebirth, the struggle between Héléna and the Inspector, and later her struggle with her husband's right-hand man, can be seen but not heard, as the soundtrack repeats the chorus from the song, 'guns don't kill people, people kill people'; the realist *polar* and the Law of the Father(s) are marginalized by mythical resolutions.

The pleasure of the film for the spectator, then, is the way it at one and the same time establishes a nostalgically French generic frame, while breaking, rather than redefining, the rules of the genre. Indeed, it is the film's excessive rule-breaking which differentiates it from the redefinitions typical of genre films. That excess functions on different levels, but is always anchored in polarities: French/American, above ground/below ground, *polar/look*, realism/pastiche. But excess and polarity do not necessarily mean irremediable fracture. *Subway* manages to be both modishly modern in its brashness and oversimplification of social issues, and nostalgic in its attempt to recover the magical innocence of maternal engulfment, the 'lost voice' of inarticulate babbling as an escape from those issues. Although generically a world apart, there is little difference between the *cinéma du look* and a retro-nostalgic film such as *Un dimanche à la campagne* where the positioning of the spectator is concerned. To the extent that spectators are likely to identify themselves with Fred, the film places them in the comfort of pleasurably masochistic dispossession, a pre-Oedipal fantasy where problems like death can be magically overcome by singing. Although it may sound patronizingly moralistic to say so, that dispossession is pleasurable because it is predicated on the abdication of responsibility: an anomic retreat from the difficult and necessary negotiation of community.

12

Mauvais Sang:
The Flight of the Female

'MAUVAIS Sang' is, famously, the first major section of Rimbaud's *Une saison en enfer*. This is a collection of prose poems of revolt and disillusion in which Rimbaud rejects the society he lives in and harks back to more 'primitive' ancestors, longing for an escape which he knows he cannot have. The collection ends in what one of the editors of his work has called 'a desperate serenity' (Rimbaud 1972: 958). The film of the same title thus immediately establishes its pitch: iconoclastic revolt, disillusion, regret.

Rimbaud is not the only intertext, and I shall be exploring the significance of the many other intertexts in the first part of this chapter, before discussing the noirish intersection between sexuality and revolt. But here I would like to stress the iconoclastic element, since this film caused a considerable sensation when released, as can be judged by some of the comments made by reviewers:

A shock. The shock you feel each time you are faced by something you have never seen before. *Mauvais Sang* . . . is a film in a category of its own. Not even that, because it is precisely not 'separate', nor 'original', nor 'marginal', nor anything like that. *Mauvais Sang* is a new film, a film which is more (*un film plus*). A film which hacks away at the norms (*érafle salement les convenances*) and which violently twists the beaten tracks of the canons which we are used to. A film which gives on to an unexplored universe and which seems to take a malign pleasure in defying description. As if the matter of cinema had never been kneaded, sculpted, polished like this before. (Yvoire 1986: 94)

Totally amazing (*éblouissement absolu*). To speak about it, you need to stress the original meaning of words which have become hackneyed, weakened: poetry, inspiration, dazzling composition (*fulgurance du plan*), in a word: emotion. (Philippon 1986: 15)

Although it is true that the film in plastic terms is quite unlike most contemporary productions, resembling early Godard, it is also true that the praise heaped upon the film in the mid-1980s was at least partly due to the lack of readily identifiable auteurs. It is significant in this respect that the film appeared in the year when French audiences for American films overtook those for French films. Some commentators were well aware of the film's conjunctural importance:

Our enthusiasm . . . is in relation to recent disappointments and overdone reputations: phoney Orson Welles, or all those commendable copies by good students which represent the majority of first films today. (Dazat 1986: 15)

Why does *Mauvais Sang* ring true while a film like *37°, 2 le matin* ring false? . . . Because in *Mauvais Sang* there is a real cinematic writing (*véritable écriture*). (Girard 1987: 67)

What many critics appreciated was the extreme awareness of film culture demonstrated in the film, mainly by virtue of constant intertextual reference. This is so obtrusive that it became one of the focuses for discussion of the film.

INTERTEXTUALITY, EXCESS, AND NOSTALGIA

It would be tedious to do more than simply briefly gesture at some of the major intertexts in the film (which, of course, are not exhaustive):

> Tintin: *L'Étoile mystérieuse* (1947): Halley's comet and the heat.
> Anna Karina in Godard's *Pierrot le Fou* (1965)/*Vivre sa vie* (1962): Binoche.
> Louise Brooks in Pabst's *Pandora's Box* (1928): Binoche.
> Lillian Gish in King Vidor's *La Bohème* (1926): Binoche.
> Gloria Swanson in Billy Wilder's *Sunset Boulevard* (1950): the American woman.
> Chaplin (Paulette Goddard): mother and child sequence.
> Cocteau, *Orphée* (1950): Alex and Lise on the motorbike.
> Buñuel, *L'Âge d'or* (1930): Alex's ventriloquism.
> Grémillon, *La Petite Lise* (1930): extract from the film.
> Truffaut, *Les 400 coups* (1959): the final run down the tarmac.

As one commentator said, the film 'collapses under the weight of its references' (Noël 1986: 59). This view of intertextuality, as what I called a centrifugal, dislocative force in the chapter on *Subway*, can be seen as a central function in postmodern discourse, constituting what Jameson calls the 'schizophrenic experience', which he defines as 'an experience of isolated, disconnected, discontinuous material signifiers which fail to link up into a coherent sequence' (Jameson 1985: 119).

Other films from the *cinéma du look* also revel in intertextual references (*Subway*, for example). During the 1980s, commentators tended to differentiate between Carax on the one hand, and Beineix and Besson on the other, Carax being praised for example by the influential *Cahiers du cinéma*, while Beineix was vilified. Carax somehow managed to 'transcend' his references in d'Yvoire's view, who mentions

All sorts of references which [Carax] seems to exhibit all the better to go beyond them. The film transcends [difficulties] rather than avoiding them or getting round them. Leos Carax systematically refuses to take the easy way out. He does not want to be restricted to a genre film. He does not want to do what everybody else is doing. If aestheticism is there in *Mauvais Sang*, it makes no concessions (*il n'est jamais caressé dans le sens du poil*), it never tries to curry favour (*jamais démagogique*). With the risk of frustrating the spectator. (Yvoire 1986: 98)

By the end of the 1980s, differences between them seemed less obvious than the similarities. They and Besson were called 'neo-baroque' directors by Bassan and the term has remained. It was taken up by Prédal, for example, in his history of the French cinema, where he points out that although Carax is generally shunned by a larger public, unlike Beineix and Besson, nevertheless they all have the attraction to the image, rather than the sequence (as might be the case with Godard), in common (Prédal 1991: 462). I would further suggest that what links them all, as I tried to show in the chapters on Besson and Beineix, is nostalgia. Carax may well have said that *Mauvais Sang* is a film which loves the cinema, and which hates the cinema of today (Carax 1986: 32), and thereby have seemed to suggest an aversion to the postmodern style of a Beineix or a Besson, but intertextuality in *Mauvais Sang*, as Forbes remarked, shows a yearning for innocence which is too much like the nostalgia shown in *Diva* or *Subway* for the differentiation she made between them at the time of *Mauvais Sang*'s release in the UK now to hold true:

Through the expressiveness of face and body, of a language beyond or anterior to words . . . Carax goes back to the origins of the cinema as well as to a state of emotional innocence temporarily captured in a look or a gesture . . . the juggling sequence in *Mauvais Sang*. This is why Carax's films make Besson's look merely slick, all gloss and no substance however accurately they capture a mood, since unlike his contemporaries Carax appears able to portray a corrupt world with an innocent eye—indeed the innocent eye of the early days of the film industry. (Forbes 1987: 293)

Besson's films may seem slick compared with Carax's, but in the end what the use of intertextuality shows more than anything else is the yearning for some kind of purity, an innocence at odds with the derisive nature not just of contemporary film production, as Forbes is here suggesting, but also of contemporary social structures.

In *Mauvais Sang*, intertextuality is excessive, and this excess itself functions as a sign of rejection. The film explodes and collapses with references to other texts, threatening to deconstruct itself beyond any recognizable narrative line. But it is precisely in the explosion that the significance of the film lies, since intertextuality here functions as a sign of marginality, most clearly indicated by the fact that the principal intertexts deal with asocial love, love outside the Law. First, there is Cocteau's *Orphée*, to which there are occasional references (the motorcycles, for example). These references are less clear than the narrative line, which resembles *Subway*'s: Orphée (Alex) leaves his wife Eurydice (Lise) for the Princess (Anna), who in *Orphée* is an agent of Death, and has to rediscover her in the kingdom of the dead, only to die when he looks at her after being told not to. Second, Alex's ventriloquism is likely to be construed as a reference to Buñuel's *L'Âge d'or*, a film specifically about *l'amour fou*, asocial/anti-social love. Third, Binoche is designed to remind the spectator of Godard's Karina, who was already designed to look like the Louise Brooks of *Pandora's Box*, which is about love in a criminal milieu. The court's son elopes with his father's mistress, is driven to crime, and she is eventually murdered in London by Jack the Ripper. And finally, in *La Petite Lise*, a scene from which is being broadcast on the television during Alex and Anna's long night together, Berthier, Lise's father, an ex-convict, takes the rap for his daughter and her lover's murder of a moneylender.

Intertexts in *Mauvais Sang* therefore function to indicate nostalgia for a golden age of cinema (anything which is not the present, since the intertexts mentioned stretch from the silent period through to the New Wave), paralleled by a golden age of innocence unsullied by the coarse realities of the principal regulating social structure, the family, and the obligations it imposes. *Mauvais Sang* is in this sense what Krutnik calls a 'transgressive adventure' in his taxonomy of film noir (Krutnik 1991: 137).

THE TRANSGRESSIVE ADVENTURE AND THE 'DISSONANT REPRESENTATION OF MASCULINITY'

It is perhaps arguable to what extent the film is a film noir, given the fracturing not just by intertexts, but by other dislocative elements. There is the insertion of narratively problematic grainy black and white footage on several occasions, for example. Then, although the dialogue is often ponderous, and wilfully precious, there are, as there are in *Vivement dimanche!*, a number of comic elements. For example, the dialogue during Alex and Anna's night together shows a predilection for Godardian puns. Alex tries to persuade Anna to stay in the butcher's shop overnight, saying that he will 'draw the windshield' ('paravent'; i.e. an object which excludes the wind), to which Anna responds negatively, saying that 'a man's gaze isn't wind'. A moment later, they are discussing the heat, which Alex explains is due to Halley's comet, to which Anna responds, punning on the phonological ressemblance between two words, 'Halley's Comet? You're joking' ('La comète de Halley . . . allez!'). The comical and the passionately intense collide together schizophrenically (to use Jameson's term) throughout this long sequence, where earlier Alex had comically managed to conjure a deluge of vegetables to Anna's delectation. Immediately after the punning dialogue Alex carries Anna over the burning hot tarmac to the accompaniment of Britten's intensely evocative Little Symphony (the 'love theme' of the film, which was first heard when Alex first caught sight of Anna reflected in the window of the bus). They communicate over the telephone, with Alex improbably hanging on to the line with all his weight as he tries to see Anna at her window, this relatively comical situation veering into the frankly comical as Alex overturns a parked Volkswagen Beetle to the quizzical gaze of an absurd-looking hotel clerk dressed in nothing more than his baggy underwear. This is hardly the stuff of film noir, with the anxious male locked in an arena of smouldering sexuality with the heady femme fatale, and this is underlined by the child-like innocence of Alex and Anna as they play together like children the following morning, covering each other with shaving-foam under the reproachful and father-like eye of Marc.

Arguably, there is a generational fracture which corresponds to the genre fracture. Alex and Anna inhabit (or try to inhabit) a world of playful uncorrupted innocence which has little to do with the tired, middle-aged noir world of Marc, Hans, and the American woman. Marc, played by the iconically oppositional actor Piccoli (who is therefore representative of 1970s cinema, as well as of the early Godard of *Le Mépris*), and the metaphorically important 'American woman' (too much like the Gloria Swanson of the already nostalgic *Sunset Boulevard* to be a coincidence), are both representatives of an old cinema, as they are of a dysfunctional world rejected by the youngsters. It is Marc and the American woman who are the anxious male and the femme fatale of film noir.

And yet, by his very rejection of this noir world, Alex also forms part of the noir element, caught in what Krutnik calls the transgressive adventure where 'the hero tends to be pitted directly against either the family or some other systematized figuration of the patriarchal order, or both' (Krutnik 1991: 137–8). Alex rejects his recently murdered father by refusing to go to the morgue, claiming that this represents freedom for him; 'at last I'm an orphan', he says over the phone to his friend Thomas, 'it's my chance to start over again'. He also rejects Marc as father-substitute, vying with him in a classic Oedipal scene for the love of Anna, the two men struggling, their faces disfigured as they are pressed against the window-pane. In this family structure, it is the American woman who functions as the mother; she says she knew Alex's father, and could have been his mother.

It is clear too that however much Anna is unlike the typical femme fatale by her passive sexuality, for example, or her lack of desire for social and financial advancement, she nevertheless functions as the attraction which ensnares Alex in an impossible revolt. Anna attracts Alex at least partly by her own unconventional attraction to Marc, and she is opposed to the loyal Lise whom Alex abandons. As Krutnik says:

The hero of the criminal adventure is . . . attracted by the woman who sets herself against convention (which is suggested in particular by the very presence of the more conventional and loyal good girl, who has either to be rejected by or lost to the hero). It is then the very danger attached to the femme fatale which makes her desirable to the hero. (Krutnik 1991: 141)

Trapped by his love for Anna, which is not returned, his hand mutilated when trying to break into a bookseller's locked container on the banks of the Seine, and warned that this could jeopardize the enterprise he is engaged in, Alex is the typical Oedipal hero of the transgressive noir adventure: 'The hero's Oedipal revolt cannot succeed, but it is this impossibility of success which intensifies the desire for transgression' (Krutnik 1991: 143).

Transgression does not necessarily mean that what is transgressed is overturned. Just as in *Vivement dimanche!*, for example, the family is re-established after the threat posed to it by a closure more typical of screwball comedy than film noir, so too in *Mauvais Sang* transgression is a dead end. Alex must die so that the family cell can be maintained. Those who are excluded are the transgressive son, Alex, and the threatening, 'bad', and therefore transgressive mother in the form of the American woman. Those who are left form a peculiarly distorted, gender-crossing, even incestuous family cell, where Marc is the 'father', Hans the surrogate 'good mother' (he has the 'feminine' characteristics of caring and attention to the way he is dressed), and Anna the mixture of wife and daughter. Such a distorted family cell is a measure of the disillusion with social structures against which the hero vainly struggles, only to fail, as fail he must, since transgression's validation is the inviolability of the Law:

The desire for transgression (and transgressive desire) exists in order to be countered, in order to justify the delimitations through which masculine identity is conventionally ordered through the Oedipus complex. Rather than simply giving voice to a frustration with the cultural parameters of masculine identity, then, the criminal adventure can be seen to represent a desire for reassurance, a desire to have demonstrated in an unequivocal manner the inescapability and inviolability of identification through, and subjection to, the Law of the Father. (Krutnik 1991: 147)

The masochistic self-effacement of the rebellious son is paralleled by the excessive *mise en scène* of Anna/Binoche in the film, which serves to reinforce patriarchal law by the fetishization of the phallic woman.

It is true that the camera tends not to focus on those parts of Binoche's body which are synonymous with male desire, such as legs (as Truffaut famously does), or breasts. On the other hand, her feet are often in close-up, and even more obvious is the fascination with Binoche's face. Vincendeau points out how '*Mauvais Sang* is a series of cartoon-like, magnified, disjointed images in which Binoche's face, shot from all possible angles including laterally and upside down, occupies a central place—rarely has an actress's face been so overtly reified' (Vincendeau 1993*a*: 24). Excessive fascination causes the film's narrative to collapse in a classic example of Mulvey's position on voyeurism, reinforcing and reinforced by the status of the protagonist as a gaze: Alex would like to be the 'voyeur du quartier' (played by Carax) who gazes silently at Anna (and who has been beaten up before by Hans). Alex says that he envies the voyeur, and that it is a 'beau métier', a job he would like.

Fetishistic voyeurism has been associated by Mulvey with masochism, and Alex is as typically masochistic, but more so, as the heroes of *Diva* and *Subway*. Like the Jules of *Diva*, he is wounded and cared for by an older male, and in his case the wound is a mutilation of what defines him as a character in the narrative, namely his nimble fingers. An equally obvious sign of castration is the absence of a 'voice', since like the Fred of *Subway*, Alex's childhood is associated with muteness. He is ironically called 'Langue-pendue' (from the idiom 'avoir la langue pendue', meaning to be talkative). This is an ironic nickname because, as Marc explains, 'the child wouldn't talk. In fact, I remember that during the first months Valérie [Alex's mother] began to think that he was dumb; he never made a sound.' Later in the film, Alex says: 'I was a frighteningly silent child, apparently. I kept silent; but that's not right. Silence keeps us.' And it is worth recalling, to underline how the film constructs Alex as the son who transgresses in an attempt to escape the Law of the Father, and in so doing recovers or attempts to recover the masochistic pre-Oedipal position, how the curious Chaplinesque sequence with Mireille Perrier and the child calls attention to itself by its dissonance and disruption of the narrative. Alex stumbles along, inexplicably tottering like the child who stumbles towards his mother.

The narrative, then, is a typical noir narrative which reinforces patriarchal law by the effacement of the transgressive son and the normalization of the family structure. Intertextual references combined with excessive fetishization of Binoche both structure a nostalgic response, supporting the normalization of the family and the traditional view of the female in structures of perception. These references also disrupt the narrative, contributing to the self-effacement of the protagonist, who is reduced to a gaze. The protagonist is replaced by the fetishized woman, mirroring contemporary French male anxiety. This argument is graphically illustrated by one of the film's metaphorical machines, the pun on 'le vol': theft and flight.

Vol/Vol

Flying is associated with *l'amour fou*, as is clear during the parachute sequence. Anna jumps from the plane, but the parachute line does not release, and she loses consciousness. Alex 'rescues' her by climbing down the line and taking her in his arms, whereupon Marc cuts the line. Alex and Anna drift down to earth in a series of long-distance shots, into which are inserted two clumsy studio close-ups, curiously at odds with the more realistic long-distance shots of the couple. The sequence is a metaphor for mad love: they are floating in silence during the two close-ups where they appear almost motionless, and accompanied by the whistling of the wind in the long-distance shots as it rushes them across the screen. It is a world which is midway between fantasy (the silence and immobility of the clumsy studio shots) and a heady reality.

The sequence is linked visually to the stealing of the serum. The shot which follows the clumsy studio shots is an extraordinary overhead shot of the two as they float down, clasped together at the centre of the web of the parachute's lines. The web of red laser beams which protects the serum recalls the web of the parachute strings, suggesting the key position of the serum. It is the final term in a series predicated on desire: Thomas loves Lise who loves Alex who loves Anna who loves Marc who wants something which will restore his masculinity in the face of the threat presented by the American woman. The serum is the phallus, as the flask into which Alex places it with its self-evidently phallic form makes abundantly clear. The parallel sequences therefore suggest that the serum resolves the tension between asocial *amour fou* and patriarchal law.

It will cure those suffering from the disease caused by making love without being in love. 'True love' is thus literally encapsulated in patriarchal law; the parachute's web of passion is the same as the laser's web of property.

The sequence which deals with the theft of the serum is still more complex, however. The theft of the serum is presented in such a way, both narratively and in the *mise en scène*, as to suggest that it is not just Marc, but also Alex's masculinity which is dependent on it. Its theft will prove that he is as good as his father was with his fingers, and if he has gone ahead with it despite his urge to dissociate himself from his father, it is to 'win' Anna's love. Alex injects this metaphor for a desired masculinity into an egg, which is placed inside a Russian doll. This curiously over-determined detail can be interpreted as the return to the pre-Oedipal (the egg within the belly of the doll), and the submission/self-effacement of the male.

Anna takes his place when she takes off along the runway in the final shot of the film. Alex, meanwhile, has been not simply annihilated, but doubly mutilated/castrated (his hand and the bullet wound), and re- or dis-organized, as the pun on the bullet-hole suggests. The statement which causes much mirth as they drive towards the aerodrome, 'j'ai un trou de balle dans le ventre', means both 'I have a bullet-hole in my stomach' and 'I have an arse-hole in my stomach'. Since Alex's stomach is where his mouth is as a ventriloquist, Alex has lost his voice, and his body is literally dis-organized as the organs are renamed and relocated in ectopic anarchy, a parody of the female-as-object, of which the surrealist Hans Bellmer's disarticulated doll is a good example. To recall the pun on 'vol' (flight/theft), Anna steals his place and his speed; he is seen half-running half-jumping at full pelt on several occasions in the film, whereas on the whole she is passive and immobile. In the final speeded-up shot of the film Anna flies away, a blurred, vanishing fetish who has killed off her voyeurs.

I began with Rimbaud, and it seems appropriate to end with what the pun on 'le vol' would recall to many French spectators: a well-known text by the feminist writer Hélène Cixous. 'La Noire vole' (literally, the black woman flies/steals) was published in 1975 and is structured on precisely the same pun, which Cixous uses to effect in expressing the mood of liberation felt by many women during the 1970s:

I never knew when I flew/stole in my dreams or in reality . . . whether I was drawn to flying/thieving for the pleasure of flying (of detaching my body from its earthbound obligations, of floating free . . . of fucking up the law of gravity and categories; of avoiding, as I escaped from the human race, the summons of the proper) or for the pleasure of thieving (of taking without paying; of derailing values, of misusing the Stock Exchange; and also, in thieving, not only the pleasure of displacing things, of renaming them, of reframing them, of disorganizing the world to reconstruct it according to my fancy, but more the pleasure of changing myself completely; and even of stealing myself from myself). (Cixous 1975: 48)

The pun on 'trou de balle' neatly summarizes my argument, since it both indicates the curious dislocation of tone, both tragic and comic, paralleled by other dislocations of style and genre, at the same time as it characterizes the derisively masochistic self-effacement of the noir male faced with the predatory flight of 'la noire vole'.

13

The Comic Film

IT's no exaggeration to say that comic films are the most popular French genre. Of the six best-selling films of the 1980s overall, five were comedies, with Coline Serreau's *Trois hommes et un couffin* (1985) the best-selling film of the decade with some 10 million spectators in France, previously outdone only by two other comedies in the 1960s, both starring the then very popular pair of comedians Bourvil and Louis de Funès, and both directed by Gérard Oury, *La Grande Vadrouille* (1966, 17,226,000 spectators) and *Le Corniaud* (1965, 11,724,000 spectators).

These two films are good examples of the more traditional type of comic film, usually called vaudeville or *boulevard*, because of its roots in theatre and music hall (theatres in Paris were found on the Grands Boulevards). Grounded in situation comedy, mainstream comic film of the vaudeville type could be said to have no substantial psychological or moral pretensions. During the 1980s, it was losing its domination. Its best-known exponents during the 1970s were Philippe de Broca (*Le Magnifique*, 1973), Georges Lautner, with a run of police comedies, Yves Robert (*Un éléphant ça trompe énormément*, 1976), Claude Zidi. Apart from Lautner, whose *Le Guignolo* (1979) with Jean-Paul Belmondo was the third best-selling film of 1980 and whose *Le Professionnel*, again with Belmondo, was the best-selling film of 1981 with close to 4 million spectators, only Zidi did particularly well during the 1980s, *Inspecteur La Bavure* (1980), with Coluche and Depardieu, and *Les Ripoux* (1984), a police comedy with Thierry Lhermitte and Philippe Noiret, getting around 2 million spectators.

Situation comedy was not always without some socio-critical intention, however, as can be seen in the films of Gérard Oury and Jean-Pierre Mocky, typical of a more sophisticated type of vaudeville. Oury's *Aventures de Rabbi Jacob* (1973) had been a satire on racism, and *L'As des as* (1982), in which Jean-Paul Belmondo plays an Olympic coach in 1936 who saves a young

Jewish boy from the Nazis, showed a similar preoccupation with anti-Semitism. *L'As des as* was the best-seller of 1982. Two of Oury's subsequent films of the 1980s similarly had either fanaticism (*La Vengeance du serpent à plumes*, 1984) or racism (*Lévy et Goliath*, 1987) at their core.

Mocky's work is more mordantly satirical than Oury's, anarchistic in conception (his *Y a-t-il un Français dans la salle?* (1982), a satire on politicians, is a case in point), and also in realization, since his films are made rapidly with little attention to detail. He has made an average of one film a year for thirty years since the 1960s, sometimes two films a year in the 1980s. *Une nuit l'Assemblé Nationale* (1988), for example, another political satire, was made between the two rounds of the legislative elections. His films usually have around 200,000 spectators in Paris and area, which is about half as many as Oury's *La Vengeance du serpent à plumes* or *Lévy et Goliath*. As Brisset comments, Mocky 'tries his hardest to shock and provoke, but his anarchistic approach sometimes leaves his spectators bemused because they do not necessarily share his sense of the burlesque' (Brisset 1990: 103).

One of the scriptwriters for the traditional comic film during the 1970s was Francis Veber, who scripted films by de Broca (*Le Magnifique*, 1973), and more especially Édouard Molinaro, including the immensely successful *La Cage aux folles* (1978). Veber was, as Siclier comments, the great revelation of 1980s comic cinema (Siclier 1991: 148), with a very successful trilogy starring Pierre Richard and Gérard Depardieu: *La Chèvre* (1981), *Les Compères* (1983), and *Les Fugitifs* (1986; the second most popular French film of that year. Veber also directed the Hollywood remake in 1989, *Three Fugitives*). The most significant aspect of these three films is that, for all their refinement of the traditional psychology of comic types, they still work on the very traditional basis of a pair of well-known male actors, as did many other lesser comic films of the 1980s (e.g. Michel Serrault and Michel Piccoli in Jacques Rouffio's *Mon beau-frère a tué ma sœur*, 1986, or Thierry Lhermitte and Jean Yanne in Gérard Mordillat's *Fucking Fernand*, 1987). Even the best-selling film of 1984, *Marche à l'ombre*, although it was directed by and starred one of the principal figures of the new *café-théâtre* type of comedy, Michel Blanc, was a very traditional road movie focusing on a pair of male losers. The opinion of critics during the 1980s was that the traditional comic film had exhausted its creative potential, even if many of the films mentioned so far were immensely successful in statistical terms.

A new type of comic film, however, based on the *café-théâtre*, seemed, at least for a time, to suggest a renewal. The *café-théâtre* phenomenon, which began in the 1960s but flourished in the wake of the May 1968 events, has been amply chronicled elsewhere (see Forbes 1992: 174–5 for a brief history, Merle (1985) for a longer history, and Grenier (1994) for a hagiographic blow-by-blow account of the most successful group, Le Splendid). The shows were based on a collection of comic sketches and gags, and were satiric and anti-conformist, tending to criticize anything which smacked of conformism to received ideas, whether left- or right-wing. They were particularly harsh on stereotypes of any sort, hence the frequent recourse to catchphrases or popular speech, recycled to absurdist effect.

The first major film success of the group which derisively called itself Le Splendid was *Les Bronzés* (1978), directed by Patrice Leconte, which satirizes the Club Méditerranée. Their second success was a film version of perhaps their most sucessful stage show, *Le Père Noël est une ordure* (1982), directed by Jean-Marie Poiré. Leconte and Poiré are the two directors who made the film versions of Le Splendid's shows, which ended in 1982 with Jean-Marie Poiré's *Papy fait de la résistance*. *Le Père Noël est une ordure* is set in the offices of SOS Détresse Amitié, a Samaritan help-line, on Christmas Eve. The following extract from the beginning of the film will give an idea of the derisive and frequently black humour of this type of comedy. Pierre (Thierry Lhermitte) and Thérèse (Anémone) are sexually repressed do-gooders, Pierre in particular being extremely prim. His catchphrase in the film is 'c'est cela' ('that's right', a pedantic version of the more common 'c'est ça'), which he frequently repeats.

[*Pierre, sitting at desk, takes the phone off the hook and rubs the mouthpiece. Close-up on a notice by the phone* ('Wiping the phone with the sponge is quickly done, and it makes people feel good, especially when the flu is about!')]: Good, good, good, good. Not too many calls, Thérèse?

Thérèse: No, nothing serious. Routine really. Just one call since 6 p.m.

Pierre: That's right, that's right. Thérèse [*answers phone*]: Hello, SOS Distress Friendship. I'm listening.

Man in booth: Hello, SOS Distress. Hello?

Thérèse: Hello? I can't hear you.

Man in booth [*holding gun to his head*]: Hello, SOS Distress. I'm at the end of the line. What should I do?

Thérèse: Hello? Press the button [*man pulls the trigger and shoots himself*].

Thérèse: Hello? Call back from a booth which is working.

Pierre: I say, Thérèse. A single call since 6 p.m., for Christmas Eve is really quiet.

Thérèse: Well, in a way, so much the better.

Pierre: That's right, that's right. So much the better for them. Because for us, in the meantime, it's really very quiet. [*He checks that the phone is on the hook. He mutters to himself.*] Telephone on the hook . . . Yes. [*To Thérèse*] Because sometimes the phone is off the hook, and so it doesn't ring, because the phone is off the hook. What.

Thérèse [*holding up three-fingered gloves*]: Well I've almost finished the gloves for my little lepers of Djakarta. I think it's completely useless. That's the Red Cross for you, they tell me to knit three-fingered gloves. Don't you think it would have been quicker to make mittens?

Pierre [*stifling laughs*]: Of course, of course. But Thérèse. If you'll allow me. A good pair of socks, and there you go! [*Laughing primly*] One does say such silly things sometimes!

As Forbes points out, 'it was probably inevitable that when these plays were produced for large audiences in the cinema, often a number of years after their first theatrical production, they lost some of their cutting edge' (Forbes 1992: 175). French critics towards the end of the decade showed considerable disillusion, both with *café-théâtre* proper, dismissed by Merle as nothing more than 'tics et radotages (*drivel*)' (Merle 1985: 35) during the 1980s, and also with its film versions. 'Tired *boulevard* tricks in modish dress', writes one in a retrospective piece on 1980s cinema in the *Revue du cinéma* (Chevassu 1988: 59); 'the costumes have changed, the language is deliberately up-to-date, but the plots and the situations are just the same as they ever were [in traditional comic films]' (ibid.).

The three films in this part of the book are connected to the two major types of comic film outlined above, but not directly. Comedy, as the most popular French genre, is no doubt too tied to its social and political context to be readily exportable, and as a consequence many of the more staple comic films already mentioned have never been distributed in the UK or USA. Curiously though, some major comic films were distributed abroad during the 1980s, and it is on three of these that the final part of the book will focus.

Trois hommes et un couffin, no doubt because it was the decade's best-seller, was not just distributed abroad, but also had a remake in the USA (*Three Men and a Baby* (1987), directed by Leonard Nimoy). Much of the work done on the film has focused on cultural differences between the two versions, despite the fact that, as Chevassu points out, the French film is 'closer to American comedy than to French comedy' (Chevassu 1988: 61).

Although none of the films connected directly to the shows of Le Splendid were distributed abroad, the first two films of Étienne Chatiliez have been. *La Vie est un long fleuve tranquille* (1987) was the third best-selling French film of 1988; indeed, it was the only French comic film and the only comic film of the twenty-five films with more than 1 million spectators, managing more of them than Bertolucci's *The Last Emperor* (2,354,000 spectators) and *Crocodile Dundee II* (2,281,000 spectators). Some critics have suggested that the film's humour is less related to *café-théâtre* than to pre-war French film with 'strong secondary characters and basic irreverence. [Chatiliez] is less heir to *Les Bronzés* than to Prévert and Carné's *Drôle de drame*' (Heymann 1988). Nevertheless, Chatiliez's frequent references to a fundamentally derisive style of humour suggests the contrary. He says, for example, that he and his co-scriptwriter, Florence Quentin (who had previously been an assistant for Pialat), 'wanted to speak of how derisive life is' (Chatiliez 1987: 122), meaning by this that he wished to counter the 1980s spirit whereby 'people help others to give themselves a good conscience and to be forgiven for not liking anybody' (Chatiliez 1988*b*), his aim therefore being 'to make people laugh while deriding what surrounds them' (Chatiliez 1988*c*: 5). It is not just the derisive aspect of the film's humour which places Chatiliez's films in the *café-théâtre* tradition. The casting of Tsilla Chelton as the eponymous heroine of his second feature, *Tatie Danielle* (1990), also suggests a link, since Chelton acted as coach and mentor for the members of Le Splendid 1970–3 (see Grenier 1994: 61–5).

Blier is arguably one of the key figures of the 1980s, although he made several important films in the 1970s, notably *Les Valseuses* (1973) and *Buffet froid* (1979), both of which starred Gérard Depardieu. *Les Valseuses* starred not just Depardieu, but two other actors with origins in the *café-théâtre*, Miou-Miou and Patrick Dewaere. These actors were part of the Café de la Gare, which, with Le Splendid, was the best known of the *café-théâtres*. Blier was to use Depardieu again in an almost self-parodic remake of *Les Valseuses*, *Tenue de soirée* (1986), with Miou-Miou and Michel Blanc (originally from the group of Le Splendid). *Tenue de soirée* is the final film to be considered in the following part of the book. As Forbes has pointed out, Blier's humour, as might be expected given the actors mentioned, is heavily influenced by *café-théâtre* (Forbes 1992: 175), the derision here being not so much the dismantling of stereotypes as their subversion: Depardieu plays a gay, and eventually transvestite, burglar smitten by the unlikely charms of Michel Blanc. The situation allows Blier to question Depardieu's star image at the same time as received notions of masculinity at the end of the 1980s.

Beyond their links, then, either direct or indirect to the two main types of comic film mentioned above, the films in this section have been chosen because of their focus on men and sexuality. The function of comedy is at one and the same time to express a problematic male identity and to alleviate male apprehension in laughter. As was the case with the *polar*, women characters are repatriated within the Law, or, failing that, excluded or ridiculed, as the men tread a precarious path towards a redefinition of their roles.

14

Trois hommes et un couffin:
Hysterical Homoeroticism

COLINE SERREAU'S *Trois hommes et un couffin* was one of the more surprising successes of the 1980s, with some 10 million French spectators, making it the third best-seller of the post-war period (after two 1960s comedies by Oury). Partly because of the Hollywood remake, it has been much commented on by American critics working in the feminist paradigm. This is less due to Serreau's feminist credentials than to the fact that it has a female director who seems to be registering a profound social change in masculine roles, while at the same time exhibiting misogynistic tendencies. These tendencies have been well documented; this chapter will review them, and then focus on male bonding and homoeroticism.

Before doing so, it is worth placing the film in its context so that some measure of its extraordinary success can be taken. Serreau began her career as a minor actress in the mid-1970s, and had only made three films before *Trois hommes et un couffin*. The first, *Mais qu'est-ce qu'elles veulent?* (1975), was a documentary on the condition of women. The second, *Pourquoi pas!* (1977), was also in the spirit of May 1968 and feminism. Like *Trois hommes et un couffin*, it is a comedy focusing on a threesome, a woman breadwinner, a domesticated man, and a male artist. Interestingly, given the subject of *Trois hommes et un couffin*, it concluded that bisexuality was a possibility for a man. *Qu'est-ce qu'on attend pour être heureux?* (1982), again in the post-1968 spirit, is an allegory of exploitation, focusing on the revolt of technicians and actors against the director of an advertising film. For the spectators of *Trois hommes et un couffin*, Serreau would therefore have carried the connotations of post-1968 feminist. Neither her profile nor her status, however, can be adduced for the huge success of *Trois hommes et un couffin*. This is also true of the actors. Dussollier was a minor character actor in the 1980s. Although he had made some twenty films before *Trois hommes et un couffin*, including a few lead roles in films by minor directors, he had always played minor or secondary roles in the films by the better-known directors, such as Chabrol in the mid-1970s, Rivette and Rohmer in the early 1980s; one exception to this, however, is a major role in Resnais's *L'Amour à mort* (1984). Giraud had only made two films with minor roles, and Boujenah only one, although admittedly the lead, in Saint-Hamant's *Mais qu-est-ce que j'ai fait au bon dieu pour avoir une femme qui boit dans les cafés avec les hommes?* (1980), a comedy about a weak man whose wife leaves him when he tries to be firm with her. *Trois hommes et un couffin*'s success cannot be put down to the reputation of the director or the actors. Nor, finally, can it be attributed to promotion, since it was handled by a small-time producer, Jean-François Lepetit, whose Flach Films had been established only a year before, and had only produced or co-produced two films, Doillon's *La Vie de famille* (1985) and Hansel's *Dust* (1985; see Tavenas and Volard 1989: 225–6).

If the film was so successful, it is clearly because it touched a nerve in French spectators. What Modleski says of the American remake is probably also true of the French film, as are several of her points, which I shall discuss in this chapter. She points out that women spectators 'are as amused and deeply touched by the film as men are', pointing out that in her experience

Much of the laughter at the beginning of the film was aimed at the men for the incompetence they displayed in dealing with the child, although by the end, the pathos of the situation had clearly overwhelmed all other response. No doubt, too, the film speaks to a legitimate desire on the part of women for men to become more involved in interpersonal relationships, to be more nurturant as individuals, and to assume greater responsibility for childcare. (Modleski 1988: 79–80)

This is borne out by French advertising campaigns of the time, especially the Cadum advertisement mentioned above in the section on the *polar*, featuring a 'pregnant' male. The film's success, therefore, was largely due, it would seem, to its articulation and problematization of changing gender roles.

That articulation, as many critics have pointed out, is fundamentally conservative. Modleski's view is that the film is regressive, not least because it marginalizes women. The effect of a film like *Trois hommes et un couffin*, she argues, 'is simply to give men more options than they already have in patriarchy: they can be real fathers, "imaginary" fathers, godfathers, *and*, in the older sense of the term, surrogate mothers' (Modleski 1988: 80; her emphasis). Fischer points out that misogyny in the comic film is well established from Chaplin onwards in so far as it involves the erasure of women by the male hero or, more frequently, heroes; or, if women are present, by the erasure of their maternal function, most often seen in the assumption of the maternal role by the male hero. Fischer's analysis of the film shows (and her comments are echoed by many of the reviews of the time) how the film promotes men as superior 'mothers' to women, vilifying or degrading the women in the film, and even fantasizing the biological assumption of the maternal function when Jacques stuffs a pillow under his pullover, a scene echoed in the American remake, as well as in the advertising campaigns mentioned above. Modleski interprets the fantasy as a paradoxical combination of envy and fear of feminization: 'men can want to *be* women and still hate and fear them ... This envy is in fact concomitant with a fear of feminization, even though existing in logical contradiction to it, so that male identification with woman is hedged about with many varieties of "masculine protest" ' (Modleski 1988: 70; her emphasis).

MASCULINE PROTEST

One of the ways in which this 'protest' manifests itself in the film is the hysterical mobility of the men, who constantly run from one end of the flat to the other, as if to escape the domesticity it represents, and the calm of nurture to which they are frequently 'condemned' when they have to feed Marie. Jacques, as the most professionally (and sexually) mobile of the three, manifests this attempted escape additionally by his protests at being 'grounded'. The décor is organized in such a way that it accentuates at one and the same time the flat's labyrinthine domestic space as well as the Dutch interior perspectives which emphasize the men's breakneck sprints. These sprints are clearly part of the grammar of the farce genre, but they also 'prove' that the men are real men, and not 'just' 'mothers' caught in the domestic uterine labyrinth.

Another, more obvious way of registering protest, which is also superficially part of the film's grammar, is the constant and loud arguments the men have, either with intruders (whether these be gangsters, guests, or nanny), or, more frequently, between themselves. That such arguments are inimical to the nurturing role is stressed by the most comical of them, when the three men begin arguing over Marie's cradle after singing her to sleep, and march off to Pierre's room to air their conflicting opinions. The incident is double-edged, however. By marching off determinedly to 'have an argument', they are showing that they are 'real men'. This is presumably to compensate for the three-part rendering of 'Au clair de la lune' to send Marie to sleep, which the audience is at least partly supposed to judge through Jacques's girlfriend's eyes. On hearing the singing, she comments, unaware of the baby's presence (a fact which in itself is hardly believable), that 'Jacques is totally nuts'. Jacques, and the others, are 'nuts' because they are nurturers, as is stressed by the departure of Jacques's girlfriend, whom he had abandoned in bed; they have preferred the baby to her, nurturing to sex, in a comic reversal of stereotypical male lust. On the one hand, then, the men's argument tells the audience that they are 'real men', but on the other, since, like almost all of their arguments in the film, it is about nurturing, it allows them to be both 'real men' as well as nurturers.

This split role is emphasized in this sequence by the standard melodramatic device of the mirror. As Jacques goes from his bedroom and sex to Marie's bedroom and nurturing, he is seen in the mirror which lies midway. This detail might not seem so remarkable were it not for the fact that it occurs throughout the film. Whenever Pierre and Michel have to assume the nurturing role before Jacques's return from Thailand, they too are reflected in one of the various mirrors which adorn the walls of the flat.

A final contradictory way of registering protest at the assumption of the female role is what at first sight appears to be clumsily grafted onto a domestic comedy plot, namely the drugs plot. Durham suggests that these two plots are significantly gendered and incompatible. On the one hand, there is 'a male story of action and adventure, of opposition to law and order', and on the other 'a female plot of domesticity, of compliance with societal norms and values' (Durham 1992: 775). The drugs plot functions primarily as a means of reinstating the threatened masculinity of the trio (and less, as Durham suggests at a later stage of her argument, as an ironic comment on the illegitimacy of both drugs trafficking and the assumption of the maternal role by men; see Durham 1992: 780). Nevertheless, it is contradictory in its function, since it leads the most anti-female of the trio (Pierre, who says at one point that it has always been understood that if a female came to live in the flat more than one night, he would immediately leave) to display 'maternal' concern at Marie's welfare when the flat has been ransacked by the gangsters.

THE DRUGS PLOT AND
OEDIPAL CONFIGURATIONS

The drugs plot may well help prove that the men are 'real' men, but when examined more closely, its function appears considerably more complex. The drugs plot locks the trio in a regressive Oedipal configuration, as well as accentuating their homoerotic bonding, as we shall see. Modleski suggests that the drugs plot crystallizes the rejection of the symbolic father. Although her comments are directed at the American film, they are just as true of the French film, which 'is centered around a paradox: in order for the men to be the kind of fathers they want to be (fathers who also take on the role of mothers, of nurturers), the men actually have to deny the father who represents the law' (Modleski 1988: 75). In the process, as Modleski succinctly puts it, 'they refuse to grow up' (Modleski 1988: 75), as can be seen in the hyperactivity generated by the drugs plot, with even more frantic running around, and even more hysterical shouting than usual. It is their relationship with the police, however, which crystallizes their refusal of the law.

This begins as farce when the gendarme interrupts Pierre's discussion with the gangsters. Apart from forcing Pierre into connivance with the gangsters, a 'bond' which is outside the law, the sequence generates comedy because the patriarchal figure loses control of the situation (the gangsters escape when Pierre tries to walk off unnoticed), as is made clear by the gendarme's comment that he 'doesn't like being made a fool of'. The French expression is not just more vulgar, it is more apposite given the Oedipal conflict involved, since it is 'se foutre de ma gueule', suggesting etymologically that the men are ridiculing the policeman by ejaculating in his face. Pierre receives his come-uppance, as it were, when the gendarme accompanies him to the flat and listens in to the telephone conversation Pierre has with Jacques. Both men stand in front of the mirror, which as we have seen is nearly always a sign of the split or splitting masculine role. Indeed, at this point Pierre is the abandoned 'mother' holding his child, unable to castigate Jacques because the policeman is listening in. The policeman is also in the mirror, but only partially so, the prying patriarchal father who has caught out the errant son, who can only voice the lament of an abandoned 'wife' as on the other end of the line Jacques tells him that he is 'on to a good thing', by which he means a woman. Authority figures will subsequently multiply as in a bad dream. The gendarme returns with two plain clothes policemen, and after the wrecking of the flat by the gangsters, four policemen come to carry on searching. In the course of the three invasions by the police, Michel and more particularly Pierre increasingly take on the maternal role. This is underlined in the first two sequences by the references to making up the baby's bottle and changing her. In the final sequence, after the flat has been ransacked, it is underlined partly by costume, since the two men are in their dressing gowns, but also by a curious *mise en scène* in the bedroom. The detective politely asks Pierre first to take the cradle off the bed, and then the baby out of the cradle, as he proceeds to strip both bed and cradle of bedclothes. The sequence is curious because of the comic distance established between exaggerated politeness (Pierre is after all 'a nursing mother'), and the manic stripping of the bedclothes, as if to stress the disparity between the male and female plots, and the male and female/maternal roles concurrently adopted by Pierre.

Pierre and Jacques are of course being 'punished' by the hysterically multiplying and hysterically acting policemen for their 'transgressive' assumption of the maternal role. But the transgression in question is ambiguous, as the first of these sequences with the police indicates. When the gendarme, seeing Michel, asks who he is, Pierre answers that he shares the flat with him. 'I see', says the gendarme. 'No, you don't see at all', responds Pierre irritably, realizing that the gendarme is implicitly assuming that Michel and Pierre are gay, 'three of us share the flat together', to which the gendarme answers, 'even better'. In other words, the men are being criticized as much for their homosocial bonding as for their assumption of the maternal role. Although it is true that three rather than two men 'confirm(s) the protagonists' virile hetero-sexuality (two men might be suspect) and minimize(s) the risk that child care might feminize them' (Forbes 1986: 170), a point Pierre's own comment supports, nevertheless the gendarme, and indeed the audience, might well remain sceptical. As Modleski says of the American film (and the comment could apply equally to the French film), 'we can speculate that the popularity of [the film] is partly attributable to its successful negotiation of homosocial desire—male bonding in this case being effected through the agency of a baby girl, rather than through the exchange of women, as has usually been the case' (Modleski 1988: 74). This is particularly true of the American film, as several commentators have pointed out, with its sexualization of the baby. This sexualization does not occur in the French film, but the point still holds: the men's desire for each other is displaced onto the baby, as we shall see. It is also manifested in a number of other displacements during the course of the film.

FROM THE HOMOSOCIAL TO THE HOMOEROTIC

When Jacques returns from his travels, he calls out to his flatmates, saying 'Coo-ee, I've got lots of presents for you.' Present-giving as an element of bonding occurs elsewhere in the film, for example when Pierre makes it clear that the reason it was he who stumbled on the cradle rather than Michel was because he was about to go and get Michel's croissants for him. Apart, then, from bonding through present-giving, the sequence is interesting in its implied distribution of gender stereotypes between the apparently more domesticated Michel (who works at home), and the aggressively irritable Pierre, whose 'maleness' is eventually questioned, not least by his position in the threesome, where he is more linked by the narrative and the *mise en scène* to the maternal function than Jacques. Jacques's return is, as one might expect, connoted as the return of the errant 'husband'. Not only does he compensate for his absence by offering presents, but Pierre and Michel, sitting primly and silently, refuse to acknowledge his jubilation. Michel is seated with Marie in his lap, the image of the domesticated woman, and Pierre mirrors him, with a phallic baby's bottle over his genitals (grossly echoed in the red-shaded table lamp by Michel's side), his masculinity 'castrated' by his nurturing role. The film therefore mediates homosocial bonding through traditional gender roles. On the one hand there is the 'feminine' Michel, domesticated from the start because he works at home, as several commentators have pointed out; he is mirrored by Pierre, whose aggressivity is eventually tempered by nurturing. On the other hand, there is the sexually hyperactive male, Jacques, whose mobility and sexual prowess is rarely tempered by nurturing. When he is involved in nurturing, either he is about to fly away (to Nice to try to get his mother to look after Marie), or he is climbing out of a bed which contains a woman.

Male bonding does not only occur between the three flatmates. I have already alluded to their connivance with the gangsters, aggravated by the farcical misunderstandings centring on and vehicled by the 'heroine' (a misunderstanding which is peculiarly apt in respect of women's role as objects of exchange: the female is quite literally the illicit object of male trading). That connivance is made manifest through the only form of touching males can reasonably expect in a film of this type: aggression. When the gendarme approaches, one of the gangsters grabs Pierre and threatens him, an action repeated by Michel on another gangster in the supermarket. Although hardly the masochistic and spectacular violence referred to by Neale in relation to the displaced homo-eroticism of the western, the action is nevertheless significant. More significant is the display of the men's bodies, which definitively turns the homosocial into the homoerotic.

Given the domestic context, it is 'natural' that we should see the men frequently undressed. But the development from full clothing at the beginning of the film to almost total nakedness is a gradual one, corresponding not just to the men's assumption of the nurturing role, but their acceptance of it. This acceptance is at its most apparent in the final sequence, when all three rush to the door half-naked to reassume the nurturing role which Sylvia is unable to carry out. The three men subsequently dance about half-naked in the kitchen, kissing and cuddling the baby, who here acts as a vehicle for male bonding articulated less around language than around touch, albeit displaced. There is one interesting exception to the equation of male bonding mediated through states of domestic undress; it is Jacques being stripped at the airport under suspicion of smuggling drugs. Even here, however, the editing establishes a parallel between Jacques at the airport and the other two at home as they wait for Jacques's return. The stripping by two customs officers, whom we see feeling up and down his trouser legs as he sits naked and bemused, prefigures the verbal stripping Jacques will receive from his flatmates, and his gradual if reluctant assumption of the nurturing role.

Gender stereotyping, physical aggression, and display are all vehicles for homoerotic bonding. Equally significant are a set of sequences with Marie where the homoerotic bonding displaced onto Marie, potentially unsettling, resurfaces as textual disturbance. The first is Pierre's return to the ransacked flat. It is filmed with an expressionistic Steadicam which follows Pierre through the flat, as he frantically searches for Marie. That this is a crucial sequence is indicated by the soundtrack. It is the first music to occur since the title sequence, and unlike the cool jazz of that sequence, Pierre's search is accompanied by the plangent melancholy of Schubert's String Quintet in C major. The sequence marks Pierre's acceptance of his feelings for Marie, indicated subsequently by his lack of clothes as he lies in bed while Michel changes her next to him; prior to this, Pierre had never been seen undressed. Those feelings are emphasized by a close-up of Pierre, who has discovered Marie in the toilet, and is cuddling her with relief. He is lit by an eerie blue light and covered by equally expressionistic shadows from the blind, as he whispers comfortingly to her, only to be surprised, and indeed embarrassed by Michel's arrival.

The sequence is paralleled by a second disrupted sequence. This is when Pierre surprises Michel babbling to the baby in excessively loud and high-pitched baby-talk. Whereas melodramatic excess in the first sequence was configured through a paradoxical combination of classical music and expressionistic *mise en scène*, here it is figured through the standard melodramatic device of the mirror in which Pierre can be seen, and by excessive awkwardness on the part of both men. Not only does Michel stand rigid, presumably embarrassed that Pierre may have overheard his baby noises, but excessively long and unnatural silences punctuate their otherwise banal conversation. In the following sequence, it is Pierre who baths the baby, talking to her quietly, and the contrast between their different types of address to Marie only serves to highlight the excessiveness of Michel's behaviour.

The bathing sequence is the third disrupted sequence. This time, it is neither *mise en scène* nor dialogue which ruffles what might on the surface seem more like an advertisement for a baby soap, as Pierre croons at Marie in sentimental close-up. It is rather that an attentive spectator will do a double-take, since Pierre does not bath a baby, he baths two babies, and the double-take is echoed by a literal double take of two pairs of shots. The sequence is comprised of a long introductory shot as Pierre puts Marie in the bath, followed by a superimposed shot, followed by a fade into another pair of superimposed shots, but this time with a clearly different baby. The fades and superimpositions, techniques which do not occur elsewhere in the film, are a cinematographic form of textual disturbance, paralleled by the extreme disruption caused by the 'doubled' baby.

Potentially problematic homoerotic bonding is then effected through parallel sequences of nurturing which have elements, albeit different elements, of textual disturbance, as the bonding, repressed and displaced onto Marie, returns to distort the naturalistic surface with constantly shifting but clearly excessive interferences. The final shots of the film will bring together the points I have been making.

SCHUBERT AND THE RETURN OF THE REPRESSED

Commentators have stressed the infantilization of Sylvia, the baby's mother, who is curled up asleep in the baby's cradle, her thumb in her mouth. Uncomfortably regressive, the image stresses the extent to which a woman who wants to work cannot manage by herself. Sylvia had said earlier in the film, 'my job comes first', and in one of the more interesting sequences concerning her, she is spied on by Michel who sees her change clothes and personalities from top model with high-heels to low-heeled low-status old-clothed mother. In the final sequence, it is not just Michel who stares at her, but all three men, clutching the apparel of nurturing (the baby's bedclothes, the tray for her high chair, and her bottle). But those three men are half-naked, a homoerotic bonding displaced onto the 'fallen' woman, who has fallen so far from her maternal 'destiny' that she has become the thing she engendered, a baby. Throughout this final sequence of the film, from the moment Michel opens the door to the distraught Sylvia, the music is the same plangent string quintet which had previously occurred when Pierre had frantically sought Marie in the ransacked flat. Since there is so little music in the film, the recall is significant. It clearly signals the reintegration of Marie into the men's world, just as it had done for Pierre. In the latter sequence, its melancholy functioned as a sign of threatened loss, and recognition of the loss as threat rather than as something to be desired. Why, however, is such melancholic music repeated on Marie's return, when the men are so clearly pleased at her return? The obvious answer might seem to be that fundamentally the men do not desire her return, that it forms part of the split role which has occurred narratively and in the *mise en scène* through the use of mirrors.

Of course, on one level the men are pleased to reassume the nurturing function. The narrative prior to the closing sequence sketches out an absurd 'post-partum depression': the men are aimless, Michel cannot create, and doodles pictures of Marie; Pierre clutches her toy giraffe, and refuses to eat; and, finally, Jacques, the father, refuses to work. Not only does he ask Michel, 'what am I living for?', repeated in heavy-handed melodramatic close-up, but he stuffs a pillow under his jumper, drinks too much, and launches into a drunken tirade in the company of the uncomprehending ex-policeman, referring to the Adam and Eve myth, and melancholically pointing out that male creativity is defective since 'nothing comes out of our rib', by which he means that men can create but not procreate.

The men therefore desire to reassume the nurturing role, but the music suggests that there is a fundamental problem. The loss implied by the music cannot be Marie, since she is with them. Moreover, when in the final shot she appears through the door as they gaze at the sleeping Sylvia, the music shifts from the melancholic slow movement to a faster, happier movement. The hypothesis with which I would like to finish is that despite the pleasure of male nurturing which the film vehicles, and which echoes socially changing gender roles, the film also, contradictorily, vehicles melancholy at the loss of a non-nurturing role defined as masculine. More worryingly, and certainly more regressively, the film also vehicles melancholy at the thought of the homoeroticism with which that nurturing is curiously bound up. It is as if the film is saying that if men become nurturers, even a threesome is no guarantee that they will not stop at a simple redistribution of the maternal and the paternal between the sexes, but that there will be reorientation of desire as men get in touch, literally, not just with themselves, but with each other. It is hardly surprising that the final image of the film is a freeze-frame of Marie, as if to re-establish the primacy of the desiring male gaze threatened by a pre-Oedipal utopia of a fatherless *Boy's Own* world where mothers are babies, and men are boys being mothers, and discovering how they like to touch each other after all.

15

La Vie est un long fleuve tranquille: Fallen Angels and Men Overboard

ONE of the more curious aspects of the success of *La Vie est un long fleuve tranquille* is the contradictory critical discourses which surrounded it on its release. The film was praised both for its realism, and for its caricatural elements. My argument in the first part of this chapter will be that this contradiction is essential because it allows a consensual positioning of the spectator, reinforced by elements of nostalgia inherent in the narrative. The effect of this nostalgic consensuality is to deny any political force to the derision intended by Chatiliez and his co-scriptwriter Quentin. However, in the second part of the chapter I shall be arguing that it is not so much the derision applied to social distinctions which makes the film interesting and indeed provocative, as the fixation on sex and its impact on gender relations. Although all the adult characters are ruthlessly derided in the film, it is essentially the women, with one important exception, who seem to suffer more, punished for their maternal 'instincts'. The film, like *Trois hommes et un couffin*, punishes women. Here it is either by ridicule, or by underlining their malevolence, or by engineering a tragic fall, whereas in *Trois hommes et un couffin* women are simply expelled as unworthy from the new man's assumption of the maternal role. It is true, of course, that men are also ridiculed in the film, in an apparently general and ultimately amoral derision; but, again, there is one exception, and my contention is that the most significant characters in the film are the exceptions, because they prove the rule which underlies this book: that 1980s French film is obsessively concerned with repositioning men, and keeping women in their place.

REALISM AND STEREOTYPE

Anyone reading parts of reviews of the film would have assumed that it was some kind of documentary. Its major virtue is its 'sketch of daily life' (Tranchant 1988), and its 'sociological and visual detail is right on target' (Mosca 1988: 7); indeed, for the critic of *Le Monde*, the film verges on the 'ethnographic report' (Heymann 1988). For others, however, one of the film's weaknesses is its dependence on stereotype, although here opinions are divided. For some critics, it is just the Groseilles who are examples of 'monstrosity' (Nortier 1988), while Madame Le Quesnoy is by contrast a rounded character. For others, both families are stereotypes, ressembling the comic cartoon types of Reiser, or those of the satiric magazine *Hara-Kiri* (Schidlow 1988: 24). The reviewer of the *Cahiers du cinéma*, focusing as many did on the fact that Chatiliez was a well-known director of television adverts, emphasized the lack of depth of the characters, linking it less to the notion of stereotype than to an attachment to the surface quality of the image (a charge levelled at Beineix and Besson):

Everything is in and for the image, everything is in the sound, leaving no space for anything off-screen. This is why the characters (perfect 'casting cloning' [*sic*] which leaves no surprises), like the shots, look like what they are (and nothing else). This is why they spend their time powdering themselves, making themselves up, colouring their hair, as if what they appear to be was a sign for what they are. (S. 1988: 61)

Only one or two reviewers saw that the realism was in fact hyper-realism, and that Chatiliez had persuaded 'the spectator that his caricatures, by their very excess, become real' (Benoist). Alain Schifres, who writes for *Le Nouvel Observateur*, pointed out, with his usual penchant for paradox, that the film's hyper-realism and its 'hallucinatory precision' meant that 'the characters aren't characters who remind you of real people, they are people who remind you of characters . . . His characters aren't caricatures but types' (Schifres 1988: 44).

NOSTALGIA, INNOCENCE, AND CONSENSUS

Schifres also reminds us that the characters do not just cause recognition in the spectator, but self-recognition, linked with nostalgia:

You feel that you knew them when you were younger and that there's something of them in you. There are Groseille left-wing rebels at the heart of Le Quesnoy centrists. There are non-Christian Le Quesnoys in the Mitterrand generation. There are Groseille activists among Le Pen's supporters, who lay into Arabs with more than just words. (Schifres 1988: 44)

This comment also underlines the move towards a consensual spectator position, consonant with the gradual de-bipolarization of French political life as the Socialists under Mitterrand became increasingly centrist during the 1980s. The film postulates two extreme 'types' which spectators can recognize in themselves, not in actuality, but in imagination. The consensuality vehicled by the film did not escape the reviewers of the time: 'The imaginary of the period is that there is no more class conflict, just a deep-seated contempt ... The ideal is to be comfortably upper class while keeping a foothold in the working class' (Mongin 1988); and another formulates what he suggests is every French person's 'dream': 'Rich man's son and poor man's kid, a real cultural hybrid' (Lefort 1988).

Indeed, for all the comments on the film's acid (the word which is frequently used is 'décapant', as of a corrosive chemical which removes a polished surface) and irreverent humour, there are as many which try to convince the reader of the film's ability not to offend, in other words to stake out a middle ground for comfortably middle-class spectators, who can say to themselves, 'I am neither the Groseilles nor the Le Quesnoys, but (I think) I know many who are like them, and maybe I or my family were like this once upon a time in deepest France, but I am not like that any more.' For this position to function, the irony must not be in too sharp a focus, but whether it is or not, the reviewers seemed keen to persuade their readers that the film, as one puts it, 'can be seen by all' (Gasperi 1988). The film 'spares nothing but respects everybody' (Heymann 1988), its 'irony has something soft and well-behaved about it' (Tranchant 1988), the 'sarcasm is not insulting' (Audé 1988: 76); indeed, the gags 'are never nasty, and the film has an exceptionally innocent quality' (Gasperi 1988).

The most important character in respect of consensus is Momo, the link between the two extremes. The *Cahiers du cinéma* critic accuses the character of blandness ('fadeur') (S. 1988: 61), apparently blind to the fact that it is essential that he must be bland for consensuality to function. Momo cannot be a (stereo)type like the other children in the film. He has to be sufficiently valueless and free-floating for him to be able to transfer effortlessly from one world to the other, the only signifier of the transfer being the hair he hastily rearranges in a mirror on a street-corner (accompanied by the unbuttoning of his shirt), codifying appearance rather than moral value as the (literally) crucial (crossing) issue. Although I agree with Marshall's view that *Mo*mo represents *mo*bility (Marshall 1992: 140; his emphasis), I am less certain that the masquerade in the mirror corresponds to a fragmented nation which is 'represented in terms of liminality and frontiers', and that Momo 'points the way forward to new identities based on hybridity, to a self knowingly constituted by difference and relations to others, plural and *disponible*' (ibid.). I would see the film as operating rather towards a blurring of frontiers by its excessive positioning of them as extremes in the form of the two families, as Marshall recognizes when he explores the way in which 'the two families induce both recognition and distance', the two world-views they represent preparing 'the way for a new consensus' (ibid. 139) which he optimistically locates in Momo. In the next section I shall attempt to show how Momo evinces neither blandness nor optimism. The underlying reason has to do with what any comedy will always include: sex.

SEX AND THE UPWARDLY MOBILE URCHIN

Sex and death are intimately linked in the film. Josette, Doctor Mavial's assistant and mistress, would like to take the place of Mavial's terminally sick wife, who benefits from Mavial's attentions and continued presence, whereas Josette is always left alone and lonely on festive occasions. The polarity between the two is emphasized: Josette is as voluble as Madame Mavial is the opposite, entreating Mavial to be quiet as she watches the television news account of the blowing up of Hamed's car. Her face is as unseen as Josette's face is excessively visible, an open book upon which emotions run melodramatically, particularly during the baby-swapping scene, where her face is contorted by a mixture of pain and revenge in classic cartoon style. The baby-swapping is the motor of the plot, occasioned by the death of the wife and the revenge of the humiliated mistress, whose infatuation for the doctor is such that she cannot resist the gropings of Mavial and is reduced to furtive couplings in the surgery rather than the romantic dinner for two she so yearns for. Sex coupled with death is therefore at the film's origins, and it returns as the repressed always does in a variety of forms throughout the course of the film.

The opening shot of the film, Hamed's car apparently destroyed by racist vandals, suggests deep-seated racial conflict. This is immediately negated in one of the following scenes by Hamed's presence at the Groseilles', where he is playing cards. The film is here working towards a consensus which negates racial conflict, or at least contains it within the confines of unsavoury banter. In this scene the Groseilles warn their daughter that she should not sleep with an Arab, and in a later scene with Hamed when they are arguing about what they call his 'shitty grocery store', they respond to Hamed's protestations by references to 'what the French did to the Arab grocers during the [Algerian] war'. Both dialogues suggest that they form part of a ritual which may superficially suggest the conflict encoded in the blown-up car, but in reality, just as the blown-up car will turn out to be an insurance scam designed by Hamed and Momo, so too the racist banter is overtaken by elements of consensus, made all the more clear by the opening shot of the card-playing scene, which focuses on Hamed's young son and the young Groseille daughter kissing and cuddling on the sofa, as Roselyne prepares to 'get [her cards] laid on the table'.

Roselyne's promiscuity is emphasized several times during the film. As she leaves the card-playing Groseilles, she encounters the electricity company engineers on the stairs, and the embarrassed comment by the one to his colleague, that he only knows her 'by sight', comically underlines the promiscuity mentioned during the card-playing scene. She later visits the Le Quesnoys and purposely drops her handkerchief when leaving so as to exhibit her posterior to the astonished Monsieur Le Quesnoy, commenting lewdly that he has good views from his house. Roselyne is the more blatant example of what typifies the Groseilles, a penchant for extreme physicality. It is she who says to Paul Le Quesnoy when he is about to go on holiday for a month that she will not wash during that time so as to keep his smell. The Groseille physicality is also linked to violent and abusive behaviour, witness Madame Groseille spitting and hurling her drink at the television announcer she detests, saying, 'who does she think she is with her face like an arsehole (*tronche de fion*). Slut! (*pouffiasse*)', the eldest son lasciviously rubbing his penis and murmuring, 'Well I wouldn't mind sticking her on my end.'

Sex gradually 'infects' the repressed Le Quesnoys: Bernadette, who is biologically a Groseille, dresses up in Madame Le Quesnoy's clothes and make-up, which would appear relatively innocuous were it not for Madame Le Quesnoy's exaggerated reaction: 'but what's got into you, child? Have you completely lost your senses?' Paul, the eldest Le Quesnoy, falls for Roselyne, tiring her out with his constant demand for sex amongst the thistles by the motorway. Monsieur Le Quesnoy, at the height of his wife's disarray, when she is drinking and wearing glasses, is sexually aroused, and utters one of the many phrases which became catchphrases, 'you [using the formal 'vous' form, totally inappropriate to the rest of the sentence] are giving me a hard-on' ('vous me faites bander'). The most interesting example, however, of the return of repressed sexuality is Momo.

Once integrated in the Le Quesnoy family, Momo is sexually attracted to Madame Le Quesnoy, his biological mother. This attraction begins when he sees her bathing. The scene is filmed in a way to suggest a formative sexual experience, such as the primal scene. Momo peeps through the bathroom door, and stands smitten, visibly shaken when he goes back downstairs. He subsequently offers his mother a flower picture made from shells. It is an appropriate present given the bathroom scene. The shells play on two related meanings, one verbal ('mer', the sea, related homonymically to 'mère' the mother), the other visual, since Madame Le Quesnoy ressembles Botticelli's Venus in the 'shell' of her bath. Momo's present would also seem innocuous (although in 'bad taste' for the Le Quesnoys, since it is just the type of bauble which fills the Groseilles' home), were it not for the phallic form of the picture, and for a later recall of the bath scene when Bernadette creeps into the Groseilles' flat to peep at Madame Groseille pawing at her husband and spitting vulgarly at the television presenter. The two voyeur scenes are obviously paralleled and are emphasizing repressed sexuality (Momo's displaced present) by positing its opposite extreme, aggressive sexual display by Frank.

As the location of difficult and troubled sexuality, Momo is neither bland, as the *Cahiers* critic wished readers to believe, nor does he allow much optimism, as Marshall argues. It is possible to read his crucial/crossing position as a problem for him rather than as the location of a freer, hybrid, and plural identity. True, as Marshall points out, Momo is active when mirrored, as opposed to Bernadette's passivity in the wardrobe's mirrors (or indeed that of Monsieur and Madame Le Quesnoy, who are frequently framed by mirrors or reflected in windows). True, when accosted by the policeman at the end of the film, Momo/Maurice gives his name as 'Le Quesnoy-Groseille', and tells the policeman, concerned that he might be lost, that 'he knows the way'. Both of these factors do indeed suggest confidence in a double (rather than plural) identity. But this view does not take account of the two final and problematic shots of the film. The first is the crane shot of a Chaplinesque Momo disappearing into the night down an empty street. The final shot is the sudden switch from the maudlin sentimentality of Chaplin to the grating music of Maurice Jarre's 'Paris en colère' which accompanies the triumphant Josette as she sits on the verandah of her holiday pavilion overlooking an equally empty but sunlit beach, with Mavial wheelchair-bound behind her. Marshall makes the point that the Josette/Mavial subplot, with its melodrama, is 'almost another film from the narrative of the two families Josette's *crime passionnel* in fact sets in motion' (Marshall 1992: 136). Chatiliez's comment on this pair of shots is instructive, however: 'Momo walking off is Chaplin going to his destiny. But the film isn't actually finished. What follows this image is evil-minded; worse, it spits on the hour and a half which precedes it' (Chatiliez 1988*a*: 59). Although this comment does not invalidate Marshall's point, it suggests a much more dialectical relationship between the two components. The utopian possibilities of a hybrid identity are put into question by the dystopian final shot with its image of the castrated male.

Marshall uses the apparent dichotomy between the Josette/Mavial subplot and the family narrative to comment on the film's refusal to 'examine power relationships as regards gender, a lack made all the more visible for its dominance of the Josette/Mavial subplot' (Marshall 1992: 137). It would seem, however, that the dialectic between the two components might allow for a reassessment of this view. Before passing on to this discussion, let me recall that I have established that nostalgia for the stability of the past is paradoxically, but not illogically (since to return to your roots must entail an uprooting and rerooting), conjoined with desire for mobility. This mobility is linked with sex, unsurprisingly, since sex is the embodiment of desire. I shall now turn to what the film tells us about gender relations.

THE FALLEN ANGEL IN THE HOUSE

The two mothers are clearly the focal point of the film. The film's narrative attempts to set up strong contrasts between the two families, who are a class apart, as is signalled by their surnames. Marshall, following Bourdieu, points out how the article in Le Quesnoy signals prestige, and is also a pun on the 'French bourgeois politician par excellence' (ibid. 128), Lecanuet, whereas 'Groseille' signals everything that is 'gross'. But just as the narrative will bring the two families together with the dramatic chestnut of a mistaken identity, so too the two women, despite the contrasts, are constantly paralleled, as is suggested by their Christian names, separated only by one central letter (Marielle Le Quesnoy, Marcelle Groseille). Centrality is also crucial to the maternal function by which they are more especially paralleled, as well as their organizational capacities which dominate their respective families. As Audé points out, the fathers in the two families are dependent on their wives (Audé 1988: 76), although the differences are instructive. Both men are sedentary, particularly at the start of the film when the two families are being introduced, and Monsieur Groseille will continue to be so during the course of the film, due to his invalidity, which we are told means that his wife must constantly care for him. By contrast, Monsieur le Quesnoy will be considerably more active, venturing into the outside world of work, and into the world of the Groseilles when negotiating with them. And yet, it is clear that both women are the hubs of their households. Even in the introductory scenes, Madame Groseille directs operations in the plot to outwit the electricity company engineers, secreting the winnings from the card-game in her ample bosom, while Madame Le Quesnoy manages to organize baths and the evening meal, briefly entertain the parish priest, as well as giving her husband an illusion of authority before supper, by seeking his approval to go to table.

However different the women may be by their class, and similar by their maternal function, the film's derision is directed mainly at the Le Quesnoys, and, by virtue of her central maternal function, at Madame Le Quesnoy. The revelation of the mistaken identity is received by the whole Groseille family, and commented on by Madame Groseille in typically robust fashion ('the buggers, they've stuck us with the son of the director of the electricity company'). By contrast, and typically also, the news is seen to be received indirectly in the Le Quesnoy household, as Madame Le Quesnoy startles everybody by vomiting at the news which she presumably only divulges later that evening. The physicality which the Le Quesnoy mores tend to repress thus emerges as a symptom in the mother, whose control over the family will gradually be destroyed: not only will the children import alien mores, visibly located in objects such as Paul's wrist-bands or the young daughter's exchange of her doll for a Groseille doll, but that importation and its destruction of Madame Le Quesnoy's world will be justified by the children's reference to the Le Quesnoys' oft-stated Christian values.

Thus, Madame Le Quesnoy has to accept the fact that her daughter has given away the doll given to her for Christmas in exchange for a doll which looks remarkably like Madame Groseille and Roselyne by her dyed and unkempt hair, because her daughter says 'it's a good deed to give to the poor'. Later, her young son Pierre says that she should not shout at the pregnant Marie-Thérèse, who has been insisting that she has never slept with a man; 'maybe she isn't lying, maybe she's like the Virgin', he says. When Madame le Quesnoy comments in response that she does not deserve this, her son quotes chapter and verse, in the only reference to the title of the film: 'But Mum, we have to know what suffering is. The Good Lord is testing us. Jesus suffered on the cross for us too. Life isn't a long quiet river, Mum.' It is clearly significant that it should be Madame Le Quesnoy who is located at the centre of the film's concerns by this negative reference to the title, as the Christ-like victim whose principles come back to haunt her, driving her to drink. She is eventually persuaded to go on holiday, replaced by a tin of ravioli which one of the sons comments is just as good as home-made ravioli. The angel of the house is thus humbled as her cherished principles are used to justify the dismantling of her world-view, where sex and sexuality, whether in the shape of Bernadette's dressing-up, Marie-Thérèse's 'immaculate conception', or her husband's inept admission of desire, intrude on the discretion signalled so forcefully in verbal codes (a pedantic high-register French), dress codes (the sensible pleated skirts), and cultural artefacts (the 'tasteful' paintings of children which adorn the 'tastefully' decorated walls). Not only does she fall from highly principled heights, but her function as provider of food, exemplified in the best known of the film's catchphrases, 'c'est lundi, c'est ravioli', is derided by the tin which takes over this central function.

By contrast, Madame Groseille is less harshly treated, mainly because she cannot 'fall' much lower. And yet, she too is presented in a negative manner, usually by virtue of her colourful and often self-deprecating language, such as at the end of the film when she goes to bed, saying that 'it's time to wrap up the meat in a cloth' ('mettre la viande dans le torchon'; 'viande' also has the connotation of a corpse, and 'torchon' that of a 'slut'). But her maternal function is also put into question. When Hamed comments that Momo was the only one of any worth in the family, and 'now he's gone', she bursts out in an excessive display of maternal grief, which Hamed repeatedly says is nothing but a charade ('grimaces'); given that she was prepared to sell Momo for 20,000 francs, it is difficult not to agree. Moreover, to return to the first point concerning the parallelism between the two mothers, both are turned into sex objects in a curious exchange when Momo returns to the Groseille household. Frank asks whether Momo's mother 'is a good lay', to which Momo testily responds, as the camera closes up on him dramatically, 'what about yours?' The atmosphere is momentarily tense until the Groseilles choose to interpret Momo's comment as a joke, something the spectators are unlikely to do, since they know, unlike the Groseilles, that Momo is sexually attracted to his mother.

MEN OVERBOARD

That the point of the film is as much and perhaps more the humbling of the mothers as the consensual derision of two extreme class positions can be seen by the fact that the only woman to succeed is the antithesis of the two mothers, the childless Josette, the archetypal femme fatale who, as Mavial's mistress, has rejected the maternal role of the other two. Her triumph in the final scene of the film brings together a number of strands, the principal one being the defeat of the sexually active male/Mavial. The two fathers are also derided, however.

I have already mentioned the position of Monsieur Groseille, an invalid cared for, but also dominated by, his wife, as is emphasized by the scene when Bernadette spies on them; Madame Groseille is seen from Bernadette's point of view crouched over her thin passive husband as if to devour him. As Monsieur Groseille had said earlier in the film, when the family was playing Happy Families, 'I'll never manage to make a family', an ironic underlining of his subordinate position.

Monsieur le Quesnoy starts off from a position of apparent strength at the beginning of the film, although it is clear even then to what extent his wife runs the household. His defeat occurs later. First, there is a challenge to his paternal competence when Bernadette locks herself in her room. Monsieur Le Quesnoy fumbles helplessly with the lock, and is upstaged by Momo whose expertise in picking locks is put to good use. Monsieur Le Quesnoy then enters the bedroom, only to run out immediately as Bernadette screams. He rejoins his wife, holding his hands primly over his genitals, signalling the obvious meaning of the scene, the dismantling of his authority as castration. Later in the film his paternal authority is challenged by Paul, his eldest son. Paul first of all leads his siblings to a forbidden swim in the canal, a clear initiation for all concerned, alcoholic for one of the youngest—and alcohol is linked to sex, because the promiscuous Mavial constantly swigs at bottles of wine—and more explicitly sexual for Paul. Paul then refuses to go 'canoeing in the Pouchoulon', as had previously been arranged with that other 'father', the parish priest, and sports wrist-bands while waiting to save up for a trail bike.

Water is an all too obvious signifier of (usually sexual) authority in the film. The Groseilles dream about going to live on the Riviera and their walls are covered with enlarged photographs of it, or 'cheap' reproductions of sea scenes. What the Groseilles merely dream about, the Le Quesnoys can afford, since they go on holiday with their yacht, *The Redoutable II*. Monsieur Le Quesnoy's authority is, as the canal scene might have hinted *a contrario*, located in his expertise on the water. An early scene shows him teaching the children the names of the parts of the yacht, and in the birthday scene at the beginning of the film, he is given a life-jacket by the family. At the end of the film, his son Paul, who does not have a licence, drives Roselyne back home in the car with the yacht in tow, signalling Monsieur Le Quesnoy's loss of authority. The subtext of sexual authority represented by water is given an interesting twist in the final scene with Josette and Mavial in their holiday chalet overlooking the beach. Josette beams triumphantly as she looks out to sea, while Mavial mumbles to himself wrapped in a rug on his deckchair, signalling impotence, his erstwhile promiscuous mobility taken from him. He holds a pair of binoculars on his knees; given the emptiness of both beach and sea, they emphasize the fact that even the gaze to which he has been reduced is impotent.

The men in the film are therefore 'at sea', stranded, their authority wrecked. Even Paul, who made a brief stand against his father, seems, at the end of the film, to be ready to go on the family holiday, pathetically lamenting the fact that he will be separated from Roselyne. The only male who is not derided is Momo, and I hope to have shown that his position cannot necessarily be viewed as optimistic. The women are also derided, specifically in their maternal function. Even Josette, although she triumphs over both the maternal women and Mavial, is not allowed a real triumph. She may have her man, but it is at the price of social exclusion with a castrated male. Moreover, the final scene strikes the spectator as awkward, an addition to the closure suggested by Momo's Chaplinesque walk down the empty street; like the Josette/Mavial subplot, the final scene is isolated from the remainder of the film. Not only does Josette not get a conclusive closure, but her triumph is derided by the absurdly hyperinflated soundtrack, the Maurice Jarre song 'Paris en colère', sung by Mireille Mathieu. The song, as Marshall reminds us, is about the euphoria of a collective identity overcoming oppression, in the case of the song, the oppression of the French by the Nazis. 'Josette's act', says Marshall, 'is for all women' (Marshall 1992: 136), identifying a feminist theme. But the song is so excessive in its allegorical gesture (men are like Nazis?) that it is just another derisive piece of the jigsaw, a scene which, like all the others, 'spits on the film', as Chatiliez puts it. In this puzzle of universal derision, there is no utopia possible any more. Women's roles, whether as mothers or femmes fatales, are as derided as men's weakness. Dystopia, fractured, is all that remains in the ruins of consensus.

16

Tenue de soirée:
The 'Suffering Macho'

B L I E R is often seen, like Pialat, as one of the major auteurs of the 1980s. Like Pialat, his career began in the 1960s. But more than Pialat, his films, since *Les Valseuses*, of which *Tenue de soirée* is more or less a remake, focus resolutely on the crisis of masculinity. *Tenue de soirée* in fact gathers together many of the issues linked to nostalgia and the repositioning of masculinity, and the paradoxes they engender. *Tenue de soirée* is postmodern in its amoral derision, but it is also nostalgic cinematographically, in that it harks back to the films of the 1930s and the 1950s, as well as the film whose *succès de scandale* put both Blier and Depardieu on the cinematic map, *Les Valseuses*. *Tenue de soirée* is also nostalgic in its concerns, since it is a misogynistic reply to feminism. Its misogyny is, as so often in Blier's work, a provocation, but that provocation is essential to the hazardous but in the end unsuccessful repositioning of masculinity underlying the films studied in this book. Like *Trois hommes et un couffin*, it at least has the merit of making that repositioning its unambiguous central message, even if that message is devalued by the comic genre to which the film belongs. And yet, unlike *Trois hommes et un couffin*, it is less comedy than black humour, albeit suffused with a pathos typical of Blier's films.

I shall investigate all of these apparently conflicting concerns—postmodern derision/nostalgia; misogyny/the repositioning of masculinity; comedy/tragedy—before showing how they are focused on Blanc and more particularly Depardieu, whose star persona negotiates and almost manages to resolve the film's inherent contradictions. As the locus of conflict and paradox, Depardieu is the crucial centre, etymologically stretched on the cross, as the emblematic figure of crisis for this book, the 'suffering macho' as

Vincendeau aptly puts it (Vincendeau 1993*b*: 353). It is therefore appropriate, in a book which has chosen to eschew auteurism as an instrument of analysis, to end with a star analysis, since star studies have been the major innovation in film studies since the early 1980s.

POSTMODERN DERISION

Tenue de soirée is clearly contemporary in its appeal, as is testified by its success. It was the fourth most popular French film of 1986. As Michel Blanc said, 'the film is of its time in the way it goes from derision to violence, to cynicism, with amoral characters' (Blanc 1986*a*: 12). Although there are many sequences which would exemplify this point, I would like to remain with the film's conclusion, which Blier labelled a 'pirouette' (Blier 1986*d*: 52). I shall return to this concluding sequence, because it is a source of endless fascination in its provocation and complexity. In the final shot, Blanc applies make-up to his face as the camera moves into close-up, and he twice smiles direct to the camera. Although it is unclear whether Blier meant this or the whole of the drag sequence to be the 'pirouette', the final shot arguably exemplifies all of Blanc's points. There is apparent violence done to Antoine's masculine identity (when earlier Bob asks Antoine to wear women's clothes, Antoine repeatedly says that he 'cannot do it'), as well as violence done to the film's conventions by the unexpected nod to self-referentiality. And yet that very self-referentiality is derisive because it so forcefully signals closure at the same time as distance, saying to the spectator 'this is the end, it was just a film, and I don't really believe in what I Antoine am doing, and neither should you'. The shot is also cynical. Its forceful closure wrenches the spectator back to the violence of the first sequence of the film where Antoine is humiliated by Monique in public for his lack of attractiveness. The film sketches out a revenge. Antoine may have been humiliated, but he has appropriated the seductive role of the woman as object of the gaze while cynically rejecting that status as merely a game. The film's conclusion recalls one of the final scenes of *Some Like it Hot*. Like the beginning of *Tenue de soirée*, this takes place on a dance-floor, and Joe E. Brown/Osgood later says to Jack Lemmon/Daphne in drag that 'nobody's perfect'.

NOSTALGIA AND MISOGYNY

Some Like it Hot is not the only film likely to come to mind when watching the conclusion of *Tenue de soirée*. Blier himself admitted that his conclusion consciously invited comparison with *La Cage aux folles* (1978) (Blier 1986*c*: 49), although clearly the overt camp of the vaudeville tradition is here replaced by a more modern irony. The dialogue, which for many critics is one of the film's strengths, is based on 1950s slang (Bonnet 1986: 64), and on the metaphor of burglary as rape which is recognizably Genet's, as Blier himself reminded the readers of *Elle* (Blier 1986*b*: 72). But it also recalls the scriptwriter Henri Jeanson's work in the 1930s. As many critics pointed out when the film was released, its dialogue and the actors' delivery echo Carné's *Hôtel du Nord*. It is these intertextual echoes of the 1930s which make the film nostalgic. The film is also, despite Blier's protestations, a virtual remake of his *Les Valseuses*, a key film of the 1970s. Although more of a road movie than *Tenue de soirée*, *Les Valseuses* is also about masculinity, and also focuses on a threesome, starring Depardieu and Miou-Miou in very similar roles.

It is a commonplace that Blier's films since *Les Valseuses* all have the same theme: the crisis of masculinity in the wake of feminism. A consideration of Miou-Miou's role in *Les Valseuses* and *Tenue de soirée* shows how the crisis has deepened. In *Les Valseuses*, the two men's project is to awaken the character played by Miou-Miou sexually, since she has never had an orgasm, and is apparently completely frigid. Her frigidity and status as unattainable object are signalled by her over-determined name, Marie-Ange. Her inability to have an orgasm may make her as sexually pure as the Virgin Mary and an angel rolled into one, but this is ironic since her purity is defined here as frigidity rather than as sexual abstinence; she is, as Forbes points out, 'in appearance an uninhibited girl, complete with mini-skirt and contraceptives' (Forbes 1992: 178). To the two men's consternation, they are unable to awaken Marie-Ange from her sexual slumber, which causes them to question their virility.

Whereas in *Les Valseuses* the character played by Miou-Miou was merely unresponsive, in *Tenue de soirée* she is shrilly virulent in her treatment of Antoine. The opening sequence of *Tenue de soirée*, Monique's harangue, underlines the shift of emphasis between the two films. Monique is complaining because she is not satisfied with Antoine's love for her, but wants material comforts. She obtains them thanks to Bob, and in the process is roundly humiliated in one of the film's key scenes in which she offers herself to Bob, who seeks consolation from her after a rebuff from Antoine. In this scene, she makes love to Bob, positioned on top of him, as he lies passively beneath her, and continues to do so when Antoine interrupts them:

Monique: Is this the first time you've screwed with a woman?
Bob: Of course not. I've had loads.
Monique: So what made you switch?
Bob: Boredom.
Monique: Are you bored right now?
Bob: I'm not over the moon.
Monique [*getting worked up*]: What do you bet that in five minutes you'll be begging for more?
Bob: Try, but don't count on it.
Antoine [*entering, to Bob*]: So now you like women?
Bob: Why? Is it a crime?
Antoine: No, but I'm a man.
Bob: Is that so?
Antoine: Yes it is, and I need to know what you prefer (*vers quoi tu t'orientes*).
Bob: What I prefer . . . what I prefer . . . As it happens, I'm a bit divided at the moment (*désorienté*). Aren't you?
Antoine: You both make me sick.
Bob [*to Monique*]: Come on, come on, stop buffing me up like that, your bloke's watching us.
Antoine [*leaves, returns abruptly*]: If you think you can screw both of us, you'd better know that I'm not happy about it. You'll have to choose.

Monique's humiliation in this scene is multiple. First, she prostitutes herself to Bob to ensure that she remains in his company. Second, her love-making does not interest Bob at all; he reacts with the same indifference as Marie-Ange in *Les Valseuses*. Third, although Monique claims that Bob will not be able to resist her, it is she who is unable to control herself, moaning with pleasure, not even seeing Antoine who has interrupted them. And fourth, their love-making is interrupted by Antoine, who has a jealous outburst, not in relation to Monique, as might be expected, but in relation to Bob. The *mise en scène* emphasizes her humiliation; she is shot in between the two men, losing control as they bicker about the 'disorientation' they feel in relation to their sexual identities.

Monique is increasingly punished for her refusal of Antoine's 'simple' love. She is gradually excluded from the male couple, the crucial scene in this respect being in the bedroom with the two men making love while Monique, infantilized and rejected, sleeps in a cot at the end of the bed, reminding us of a similar infantilization at the end of *Trois hommes et un couffin*. Bob sells her to a pimp, and she returns to the prostitution from which it is implied Antoine rescued her. The film is therefore considerably more misogynistic than *Les Valseuses*, in which Marie-Ange at least achieves her long-awaited orgasm.

If *Tenue de soirée* is so misogynistic, it is partly because it is a response to feminism, as Blier makes clear in an interview for *Elle*. Pointing out that the film is about 'the destruction of virility' (Blier 1986*b*: 72), he sees misogyny as directly linked to feminism: 'Feminism has lost much of its virulence. So misogyny has too. In my private life I don't think that I am misogynistic. That said I shall soon be fifty years old and I belong to the generation of men which was destabilized by feminism' (ibid.). The same dossier in *Elle* interestingly contrasts two 'views' of the film. The writer who is against the film sees the lesson of the film as women 'getting what they deserve for demanding too much' (Pringle 1986: 71).

BLANC AND THE REDEFINITION OF MASCULINITY

There is another way of considering the film, however, and it is expressed by the opposing view in the *Elle* dossier, that the film is a critique of traditional masculinity because 'the macho man is derided' (Chabrol 1986: 70). As Blier points out, the film is also about the redefinition of masculinity: 'Fragility is no longer an exclusively feminine phenomenon' (Blier 1986*c*: 50). The redefinition proposed by the film is problematic on several counts, however.

The first is that the redefinition is located principally in the character played by Michel Blanc. Blanc is a comic actor, and the connotations attached to him prior to *Monsieur Hire* (1989) were that of the risibly unattractive loser, particularly in relation to women. The most successful film of 1984 in France was *Marche à l'ombre* scripted by, directed by, and starring Blanc himself in the role of the less attractive of two losers on the road. To turn Blanc into the object of attraction in *Tenue de soirée* therefore makes his supposed femininity considerably less believable than if the role had been played by Bernard Giraudeau, as had originally been intended, despite Blanc's assertion that 'someone who is not at all seductive can very well have "a pretty little arse" [he is quoting from the film] and the other one can very well want it' (Blanc 1986*a*: 13).

The difficulty that spectators are likely to have in accepting Blanc's 'femininity' is compounded by a more general problem of identification. Blier's films are by common consent theatrical and, more especially, dreamlike (an epithet which is constantly repeated by reviewers of *Tenue de soirée*). This is achieved partly by the highly literary nature of the dialogue, partly by the characters' relationship to the décor, from which they remain curiously detached. For Michel Sineux, for example, the characters 'are not integrated [into the décor], except to play around with it as if they were strangers to it' (Sineux 1986: 73). Although this is obviously the case in *Tenue de soirée* when the three enter empty houses and proceed to rip up carpets with gay abandon, it is also, and more pointedly, the case in the three burglary sequences where the owners are present and end up brandishing guns. In all cases, the décor is immaterial to the games of desire played by the characters. It is true that in two of the three sequences, the décor seems obtrusive and therefore somehow 'significant'. In the bourgeois flat of the theatre-goers, the modern décor with its cold blue light suggests alienation and boredom; in the sequence where Bob sells Antoine, the character played by Stevenin lives in a labyrinthine mansion with marble floors and seemingly endless rooms of statues of naked men. The décor is only apparently significant, however; it is immaterial to the point of the sequences, which is the violence done to the spectators' perception of the characters. In the first sequence, the trio of catchers have been caught, and by an absurd twist of logic appear more sexually repressed than the bored bourgeois. In the second, the point of the sequence is Bob's treachery, and, more surprisingly, Antoine's masochistic submission.

That masochistic submission is characteristic of Blanc's star persona. Nevertheless, on the whole, Blanc's star persona and problems of identification make Antoine's supposed femininity difficult to accept. In addition to these two problems, there is a third, more acute problem for spectatorial identification. It is the questionable assertion implied by the film, that for a man to become more 'feminine', he must become homosexual. The way that reviewers, actors, and director cope with this problem is not to deny homosexuality, but to marginalize it. Confronted by scenes of tenderness and jealousy between two men, reviewers nevertheless state bluntly that the film is not about homosexuality, but about the need for the feminization of men. Homosexuality is merely 'a pretext, a means of pushing the subject to an extreme' (Baron 1986: 20). Blier himself suggests, tongue in cheek, that 'it's a film about the need for love. A little love wherever it comes from is better than no love at all, even if this means a bit of fooling around' (quoted in Sorin 1986: 13). One should of course not make the film out to be a sensitive portrayal of the relationship between two men merely because the two men display sensitivity towards each other. Perez points out that the representation of homosexuality is entirely stereotypical in its assumption that homosexuality leads to 'treachery and prostitution' (Perez 1986). Nevertheless, the frequently repeated assertion that the film is not about homosexuality is suspect. Michel Blanc is amongst those who make it, and his comment is revealing: 'It's not true to say that it's a film on homosexuality. What comes out of the film is that it's a nightmare' (Blanc 1986a: 12).

Blanc is referring to the dreamlike quality of the film, and the comment elaborates on the way a realist frame is gradually dislocated and displaced as dream logic takes over. Nevertheless, the way in which Blanc links the dream, with its logic of desire, and homosexuality, is very telling. The 'nightmare' is that of homosexuality. The film is like a dream, in that it vehicles desire, and that desire is the masochistic effacement of gender difference at the expense of women. If the dream turns into a nightmare, it is because the effacement of gender difference stumbles on the blockage of homosexuality and cannot go any further, as the unexpected conclusion to the film makes abundantly clear.

The conclusion appears to be tacked on to the end of the film, particularly since it comes after the dance-hall sequence which mirrors the beginning of the film and which suggests closure to the spectator. Closure is all the more suggested by the mounting hysteria of the dancing scene: Antoine is in drag and is improbably accepted by the crowd; there is an apparently fortuitous meeting with Monique, followed by the murder of Pedro, her pimp, itself followed by high melodrama in a bedroom, with a suddenly chaotic *mise en scène* based on the dislocation of space by mirrors. In the first shot, Antoine threatens Bob and his boyfriend as they lie in bed; he is mirrored twice by overhead mirrors. This already disorienting shot is followed by a second, considerably more complex shot where we see Bob and his boyfriend in bed in front of a mirror on one side of the screen; on the other side of the screen, Antoine is twice mirrored, and confusingly faces away from Bob and his boyfriend. During these two shots, Bob and his boyfriend refer to Antoine as 'she', *mise en scène* (literally) mirroring gender instability. Melodrama reverts to farce as Antoine hustles Bob into a car, but resurfaces in their conversation in the parked car where Bob is unsure whether Antoine is going to kill him. At the end of the sequence, Bob shouts nervously to Antoine: 'Shoot me in the head. That's what the head's for. Is it my brains that bother you?', to which Antoine melodramatically replies 'no. It's your soul.' When Bob, after a considerable pause which slides back into comedy as he rolls his eyes uncomprehendingly, asks Antoine, 'what's the matter with my soul?', Antoine again, and even more melodramatically, as is emphasized by a sudden shift of camera, leans forward with the gun, and says portentously and menacingly, 'it's black'. The spectator expects the film to finish with Antoine blowing Bob's brains out; after all, this had been prepared meticulously by Antoine's murder of Pedro, and his deliriously haphazard shooting in the bedroom. But the sequence switches back to the streets of Paris, with a problematic conclusion.

This corresponds to the difficulties Blier confesses to having with conclusions. It is enough of a commonplace that it even surfaces in Depardieu's letter to Blier in *Lettres volées*: 'Some people reproach you for not knowing how to finish your films. But you don't want your films to finish! (Depardieu 1988: 45). Indeed, Blier professes to be uninterested in the end of his films, saying that he usually has several conclusions to choose from, and that the end of *Tenue de soirée* was written during the making of the film and improvised at the last minute (Blier 1986*a*: 10). The conclusion is acceptable as a closure to the spectator because it apparently resolves the murderous hysteria of the previous sequences by establishing a stable but 'perverted' family: three 'women' (two of them men) prostituting themselves and an absent child whose voice figures on the soundtrack as a fantasy for both the characters and the spectators. The child is there to legitimize the redefined family structure. But this apparently acceptable closure raises many more questions than it resolves.

Its effect is to suggest that dressing up as women is just a game, because at some time a more 'normal' sexual relationship has occurred between Monique and Antoine, whose child we assume it is. Antoine's smile in the final shot confirms this hypothesis for the spectator. It could be viewed positively as camp, as 'life-as-theatre' (Babuscio 1977: 44), suggesting a fundamental critique of 'restrictive sex roles and sexual identifications' (ibid. 46). But the message is surely somewhat bleaker: homosexuality is nothing more than a masquerade, in which the heterosexual male remains the positive pole, and against which all other gender preferences are negative variations. Indeed, the positive aspects of feminine masquerade identified by Doane as 'a mask that can be worn or removed' (Doane 1991: 25) have here been appropriated by men to comic effect, neutralizing their subversive potential.

If the film had ended with the camera on Depardieu, one might have been inclined to a less pessimistic view. This is because Depardieu's star persona incorporates a 'femininity' which is said to complement his macho masculinity, unlike the masochistic submission of Blanc and the dissipation of a problematic 'femininity' in masquerade. It is because Blanc's star persona is one of submission that spectators are more likely to accept the switch from dominated heterosexual to dominated homosexual. Antoine has merely exchanged one dominating partner (Monique), for a new one (Bob); in the film's only explicit homosex scene, it is Bob who is on top of Antoine, reaching orgasm as Antoine fusses about Monique in her cot. In this respect, the film functions in the same way as *Les Valseuses* with regard to homosexuality. As Marshall points out, 'the homosexual element . . . both transgresses the norms and does not, since it is always seen as sodomy and thus mimicking the power relations the men seek in heterosexuality' (Marshall 1987: 241). Antoine's 'femininity' therefore is just like a mask; he remains fundamentally a dominated man. One can measure how much this is the case by one of Blanc's interviews, where he says that 'what's good about this film is that it shows, through a man, what a woman generally feels in relation to sexuality, a feeling of being prey. It's what makes me say that rarely has a more feminist film been made' (Blanc 1986b: 176). The laughter signalled in the text following this extraordinary and misleading statement is that, presumably, of Blanc and his male interviewer, Jean-Pierre Lavoignat. If Blanc remains resolutely a man throughout his masquerade, Depardieu, on the other hand, is another matter.

DEPARDIEU AND DERISION

Depardieu's star persona is notoriously a combination of proletarian machismo and 'femininity', of swagger and sensitivity, as the bedroom seduction scene shows. Bob sensitively strokes Antoine's bare chest, and tells him that they can spend some time together 'to chat about clothes' ('parler chiffons'). Once Monique steps out of the door, Bob strips off, looms over Antoine, and shows off his tattoo as he launches into one of the film's more brutally poetic monologues. Its sub-Genet mixture of criminality, death, and sodomy delivered in uncomfortably threatening close-up could not be more different from the sensitivity earlier displayed:

Bob: I've a tattoo which expands and contracts. When it's dormant it's a grenade, when it wakes up it's a torpedo. Like to see it?
Antoine: You're not in prison now you know.
Bob: We're all in prison, my friend. Life is a prison. The worst kind. The only way out is feet first. Don't joke about things like that. I'm going to bugger you. I'm going to bugger you and you'll come. Your asshole will quiver with joy. It's no use shouting for help. When you're free, there are no guards. No-one will come. You'll be alone with your shame. And I'll turn your shame into happiness. Offer it to you like a bouquet.
Antoine: You can speak well when you want to.
Bob: I'm inspired by your lips. By your lips and by your heart. I'm going to steal your heart and all that goes with it. I shall slip in and swipe the lot.

If Depardieu can make such a monologue convincing, it is less due to Antoine's comment that Bob is a good speaker than to the commonplace of the combination between proletarian machismo and 'femininity' which Depardieu has carefully cultivated over the years. Broadly speaking, in his early career, as Vincendeau points out, Depardieu's persona was rooted in the 'loubard' or urban delinquent. During the 1980s he assiduously cultivated its exact opposite, tradition and nostalgia, by his constantly reiterated love of the land, exemplified, in a kind of *reductio ad absurdum*, by his frequent allusions to his profession on his passport: 'vigneron', or wine grower; one of his letters in *Lettres volées*, for example, is written 'to Nature', and extols the virtues of wine-making. Hand in hand with tradition and nostalgia go his equally frequent allusions during the 1980s to his 'femininity'. For example, a star profile which appeared in *Figaro Madame* in 1981 is entitled 'Depardieu: "J'ai un côté féminin"' (Turkheim 1981: 76). And later in the 1980s, in the letter to Adjani from *Lettres volées*, he writes that when he and Adjani made *Camille Claudel*, he felt the sort of 'complicity you find between people of the same sex' (Depardieu 1988: 50), adding that he prefers to be 'on the side of women'. Whether one considers the 'loubard' outsider, or the comic roles played by Depardieu, where, as is always the case with comedy, 'comic types, as embodied by stars, evolved at focal points of social change' (Vincendeau 1993*b*: 346), both roles converge towards a similar configuration, namely, as Vincendeau aptly puts it, 'the romanticism of suffering' (ibid. 353) and a sexual identity which 'is somewhat beyond that of a mere heterosexual man' (ibid. 357).

Although Depardieu's frequent statements concerning his 'femininity' may not appear to be very different from Blanc's suggestion that when playing Antoine he knew what it was like to be 'female prey', Depardieu's star persona is such that it can make his statement convincing whereas Blanc's simply leads to incredulous laughter. The one part of the film which is unconvincing, however, is the conclusion, where Depardieu camps it up in drag. As Blier said, although he 'didn't want people to make a comparison between *La Cage aux folles* and *Tenue de soirée* ... one must give oneself the pleasure of seeing Depardieu in a fur and blonde wig' (Blier 1986*c*: 49). The excessive pleasure gained from pushing Depardieu's 'femininity' beyond the constraints set upon it by the counterbalancing effects of his 'masculinity', which here disappears beneath the wig and under the skirt, upsets the balance of masculinity in crisis in so far as it is predicated on the dialectic between 'feminine' and 'masculine' elements. That delicate balance is turned into a derisive game, literally into a charade, the dressing up of a problem in comic guise. This is all the more the case because we do not see Depardieu making himself up. If we had, it might have been easier to accept the 'suffering macho' masquerading. As it is, we see Blanc, the comical loser, masquerading. The effect is to deflect the crisis of masculinity back into the resolutely comic, and away from the balance between drama and comedy, between 'femininity' and 'masculinity' which the spectator might accept because they are normally part of Depardieu's star persona. The film's failure to maintain that precarious balance, its deflection into an unsubversive pretence at camp, is a measure of how the crisis of masculinity is too deep to be confronted adequately by mainstream cinema.

The missed opportunity is encapsulated in Depardieu's letter to Dewaere (who committed suicide in 1982) in *Lettres volées*, where he safely toys with what might have been:

> I'd have liked to have an affair with you. Don't get your hackles up. Not the sort of cheap sodomy of *Les Valseuses*. There they do it because they're bored, because they've had enough of wandering around. Blokes hug each other the more time they spend together. They screw each other because they start to have doubts about themselves . . . Homosexuality is no doubt more subtle than people say. Anyway, I don't know what it is . . . I can't help thinking, Patrick, that if you hadn't left us, it would perhaps have been you I was kissing in *Tenue de soirée*. (Depardieu 1988: 62–3)

The statement accepts the crisis of masculinity as a given (men are having doubts about themselves). Self-doubt is equated with homosexuality. And Depardieu then rather neatly claims he does not know what homosexuality is anyway, an ambiguous statement which could mean that he had never experienced it, or that he had experienced it, but did not 'connect' with it. The final cherry on the cake which he both has and eats is to fantasize a homosexual relationship with Dewaere, who is not there to answer back. The film, then, like so many discussed in this book, merely gestures at a crisis. As Bob says in the seduction scene with Antoine, there are 'just two blokes, Bob and Antoine. Just made for each other. Like the sky and the sea. Monique's just a seagull. Remove the seagull, and the scenery is still the same. It's still the sky and the sea.' Once women are conveniently out of the way, or humiliated, with the sky/masculine/Bob and the redefined sea/feminine/Antoine in the picture, the film draws back from the brink of its own temerity, and collapses in derision and nostalgia. It is the derision of Depardieu in a wig; more seriously, it is the derision in presenting 'femininity' as a mixture of prostitution and homosexuality. And, finally, it is also a regressive nostalgia, signalled by a fantasized child, a voice from the Imaginary sent to haunt male lack.

17

Conclusion

THE films of the 1980s studied in this book have shown a tendency to dwell on the discomfiture of the male. This has usually been at the expense of women characters, exemplifying Mulvey's view of mainstream cinema. Women are either relegated to the status of erotic objects, fetishized so that they will not threaten; or the male becomes the object of desire, the women being blamed or punished. For example, Le Papet is given a tragic apotheosis in *Manon des Sources*, the granddaughter being 'married off' and given little weight in the film's closure, in spite of the film's title, compared to the self-inflicted pain of the patriarch who has unwittingly caused his son's death. Alex in *Mauvais Sang* dies a hero, the 'fault' being Anna's because she did not love him. Antoine in *Tenue de soirée* 'becomes' a woman and ends up controlling the narrative's truth value by his final gaze at the camera, while Monique, who was already a 'woman', 'becomes' less than one, relegated to the position of the dog at the end of the conjugal bed. Even films by women have been problematic. *Coup de foudre* excludes the typically aggressive male while yearning for the lost father. And in *Trois hommes et un couffin*, where the men are constructed as mothers, the film yearns for their lost laddishness.

It is true that the films discussed in this book are very broadly mainstream films. Art-house films are more likely to question regressive constructions of this type, at least partly by their tendency to work with ambiguity. Godard's *Prénom: Carmen*, for example, despite its title, focuses more on the male protagonist Joseph than it does on representations of femininity, as I have shown elsewhere (Powrie 1995). One would expect a Godard film to question gender representation, of course, but the point still holds if one considers other art-house films. The narrative of the relatively successful *Le Retour de Martin Guerre* is founded on the desire of a woman and an adventurer's opportunistic, but ultimately masochistic, subservience to the identity she wishes him to assume and play out. Depardieu's Martin is a split personality whose opportunism gives way to love; he persuades himself that he really is Martin, his life becoming a masquerade which ends in a hanging. The masochistic element I have emphasized is even clearer in Claire Devers's *Noir et blanc* (1986). I began this book with a quotation from *Noir et blanc* in the form of an epigraph, and it is with this film that I shall conclude my investigation, in the hope that the epigraph will now make more sense.

The film was Devers's first feature, and won the Caméra d'Or at Cannes. Shot in fuzzy black and white 16 mm, it focuses on the sado-masochistic relationship between a shy white accountant and a surly black masseur. The narrative's unsettling nature is underlined by a claustrophobic *mise en scène* (most of the shots occur in enclosed spaces—a small apartment, the masseur's closet—whose claustrophobia is further emphasized by the lack of establishing shots), a minimalist soundtrack (there is no music), and an elliptical style. Although the film is about sado-masochism, this is mostly hinted at; we never see violence, even when the accountant asks the masseur to chain him to a rolling-machine in the film's suicidal apotheosis, where the film's style suddenly disintegrates into an almost incoherent amalgam of futurism (*2001*), materialism (the final shot of the machine which echoes *Battleship Potemkin*), and the Gothic horror of Corman's Poe adaptations. Despite this, it is the lack of spectacle which impresses most, particularly the refusal of the camera to fetishize the characters, whether male or female (with one exception, Antoine's first glimpse of the masseur, a point-of-view shot in close-up on his shoulders as he dips in and out of the club's swimming pool). Whereas women in the films discussed in this book pose problems for the spectator, women in *Noir et blanc* are de-eroticized by the camera (no close-ups) and by the narrative, since their actions are as unexplained as the men's. The friendly secretary at the health club where Antoine is working touches him in what appears to be a friendly gesture, although this is belied by his extremely aggressive reaction, which, oddly, does not seem to alter their working relationship subsequently. Antoine's wife visits the health club after Antoine has had too many 'accidents' (grazes, a broken arm) for her not to suspect something, but slaps the secretary, presumably in displaced frustration or displeasure, although her motives are never made clear either by the narrative line or by the dialogue.

The main character's motives remain unexplained until very late on in the film. Surprised by the owner of the club, Antoine and Dominique are both thrown out. Antoine goes to a hotel with the masseur, and reflects on what has happened to him. The dialogue begins as a voice-over while he sleeps, turning seamlessly into a diegetic address to Dominique upon whose face the camera focuses for most of the dialogue which follows, which startles the spectator by its unusually explicative and confessional nature:

I was too shy. Or rather, I had no curiosity. I knew nothing about myself. The idea of a massage should have scared me, but my fear left me. Like everything else in my life, it wasn't a conscious choice or effort. But from then on, the craving ruled my life. But my desire was too great. You saw through me too quickly. You could no longer resist the urge to hit me. But I have no memory or secret to confess. Not even pleasure. It always catches me unawares. I never know where to expect your hands. On my shoulder, my leg, or my waist. I discover the pleasure much later, when I move a limb or stroke a wound. I remember the first time, and it's only the memory of the pain which gives me pleasure. Afterwards.

The film gathers together the elements of the crisis of masculinity as I have explored it in this book. Women have been expunged so that the focus is resolutely on two men and their relationship. The sado-masochistic relationship is clearly implicitly sexual, 'misplaced homo-erotic desire' (Hayward 1993a: 259). Unlike *Tenue de soirée*, however, where the problem of being a man in the 1980s was displaced onto a different issue, that of sexual orientation, in *Noir et blanc* the relationship is used to explore the issue of identity directly ('I knew nothing about myself') and its interface with difference. And identity is seen as located in pain and nostalgia: 'I remember the first time, and it's only the memory of the pain which gives me pleasure. Afterwards.' Antoine's desire is a machine, in the Deleuzian sense, his pleasure the memory of the 'corps sans organe', as Dominique pummels him as if to expel the organs within. It is fitting therefore that the final scene should imply the ripping apart of his body (we do not see it; it is, as Austin points out, an aural rather than visual horror; Austin 1996: 92), on what seems to be an endless and endlessly rolling machine.

Deleuze and Guattari's *L'Anti-Œdipe*, to which I have just alluded, appeared in 1972, coincidentally the accepted date of the launching of the post-1968 French women's movement. We have seen how the crisis of masculinity is bound up with changing patterns in employment impacting on social attitudes, particularly with regard to gender roles. Additionally, *Noir et blanc* was made in 1986, the year in which French spectators seemed to reject French cinema in preference to American cinema. The film is therefore emblematic of the concerns raised in this book, the crisis of masculinity and the crisis of the French cinema. These are unspectacularly located in the pallid tortured frame of the repressed white middle-class male, Antoine, avatar of Antoine Doinel, child-hero of the New Wave, lost in a world changed beyond recognition, his only pleasure that of a remembered pain. But unlike many of the films studied in this book, *Noir et blanc* disengages itself from regressively nostalgic melodramatizing by pointing forward to one of the main concerns of 1990s French cinema, ethnicity and difference.

Filmography

THIS filmography includes films from the 1980s mentioned in this book. Where available, it gives the title of the film, the year in which it first appeared, the director, the total number of spectators in Paris and its region, the total number of spectators in France, the number of weeks the film ran, and the ranking of the film in its first full year if it had more than 1 million spectators in France. Viewing figures for Paris and the number of weeks the film ran are taken from Paul Cohen-Solal, *10 ans de cinéma en chiffres 1980–1990* (Paris: Ciné-chiffres/Le Film Français, 1991). Viewing figures for France and the ranking are taken from Stéphane Brisset, *Le Cinéma des années 80* (Paris: MA Éditions, 1990), supplemented by figures from the CNC.

Title of Film	Date	Director	Paris (1,000s)	France (1,000s)	Weeks	Rank
37°, 2 le matin	1986	Beineix	881	3,395	97	8
A nos amours	1983	Pialat	329		28	
Amour à mort, L'	1984	Resnais	157	348	36	
As des as, L'	1982	Oury	1,223	4,762	26	1
Au revoir les enfants	1987	Malle	826	3,192	57	11
Balance, La	1982	Swaim	1,069	4,134	33	11
Baule-les-Pins, La	1989	Kurys	203		8	
Bourgeois gentilhomme, Le	1981	Coggio	42		5	
Camille Claudel	1988	Nuttyens	759	2,636	54	24
Chèvre, La	1981	Veber	1,442	6,810	44	8
Chocolat	1988	Denis	289	794	23	
Choix des armes	1981	Corneau	513	1,714	13	18
Compères, Les	1983	Veber	1,954	4,754	24	7
Coup de foudre	1983	Kurys	461	1,596	23	24
Coup de torchon	1981	Tavernier	710	1,562	38	23
Dernier Métro, Le	1980	Truffaut	1,110	2,090	68	9
Détective	1985	Godard	141	382	17	
Diva	1980	Beineix	775	1,500	204	
Fourberies de Scapin, Les	1980	Coggio	164	1,781	20	15
Fort Saganne	1984	Corneau	586	2,135	21	12
Fucking Fernand	1987	Mordillat	50	215	7	

Table (*continued*)

Title of Film	Date	Director	Paris (1,000s)	France (1,000s)	Weeks	Rank
Fugitifs, Les	1986	Veber	1,014	4,474	20	12
Grand Bleu, Le	1988	Besson	1,946	9,066	138	
Grand Pardon, Le	1982	Arcady	604	2,122	18	16
Guerre du feu, La	1979	Annaud	1,173	3,644	70	
Harem	1985	Joffé	243	816	14	
Inspecteur La Bavure	1980	Zidi	768	3,611	14	12
Inspecteur Lavardin	1986	Chabrol	300	623	15	
Je vous salue Marie	1985	Godard	105	353	25	
Jean de Florette	1986	Berri	1,165	7,223	70	1
Lévy et Goliath	1987	Oury	545	2,148	10	9
Lune dans le caniveau, La	1983	Beineix	186		17	
Mais qu-est-ce que j'ai fait . . .	1980	Saint-Hamant	130		8	
Manon des Sources	1986	Berri	1,052	6,644	58	5
Marche à l'ombre	1984	Blanc	1,338	5.194	51	1
Masques	1987	Chabrol	288	708	10	
Mauvais Sang	1986	Carax	186	504	43	
Misérables, Les	1982	Hossein	597	2,960	27	10
Mon beau-frère a tué ma sœur	1986	Rouffio	85	192	6	
Monsieur Hire	1989	Leconte	240	603	22	
Noir et blanc	1986	Devers	26	45	18	
Nom de la rose, Le	1986	Annaud	1,370	4,809	74	2
Œuvre au noir, I.'	1988	Delvaux	89	193	28	
Ours, L'	1988	Annaud	1,704	8,661	34	1
Papy fait de la résistance	1983	Poiré	928	3,700	13	5
Passion	1982	Godard	95		23	
Passion Béatrice, La	1987	Tavernier	146	512	12	
Père Noël est une ordure, Le	1982	Poiré	437	1,576	14	
Police	1985	Pialat	537	1,787	13	20
Poulet au vinaigre	1985	Chabrol	258	764	15	
Prénom: Carmen	1984	Godard	170	391	12	
Professional, Le	1981	Lautner	1,192	3,981	23	1
Qu'est-ce qu'on attend . . .	1982	Serreau	39		7	
Retour de Martin Guerre, Le	1982	Vigne	289	1,134	23	33
Ripoux, Les	1984	Zidi	1,673	5,744	77	4
Sous le soleil de Satan	1987	Pialat	246	815	30	
Subway	1985	Besson	810	2,219	61	16
Tchao Pantin	1983	Berri	756	2,794	32	6
Tenue de soirée	1986	Blier	823	3,138	20	7
Terminus	1987	Glenn	58	287	5	

Table (*continued*)

Title of Film	Date	Director	Paris (1,000s)	France (1,000s)	Weeks	Rank
Thérèse	1986	Cavalier	372	1,474	59	
Tir groupé	1982	Missiaen	367	1,140	24	32
Trois hommes et un couffin	1985	Serreau	2,195	9,910	81	3
Un amour de Swann	1984	Schlöndorff	315	807	34	
Un dimanche à la campagne	1984	Tavernier	442	1,095	77	
Une nuit à l'Assemblé Nationale	1988	Mocky	78	223	7	
Une semaine de vacances	1980	Tavernier	350		18	
Urgence	1985	Béhat	223	840	8	
Vengeance du serpent à plumes, La	1984	Oury	523	2,236	10	11
Vie de famille, La	1985	Doillon	71	195	10	
Vie est un long fleuve tranquille, La	1987	Chatiliez	1,273	3,649	151	4
Vie et rien d'autre La	1989	Tavernier	476	1,505	30	
Vivement dimanche!	1983	Truffaut	475	1,113	30	36
Y a-t-il un Français dans la salle?	1982	Mocky	237		19	

Bibliography

ADAIR, GILBERT (1983), 'Vivement dimanche! (Finally Sunday!)', Monthly Film Bulletin, 50: 312–13.

—— (1984), 'Un amour de Swann (Swann in Love)', Monthly Film Bulletin, 51: 112–13.

ALLEN, DON (1986) Finally Truffaut (London: Palladin).

ARTINIAN, ARIANE, and BOCCARA, LAURENCE (1992), Femmes au travail (Paris: Hatier).

AUDÉ, FRANÇOISE (1988), 'La Vie est un long fleuve tranquille', Positif, 325: 75–6.

AUMONT, JACQUES (1989), L'Œil interminable: Cinéma et peinture (Paris: Seguier).

AUSTIN, GUY (1996), Contemporary French Cinema: An Introduction (Manchester: Manchester University Press).

BABUSCIO, JACK (1977), 'Camp and Gay Sensibility', in Richard Dyer (ed.), Gays and Film (London: BFI), 40–57.

BADINTER, ELIZABETH (1980), L'Amour en plus (Paris: Flammarion).

—— (1994a), XY: De l'identité masculine (Paris: Livre de Poche).

—— (1994b), 'La Crise de l'identité masculine', Sciences humaines, 42: 32–4.

BARON, JEANINE (1986), 'Blier, gentleman-provocateur', La Croix l'événement, 24 Apr.), 20.

BASSAN, RAPHAËL (1989), 'Trois néo-baroques français: Beineix, Besson, Carax, de Diva au Grand Bleu', Revue du cinéma, 449: 44–50.

BAUMGARTEN, RUTH (1984), 'La Vie en bleu: Swann in Love', Stills, 12 (June–July), 101.

BAZIN, ANDRÉ (1983), 'The Pagnol Case', in Mary Lea Bandy (ed.), Rediscovering French Film (New York: Museum of Modern Art), 92–3.

BEINEIX, JEAN-JACQUES (1981), Interview in Le Film français, 1855: 25–6.

—— (1982), Interview in Amis du film cinéma et TV, 312–13: 5–6.

—— (1985), 'Jean-Jacques Beineix: Le Virage', Starfix, 30: 58–9.

—— (1987), 'Interview', Séquences, 129: 40–7.

—— (1989), Interview in La Revue du cinéma, 448: 50.

BENOIST, ALAIN DE (1988), 'Un long fleuve tranquille', Figaro-Magazine (18 Mar.)

BERGALA, ALAIN (1983), 'Le Vrai, le faux, le factice', Cahiers du cinéma, 351: 4–9.

BLANC, MICHEL (1986*a*), 'La Baguette magique: Entretien avec Michel Blanc', *Cahiers du cinéma*, 382: 11–13.

—— (1986*b*), Interview, *Première*, 109: 79–80, 176.

BLIER, BERTRAND (1986*a*), 'Les Mots et les choses: Entretien avec Bertrand Blier', *Cahiers du cinéma*, 382: 8–10.

—— (1986*b*), 'J'ai fait un film d'amour', *Elle* (5 May), 71–2.

—— (1986*c*), 'Entretien avec Bertrand Blier', *Revue du cinéma*, 417: 49–50.

—— (1986*d*), 'Le Petit Blier illustré: Bertrand Blier de A à Z', *Revue du cinéma*, 417: 51–5.

BONNET, JEAN-CLAUDE (1986), '*Tenue de soirée*', *Cinématographe*, 119: 64.

BORGER, L. (1984), '*Un amour de Swann*', *Variety*, 314: 16.

BOSSÉNO, CHRISTIAN (1981), '*Diva*', *Image et son*, 361: 30.

BRISSET, STÉPHANE (1990), *Le Cinéma des années 80* (Paris: MA Éditions).

BUSS, ROBIN (1994), *French Film Noir* (London: Marion Boyars).

CANBY, VINCENT (1987), '*Jean de Florette*', *New York Times* (6 Nov.), 25.

CARAX, LEOS (1986), 'La Beauté en révolte: Entretien avec Leos Carax', *Cahiers du cinéma*, 390: 24–32.

CARCASSONNE, PHILIPPE (1981), '*Diva*', *Cinématographe*, 66: 76.

CARRÈRE, EMMANUEL (1983), 'Cinéma français: Le Triomphe du prêt-à-filmer', *Télérama*, 1739 (11 May), 5–14.

CARRIÈRE, JEAN-CLAUDE (1984), 'Debusquer les gens et les choses,' *L'Avant-scène cinéma*, 321–2: 11–17.

CHABROL, ANNE (1986), 'J'aime', *Elle* (5 May), 70–1.

CHATILIEZ, ÉTIENNE (1987), '*La Vie est un long fleuve tranquille*', *Première*, 128: 120–2.

—— (1988*a*), 'La Bonne Pointure', *Première*, 131: 56–9.

—— (1988*b*), 'Le Rire des autres, c'est une drogue', *Le Monde* (4 Feb.).

—— (1988*c*), 'Propos d'Étienne Chatiliez', *Revue du cinéma*, 436: 5–7.

CHEVASSU, FRANÇOIS (1988), '1983–1987: Petit Inventaire d'un lustre frileux', *Revue du cinéma*, 441: 58–67.

CHÉVRIE, MARC (1987), 'La Valeur-image', *Cahiers du cinéma*, 395–6: 27–30.

CIXOUS, HÉLÈNE (1975), 'La Noire vole', *La Nouvelle Critique*, 82: 48–53.

COGNARD, FRANÇOIS (1985), Dossier on *Subway*, *Starfix*, 26: 54–67.

COGNIAT, RAYMOND (1975), 'Prélude à l'intimisme', in *Bonnard Vuillard Roussel*, exhibition catalogue (Brussels: Musées Royaux des Beaux-Arts de Belgique) 7–8.

CONRAD, JOSEPH (1968), *Lord Jim* (New York: W. W. Norton).

CORDERO, CHRISTINE (1994), *Le Travail des femmes* (Paris: Le Monde-Éditions).

CUEL, FRANÇOIS (1981), '*Diva*', *Cinématographe*, 66: 76.

DANEY, SERGE (1993), *Le Salaire du zappeur* (Paris: POL: 1st edn. Paris: Ramsay, 1988).

DARKE, CHRIS (1993), 'Rupture, Continuity and Diversification: *Cahiers du cinéma* in the 1980s', *Screen*, 34: 362–79.

DAZAT, OLIVIER (1986), 'Leos Carax est-il génial?', *Cinématographe*, 124: 15.

DEDET, YANN (1985), 'La Mémoire des rushes: Entretien avec Yann Dedet', *Cahiers du cinéma*, 375: 21–3.

DELEUZE, GILLES, and GUATTARI, FÉLIX (1972) *L'Anti-Œdipe: Capitalisme et schizophrénie* (Paris: Minuit).

DEPARDIEU, GÉRARD (1988), *Lettres volées* (Paris: Livre de Poche).

DEVARRIEUX, CLAIRE (1992), 'Face à face: Jean-Luc Godard/Maurice Pialat', Sergio Toffetti and Aldo Tassone (eds.), in *Maurice Pialat: L'Enfant sauvage*, (Turin: Lindau), 201–13. Edited dialogue first published in *Le Monde*, 16 Feb. 1984.

Diva, (1991) *L'Avant-scène cinéma*, 407.

DOANE, MARY ANNE (1980), 'Misrecognition and Identity', *Cine-tracts*, 11: 25–32.

—— (1991), *Femmes Fatales: Feminism, Film, Psychoanalysis* (New York: Routledge).

DOUIN, JEAN-LUC (1984), 'Un dimanche à la campagne: Á l'ombre de Monsieur Ladmiral', *Télérama*, 1787: 20–1.

—— (1988), 'Au nom du père', in Jean-Luc Douin, *Tavernier* (Paris: Edilig), 59–62.

DURHAM, CAROLYN A. (1992), 'Taking the Baby out of the Basket and/or Robbing the Cradle: "Remaking" Gender and Culture in Franco-American Film', *French Review*, 55: 774–84.

DYER, RICHARD (1990) *Now You See It: Studies on Lesbian and Gay Film* (London: Routledge).

ELLIS, JOHN (1982), 'The Literary Adaptation: An Introduction', *Screen*, 23: 3–5.

FISCHER, LUCY (1991), 'Sometimes I Feel Like a Motherless Child: Comedy and Matricide', in Andrew Horton (ed.), *Comedy/Cinema/Theory* (Berkeley and Los Angeles: University of California Press), 60–78.

FLINN, CARY (1992), *Strains of Utopia: Gender, Nostalgia, and Hollywood Film Music* (Princeton: Princeton University Press).

FORBES, JILL (1984), 'Alas, poor Swann', *Sight and Sound*, 53: 221–2.

—— (1986), '*Trois hommes et un couffin*', *Monthly Film Bulletin*, 641: 169–70.

—— (1987), 'Omegaville', *Sight and Sound*, 4: 292–3.

—— (1991), 'The *Série Noire*', in Brian Rigby and Nicholas Hewitt (eds.), *France and the Mass Media* (London: Macmillan), 85–97.

—— (1992), *The Cinema in France after the New Wave* (London: BFI/Macmillan).

FREUD, SIGMUND (1957), 'Mourning and Melancholia', *The Standard Edition of the Complete Psychological Works of Sigmund Freud*, vol. xiv (London: Hogarth Press), 243–58.

FRODON, JEAN-MICHEL (1995), *L'Age moderne du cinéma français: De la Nouvelle Vague à nos jours* (Paris: Flammarion).

—— and Loiseau, Jean-Claude (1987), *Jean de Florette: La Folle Aventure de Film* (Paris: Herscher).

GASPERI, ANNE DE (1988), 'Gare aux tourbillons!', *Le Quotidien de Paris* (8 Feb.).

GIRARD, MARTIN (1987), '*Mauvais Sang*', *Séquences*, 129: 68–9.

GLEDHILL, CHRISTINE (1980), 'Klute 1: A Contemporary *Film Noir* and Feminist Criticism', in E. Ann Kaplan (ed.), *Women in Film Noir* (London: BFI), 6–21.

—— (1985), 'Melodrama', in Pam Cook (ed.), *The Film Book* (London: BFI), 73–84.

GODARD, JEAN-LUC (1985), *Jean-Luc Godard par Jean-Luc Godard* (Paris: Éditions de l'Étoile).

GRAS, PIERRE (1985), 'DE *L'Enfance nue* à *A nos amours*', *Revue du cinéma*, 408: 76–82.

GRENIER, ALEXANDRE (1994), *Génération Père Noël: Du Splendid à la gloire!* (Paris: Belfond).

GUÉRIF, FRANÇOIS (1981), *Le Cinéma policier français* (Paris: Veyrier).

—— (1987), 'François Truffaut et la Série Noire', *L'Avant-scène cinéma*, 362–3: 5–9.

—— and Mérigeau, Pascal (1982), 'Pour quelques polars de plus . . .', *Image et son*, 368: 67–74.

HAGEN, W. M. (1988) 'Performance Space in *Diva*', *Literature and Film Quarterly*, 6: 155–9.

HAYWARD, SUSAN (1993*a*), *French National Cinema* (London: Routledge).

—— (1993*b*), 'State, Culture and the Cinema: Jack Lang's Strategies for the French Film Industry', *Screen*, 34: 380–91.

HEYMANN, DANIÈLE (1988), 'L'Inné narrable', *Le Monde* (4 Feb.).

HIGSON, ANDREW (1993), 'Re-presenting the National Past: Nostalgia and Pastiche in the Heritage Film', in Lester Friedman (ed.), *Fires Were Started: British Cinema and Thatcherism* (Minneapolis: University of Minnesota Press), 109–29.

HOLMLUND, CHRISTINE (1991), 'When is a Lesbian not a Lesbian? The Lesbian Continuum and the Mainstream Femme Film', *Camera Obscura*, 25–6: 144–79.

IRIGARAY, LUCE (1985), *This Sex Which Is Not One*, trans. Catherine Porter with Carolyn Burke (New York: Cornell University Press).

JAMESON, FREDRIC (1985), 'Postmodernism and Consumer Society', in H. Foster (ed.), *Postmodern Culture* (London: Pluto), 111–25.

—— (1990), '*Diva* and French Socialism', in *Signatures of the Visible* (New York: Routledge), 55–62.

—— (1993), 'Postmodernism, or the Cultural Logic of Late Capitalism', in Thomas Docherty (ed.), *Postmodernism: A Reader* (New York: Harvester Wheatsheaf), 62–92.

JANKÉLÉVITCH, VLADIMIR (1974), *L'Irréversible et la nostalgia* (Paris: Flammarion, 'Champs').

JEANCOLAS, JEAN-PIERRE (1983), *15 ans d'années trente: Le Cinéma des Français 1929–1944* (Paris: Stock, 'Cinéma').

JOUVE, CHRISTIANE (1983), 'Spectables', *Lesbia* (June), 28.

KAUFMANN, JEAN-CLAUDE (1992), *La Trame conjugale: Analyse du couple par son linge* (Paris: Nathan).

—— (1994), *La Vie du couple* (Paris: Presses Universitaires de France).

KELLY, ERNECE B. (1984), '*Diva*: High Tech Sexual Politics', *Jump Cut*, 29: 39–40.

KEMP, PETER (1984), 'Week in View', *Sunday Times* [Magazine], 8330 (1 Apr.), 51.

KERMABON, JACQUES, and SHAHANI, KUMAR (1991), *Cinema and Television: Fifty Years of Reflection in France* (Hyderabad: Sangham).

KLEIN, MELANIE (1986), 'Mourning and its Relation to Manic-Depressive States (1940)', in *The Selected Melanie Klein*, ed. Juliet Mitchell (Harmondsworth: Penguin), 146–74.

KRUTNIK, FRANK (1991), *In a Lonely Street: Film Noir, Genre, Masculinity* (London: Routledge).

KURYS, DIANE (1983*a*), 'Diane Kurys: "Ce sont les détails qui font un film" ' (interview), *Le Matin* (9 Apr.), 26.

—— (1983*b*), Interview in *Masques: Revue des homosexualités*, 18: 118–23.

LARDEAU, YANN (1983), 'Série B comme Barbara: *Vivement dimanche!*', *Cahiers du cinéma*, 351: 56.

—— (1984), 'Le Dimanche d'un tâcheron', *Cahiers du cinéma*, 359: 36–7.

LE FANU, MARK (1984), '*Swann in Love*', *Films and Filming*, 30: 37–8.

LEFORT, GÉRARD (1988), 'Étienne Chatiliez, la farce profonde', *Libération* (3 Feb.).

LE GUAY, PHILIPPE (1983), '*Vivement dimanche!*', *Cinématographe*, 92: 37–9.

LERNER, LAURENCE (1972), *The Uses of Nostalgia: Studies in Pastoral Poetry* (London: Chatto & Windus).

LOWENTHAL, DAVID (1985), *The Past is a Foreign Country* (Cambridge: Cambridge University Press).

MAILLET, DOMINIQUE (1983), '*Un dimanche à la campagne*', *Première*, 80: 84.

MARSHALL, BILL (1987), 'Stars: Deneuve and Depardieu: Aspects of Class and Identity', in Jeff Bridgford (ed.), *France: Image and Identity* (Newcastle upon Tyne: Association for the Study of Modern and Contemporary France), 234–51.

—— (1992), 'Carnival, Consumption and Identity in *La Vie est un long fleuve tranquille*', in R. A. Chapman and N. Hewitt (eds.), *Popular Culture and Mass Communication in Twentieth-Century France* (Lewiston, NY: Edwin Mellen Press), 126–41.

MARTIN, MARCEL (1988) 'Le Cinéma d'auteur', *Revue du cinéma*, 441: 70–2.

MATIGNON (1985), 'Femmes: Citoyennes à part entière, *Lettre de Matignon*, 173 (12 Nov.), 2–3.

MENKES, S. (1984), 'A Priceless Parade of Props', *The Times* (3 Apr.), 51.

MERCK, MANDY (1986), '*Lianna* and the Lesbians of Art Cinema', in Charlotte Brunsdon (ed.), *Films for Women* (London: BFI), 166–75.

MÉRIGEAU, PASCAL (1982), '*La Balance*', *Revue du cinéma*, 378: 38.

MERLE, PIERRE (1985), *Le Café-théâtre* (Paris: Presses Universitaires de France).

MERMET, GÉRARD (1985), *Francoscopie* (Paris: Larousse).

METZ, CHRISTIAN (1975), 'The Imaginary Signifier', *Screen*, 16: 17–46.

MODLESKI, TANIA (1988), 'Three Men and Baby M', *Camera Obscura*, 17: 69–81.

MONGIN, OLIVIER (1988), 'Portrait de groupe aquatique', *Esprit*, 138.

MOSCA, BERTRAND (1988), '*La Vie est un long fleuve tranquille*', *Première*, 131: 7.

MULVEY, LAURA (1975), 'Visual Pleasure and Narrative Cinema', *Screen*, 16: 6–18.

—— (1981), 'Afterthoughts on "Visual Pleasure and Narrative Cinema" Inspired by *Duel in the Sun* (King Vidor, 1946)', *Framework*, 15–17: 12–15.

MURAT, PIERRE (1986), 'Triste Garrigature', *Télérama*, 1911 (3 Sept.), 22–4.

NEALE, STEVE (1980), *Genre* (London: BFI).

—— (1983), 'Masculinity as Spectacle: Reflections on Men and Mainstream Cinema', *Screen*, 24: 2–16.

NOËL, BENOÎT (1986), '*Mauvais Sang*', *Cinématographe*, 125: 59.

NORTIER, VIVIANE (1988), 'Fils de pub', *La Dépêche* (10 Feb.).

NOWELL-SMITH, GEOFFREY (1977), 'Minnelli and Melodrama', *Screen*, 18 (Summer), 115–18.

OWEN, MICHAEL (1983), 'Many a Slap for Miss Ardant', *Standard* (18 Nov.), 27.

PAGNOL, MARCEL (1988), *The Water of the Hills* trans. W. E. van Heyningen (London: Pan Books).

PALLY, MARCIA (1984), 'World of our Mothers', *Film Comment*, 20: 11–17.

PARENT, DENIS (1989), *Jean-Jacques Beineix: Version originale* (Paris: Barrault Studio).

PARRA, DANIEL (1984), 'Entretien avec Bertrand Tavernier', *Revue du cinéma*, 393: 62–4.

PEREZ, MICHEL (1986), 'La violette et le taureau', *Le Nouvel Observateur* (25 Apr.).

PHILIPPON, ALAIN (1986), 'Sur la terre comme au ciel', *Cahiers du cinéma*, 389: 14–17.

PIALAT, MAURICE (1985*a*), 'Les Rayures du zèbre', *Cahiers du cinéma*, 375: 15–20.

—— (1985*b*) 'Le Style, ça ne se cherche pas, ça se trouve', *Première*, 102: 70–2, 144.

—— (1985*c*), 'Entretien avec Maurice Pialat', *Positif*, 296: 5–11.

POWRIE, PHIL (1988), 'Marketing History: *Swann in Love*', *Film Criticism*, 12: 33–45.

—— (1995), '*Prénom: Carmen* and Male Sexuality', *Forum for Modern Language Studies*, 21 (Jan.), 64–73.

PRÉDAL, RENÉ (1991), *Le Cinéma des Français depuis 1945* (Paris: Nathan).

PRINGLE, COLOMBE (1986), 'Je déteste', *Elle* (5 May), 70–1.

PROUST, MARCEL (1983), *Remembrance of Things Past*, 3 vols., trans. C. K. Scott Moncrieff and T. Kilmartin (Harmondsworth: Penguin).

RABOURDIN, DOMINIQUE (ed.), *Truffaut par Truffaut* (Paris: Chêne).

RAMASSE, F. (1981), '*Diva*', *Positif*, 243: 68.

RENTSCHLER, ERIC (1984), *West German Film in the Course of Time: Reflections on the Twenty Years since Oberhausen* (New York: Redgrave Publishing Company).

REVIE, IAN (1994), 'Paris Remythologized in *Diva* and *Subway*: *Nanas néopolarisées* and *Orphées aux enfers*', in *Mythologies of Paris* (Stirling: Stirling French Publications), 2, 28–43.

RIMBAUD, ARTHUR (1972), *Œuvres complètes* (Paris: Gallimard).

ROBINSON, DAVID (1984), 'Magical Fragment of Remembrance', *The Times* (6 Apr.), 15.

RODDICK, NICK (1983–4), 'Doodling: *Vivement dimanche!*', *Sight and Sound*, 53: 61.

RODOWICK, DAVID NORMAN (1991), *The Difficulty of Difference: Psychoanalysis, Sexual Difference, and Film Theory* (London: Routledge).

S., F. (1988), '*La Vie est un long fleuve tranquille*', *Cahiers du cinéma*, 404: 61.

SAINDERICHAIN, GUY-PATRICK (1981), 'Diva', Cahiers du cinéma, 322: 66.

SAINT-MARC, C. (1988), 'La Compétance relationnelle du père: Son influence sur le développement socio-personnel du jeune enfant', Revue française des affaires sociales, special number, 'Pères et paternité (Nov.).

SANZIO, ALAIN (1983), 'Coup de foudre', Masques: Revue des homosexualités, 18: 124–5.

SCHIDLOW, JOSHKA (1988), 'La Vie est un long fleuve tranquille', Télérama, 1986 (3 Feb.), 24.

SCHIFRES, ALAIN (1983), 'Les Dessous de la "pub" à la télévision', Le Nouvel Observateur, 975: 42.

—— (1988), 'A la tienne Étienne', Le Nouvel Observateur (25 Mar.), 42–4.

SICLIER, JACQUES (1991), Le Cinéma français, ii: De Baisers volés à Cyrano de Bergerac (Paris: Ramsay Cinéma).

SILVERMAN, KAJA (1984), 'Dis-embodying the Female Voice', in Mary Ann Doane, Patricia Mellancamp, and Linda Williams (eds.), Re-Vision: Essays in Feminist Film Criticism (Frederick, Md.: University Publications of America/American Film Institute), 131–49.

—— (1992), Male Subjectivity at the Margins (London: Routledge).

SINEUX, MICHEL (1986), 'Tenue de soirée', Positif, 304: 72–3.

SMITH, STEVE (1993), 'Godard and Film Noir: A Reading of A bout de souffle', Nottingham French Studies, 32: 65–73.

SORIN, RAPHAËL (1986), 'Hétéro, homo, travelo', Le Matin (21 Apr.), 13.

STACEY, JACKIE (1994), Star Gazing: Hollywood Cinema and Female Spectatorship (London: Routledge).

STAM, ROBERT, BURGOYNE, ROBERT, and FLITTERMAN-LEWIS, SANDY (1992), New Vocabularies in Film Semiotics: Structuralism, Poststructuralism and Beyond (London: Routledge).

STAROBINSKI, JEAN (1966), 'The Idea of Nostalgia', Diogenes, 54: 81–103.

STRAAYER, CHRIS (1990), 'Voyage en douce, Entre nous: The Hypothetical Lesbian Heroine', Jump Cut, 35: 50–7.

STUDLAR, GAYLYN (1990), 'Masochism, Masquerade, and the Erotic Metamorphoses of Marlene Dietrich', in Jane Gaines and Charlotte Herzog (eds.), Fabrications: Costume and the Female Body (New York: Routledge), 229–49.

TASKER, YVONNE (1993), Spectacular Bodies: Gender, Genre and the Action Cinema (London: Routledge).

TAVENAS, STÉPHANE, and VOLARD, FRANÇOIS (1989), Guide du cinéma européen: Les Sources de financement, de la production, les producteurs, les distributeurs (Paris: Ramsay/Eurocinéma).

TCHERNIA, PIERRE (1989), 80 grands succès du cinéma policier français (Paris: Casterman).

TESSON, CHARLES (1985), 'Pour la peau d'un film', Cahiers du cinéma, 371–2: 117–19.

TOMALIN, C. (1984), 'Proust Goes to the Movies', *Sunday Times* (25 Mar.), 39.

TOUBIANA, SERGE (1991), 'Trajectoire en 20 points', *Cahiers du cinéma*, 443–4: 42–8.

TRANCHANT, M.-N. (1988), 'Carnet de croquis', *Le Figaro* (5 Feb.).

TRÉMOIS, C.-M. (1983), '*Vivement dimanche!* Fantasia chez Truffaut', *Télérama*, 1752 (10 Aug.), 13.

TRUFFAUT, FRANÇOIS (1968), *Hitchcock* (London: Secker & Warburg).

—— (1976), 'A Certain Tendency of the French Cinema', in Bill Nichols (ed.), *Movies and Methods*, vol. i (Berkeley and Los Angeles: University of California Press), 224–34.

TULARD, JEAN (1990), *Guide des films*, 2 vols. (Paris: Laffont).

TURKHEIM, HÉLÉNE DE (1981), 'Depardieu: "J'ai un côté féminin" ', *Figaro Madame* (28 Nov.), 76–8.

Un amour de Swann (1984), *L'Avant-scène cinéma*, 321–2.

VIDAL, JEAN-MARC (1989), 'Les Papas s'affichent', *Avantages* (10 July), 112–13.

VINCENDEAU, GINETTE (1990), 'Therapeutic Realism: Maurice Pialat's *A nos amours* (1983)', in Susan Hayward and Ginette Vincendeau (eds.) *French Film: Texts and Contexts* (London: Routledge), 257–68.

—— (1993*a*), 'Juliette Binoche: From Gamine to Femme Fatale', *Sight and Sound*, 3: 22–4.

—— (1993*b*), 'Gérard Depardieu: The Axiom of Contemporary French Cinema', *Screen*, 34: 343–61.

VIRENQUE, ANTOINE (1990), *L'Industrie cinématographique française* (Paris: Presses Universitaires de France).

Vivement dimanche! (1987), *François Truffaut et la Série Noire: Tirez sur le pianiste (1960), Vivement dimanche! (1983)*, *L'Avant-scène cinéma*, 362–3.

WARNOD, JEANINE (1988), *Vuillard* (Paris: Flammarion).

WILLIAMS, CHARLES (1963), *Vivement dimanche!*, trans. Marcel Frère (Paris: Gallimard).

YAKIR, DAN (1984), Interview with Bertrand Tavernier, *Film Comment*, 20: 18–22.

YVOIRE, CHRISTOPHE D' (1986), '*Mauvais Sang*', *Cinématographe*, 124: 94–9.

Index

The index lists proper names and film titles

A bout de souffle (1959) 122–4
A nos amours (1983) 96
A tout casser (1968) 105
Adjani, Isabelle 3, 8, 12, 127, 181
Age d'Or, L' (1930) 131, 133
Akerman, Chantal 24
Amour à mort, L' (1984) 148
Anémone (Anne-Aymone Bourguignon) 143
Annaud, Jean-Jacques 3
Another Country (1984) 13
Apollinaire, Guillaume 9
Arcady, Alexandre 6, 75
Ardant, Fanny 84, 88, 91, 127
Arroseur arrosé, L' (1895) 93
As des as, L' (1982) 79, 141–2
Au revoir les enfants (1987) 15
Aurenche, Jean 21, 48
Aventure c'est l'aventure, L' (1972) 105
Aventures de Rabbi Jacob (1973) 141
Aznavour, Charles 105

Baisers Volés (1968) 85
Balance, La (1982) 77, 96, 99, 100–2, 107–08
Balzac, Honoré de 76
Barthes, Roland 23
Battleship Potemkin (1925) 184
Baule-les-Pins, La (1989) 15
Baye, Nathalie 96, 98, 100, 105
Bazin, André 52–3, 81–2
Becker, Jacques 85
Beethoven, Ludwig van 112
Béhat, Gilles 6, 75
Beineix, Jean-Jacques 6, 75, 77–83, 110–11, 115–19, 132, 160
Belle Noiseuse, La (1991) 39
Bellmer, Hans 139
Belmondo, Jean-Paul 79, 141
Bernanos, Georges 14
Berri, Claude 3, 8, 20, 50–4, 56, 61
Bertolucci, Bernardo 145
Besson (painter) 39

Besson, Luc 3, 6, 77–8, 132, 160
Binoche, Juliette 131, 133, 136–8
Blanc, Michel 142, 146, 171–2, 175–7, 179, 181
Blier, Bertrand 6, 145–6, 171–3, 175–8, 181
Blow Out (1981) 110, 119
Bob le flambeur (1956) 77
Bohème, La (1926) 131
Boisset, Yves 6
Bost, Pierre 21, 38, 48
Botticelli, Sandro 32, 34, 164
Boujenah, Michel 148
Bourgeois gentilhomme, Le (1981) 14
Bourvil (André Raimbourg) 141
Bral, Jacques 6
Brideshead Revisited (1981) 13
Britten, Benjamin 134
Broca, Philippe de 141–2, 191
Brochet, Anne 14
Bronzés, Les (1978) 143, 145
Brooks, Louise 131, 133
Brown, Joe E. 172
Buffet froid (1979) 145
Buñuel, Luis 131, 133

Cage aux folles, La (1978) 142, 173, 181
Caillebotte, Gustave 42
Camille Claudel (1988) 3, 181
Camille ou la comédie catastrophique (1971) 99
Carax, Leos 5, 78, 132–3
Carné, Marcel 111, 124, 145, 173
Caro, Marc and Jeunet, Jean-Pierre 6
Cavalier, Alain 38
César (1936) 51
Cézanne, Paul 42
Chabrol, Claude 80, 96, 148
Chambre Verte, La (1978) 85
Champaigne, Philippe de 38
Chandler, Raymond 76
Chaplin, Charlie 131, 137, 149, 165, 170

Chariots of Fire (1981) 12
Château de ma mère, Le (1990) 16
Chatiliez, Etienne 80, 145, 159–60, 165, 170
Chelton, Tsilla 145
Cherchez l'idole (1964) 105
Chéreau, Patrice 8
Chèvre, La (1981) 142
Chinoise, La (1967) 107
Chocolat (1988) 15
Choix des armes (1981) 96
Citizen Kane (1941) 79, 111, 116
Cixous, Hélène 139
Cocteau, Jean 122, 124, 131, 133
Coggio, Roger 13
Coluche (Michel Colucci) 141
Como, Perry 63
Compères, Les (1983) 142
Conrad, Joseph 105
Corbucci, Sergio 105
Corman, Roger 184
Corneau, Alain 7, 96
Corniaud, Le (1965) 141
Coup de foudre (1982) 15, 21, 27, 62–74, 183
Coup de torchon (1981) 15, 21
Crocodile Dundee II (1988) 145
Cyrano de Bergerac (1990) 14

Dedet, Yann 104
Déjeuner sur l'herbe (1959) 41
Deleuze, Gilles 25, 46, 185
Delicatessen (1991) 6
Delon, Alain 29, 77
Delvaux, André 14
Deneuve, Catherine 55
Denis, Claire 15
Depardieu, Gérard 14, 18, 50, 57, 77, 81, 96–7, 102–4, 141–2, 145–6, 171, 178–82, 184
Dernier métro, Le (1980) 15, 85
Desert Hearts (1986) 62
Détective (1985) 79, 96, 98–9, 105–8
Deux Anglaises et le continent (1971) 99
Devers, Claire 184
Deville, Michel 6
Dewaere, Patrick 146, 182
Diva (1980) 6, 20, 75, 77, 79–83, 109–20, 125, 132, 137
Doillon, Jacques 148
Drôle de drame (1936) 145
Ducreux, Louis 39

Dussollier, André 147–8
Dust (1985) 148
Duval, Daniel 100

Eco, Umberto 14
Enfants du Paradis, Les (1945) 111

Fanny (1932) 51
Feuillade, Louis 76, 111
Forster, E.M. 13, 21
Flach Films 148
Fort Saganne (1984) 7
Fourberies de Scapin, Les (1980) 13–14
Franju, Georges 85
Freud, Sigmund 24–5, 44, 55
Fucking Fernand (1987) 142
Fugitifs, Les (1986) 142
Funès, Louis de 141

Gaumont-Pathé 2, 81
Genet, Jean 173, 180
Germinal (1993) 8
Giono, Jean 51
Giraud, Roland 148
Giraudeau, Bernard 176
Gish, Lillian 131
Glenn, Pierre William 3
Gloire de mon père, La (1990) 16
Godard, Jean-Luc 6, 38, 78–9, 81–2, 92, 96, 98–9, 106–8, 122–3, 130–5, 183
Goddard, Paulette 131
Gorecki, Henryk Mikolaj 104
Grand Bleu, Le (1988) 3
Grand Pardon, Le (1982) 75
Grande Vadrouille, La (1966) 141
Granier-Defferre, Pierre 6
Gregorio, Eduardo de 100
Grémillon, Jean 131
Gueule ouverte, La (1973) 100
Guerre du feu, La (1979) 3
Guignolo, Le (1979) 141

Hallyday, Johnny 96, 99, 105
Hammett, Dashiell 76
Handful of Dust, A (1987) 13
Hansel, Marion 148
Harem (1985) 3
Henze, Hans Werner 19
Hitchcock, Alfred 84, 94
Hofer, Johannes 16
Homme qui aimait les femmes, L' (1977) 85

Horloger de Saint-Paul, L' (1974) 21
Hossein, Robert 14
Hôtel du Nord (1938) 173
Howard's End (1992) 13
Hugo, Victor 14, 71, 76, 86–7, 94
Huppert, Isabelle 64
Hussard sur le toit, Le (1995) 8

Indochine (1991) 7
Inspecteur La Bavure (1980) 141
Inspecteur Lavardin (1986) 96
Irigaray, Luce 66
Irons, Jeremy 35

Jarre, Maurice 165, 170
Je vous salue Marie (1985) 98
Jean de Florette (1986) 3, 16, 18–20,
   26–7, 50–61
Jeanson, Henri 173
Joffé, Arthur 3
Jofroi (1934) 51
Journeys From Berlin/71 (1980) 24
Juge et l'assassin, Le (1976) 21

Karina, Anna 131, 133
King Lear (1987) 98
Klein, Melanie 44–5, 62, 73–4
Kristeva, Julia 23
Kurys, Diane 15, 21, 63–4, 66

Lang, Jack 2
Last Emperor, The (1988) 145
Lautner, Georges 141
Léaud, Jean-Pierre 107
Lecanuet, Jean 166
Leconte, Patrice 143
Lelouch, Claude 105
Lemmon, Jack 172
Léotard, Philippe 96, 98–9
Lepetit, Jean-François 148
Leterrier, François 100
Lévi-Strauss, Claude 109, 125
Lévy et Goliath (1987) 142
Lhermitte, Thierry 141–3
Lianna (1983) 62
Little Dorrit (1987) 13
Lumière, Auguste 93
Lune dans le caniveau, La (1983) 81

Magnifique, Le (1973) 141–2
Mais qu'est-ce qu'elles veulent? (1975)
   147
Mais qu-est-ce que j'ai fait au bon dieu

*pour avoir une femme qui boit dans
les cafés avec les hommes?* (1980)
148
Malle, Louis 15
Manet, Edouard 39–41, 43, 45–6
Manon des Sources (1952) 50
Manon des Sources (1986) 3, 15–16,
   19–20, 27, 50–61, 183
Marceau, Sophie 96–7
Marchand, Guy 63
Marche à l'ombre (1985) 142, 175
Mariée était en noir, La (1967) 85
Marius (1931) 51
Masques (1987) 96
Mathieu, Mireille 170
Maurice (1987) 13
Mauvais Sang (1986) 79, 130–40, 182
Melville, Jean-Pierre 77
Mémoire courte, La (1979) 100
Mépris, Le (1963) 92, 135
Merchant, Ismael and Ivory, James 21
Miller, Claude 99
Miller, Glenn 63
Miou-Miou (Sylvette Herry) 64, 146,
   173
Misérables, Les (1982) 14
Missiaen, Jean-Pierre 75
Mitterrand, François 109, 161
Mocky Jean-Pierre 141–2
Molière 13
Molinaro, Edouard 142
Monet, Claude 42
Mon beau-frère a tué ma soeur (1986)
   142
Monsieur Hire (1989) 175
Montand, Yves 50
Mordillat, Girard 142

Nikita (1990) 121
Nimoy, Leonard 145
Noir et blanc (1986) 26, 184–6
Noiret, Philippe 141
Nom de la rose, Le (1986) 3, 14
Nuttyens, Bruno 3

Œuvre au noir, L' (1988) 14
Ombre des châteaux, L' (1976) 100
Orphée (1950) 122, 124–5, 131, 133
Ours, L' (1988) 3
Oury, Gérard 141–2, 147

Pabst, Georg Wilhelm 131
Pagnol, Marcel 16, 50–61

Palma, Brian de 110
Pandora's Box (1928) 131, 133
Papy fait de la résistance (1982) 143
Passage to India, A (1985) 13
Passion (1982) 38–9
Passion Béatrice, La (1987) 14
Peau Douce, La (1964) 85
Père Noël est une ordure, Le (1982) 143–4
Perrier, Mireille 137
Perrin, Jacques 6
Petite Lise, La (1930) 131, 133
Phantom Lady (1944) 85
Pialat, Maurice 14, 77, 96–8, 100, 145, 171
Piccoli, Michel 135, 142
Pierrot le Fou (1965) 131
Poe, Edgar Allan 184
Poiré, Jean-Marie 143
Poiret, Jean 96
Police (1985) 77, 96–9, 102–5, 107–08
Police (group) 125
Poulet au vinaigre (1985) 96
Pourquoi pas! (1977) 147
Prénom: Carmen (1984) 98, 183
Prévert, Jacques 145
Professionnel, Le (1981) 141
Proust, Marcel 14, 18–19, 22, 29–32, 34

400 coups, Les (1959) 85, 131
Qu'est-ce qu'on attend pour être heureux? (1982) 147
Que la fête commence (1975) 21
Quentin, Florence 145, 159

Rainer, Yvonne 24
Rappeneau, Jean-Paul 8, 80
Ravanne 39
Règle du Jeu, La (1939) 85
Reine Margot, La (1994) 8
Renoir, Auguste 39–42, 45
Renoir, Jean 21, 41, 48, 85
Resnais Alain 148
Retour de Martin Guerre, Le (1982) 14, 183
Richard, Pierre 142
Rimbaud, Arthur 130, 139
Ripoux, Les (1984) 6, 141
Rivette, Jacques 39, 148
Robert, Yves 16, 141
Rohmer, Eric 148
Rolling Stones, The 125

Room with a View, A (1986) 13
Rouffio, Jacques 142
Rousseau, Jean-Jacques 19

Sabotage (1936) 84
Saboteur (1942) 84–5
Saint-Hamant, Jan 148
Sartre, Jean-Paul 125
Sassinot de Nesles, Yvonne 18
Schlöndorff, Volker 20, 22, 33
Schubert, Franz 155–6
Scott, Ridley 24
Série noire (1979) 96
Serra, Eric 125
Serrault, Michel 142
Serreau, Coline 6, 141, 147
Seven-Year Itch, The (1955) 111
Sinatra, Frank 125
Siodmak, Robert 85
Socrates 125
Some like it hot (1959) 172–3
Sous le soleil de Satan (1987) 14
Spécialiste, Le (1969) 105
Speilberg, Steven 123
Stevenin, Jean-François 236
Sting 125
Subway (1985) 20, 24, 79, 121–9, 132–3, 137
Sunset Boulevard (1950) 131, 135
Superman 3 63
Swaim, Bob 96–7
Swanson, Gloria 131, 135

Tatie Danielle (1990) 145
Tavernier, Bertrand 7, 14–15, 17, 20–1, 39–41, 43, 48, 79, 100
Tchao Pantin (1983) 50
Tenue de soirée (1986) 6, 146, 171–82, 185
Terminus (1987) 3
Thelma and Louise (1991) 24
Thérèse (1986) 38–9
Thomas l'Imposteur (1964) 85
Three Fugitives (1989) 142
Three Men and a Baby (1987) 145
Tintin 131
Tir groupé (1982) 75
Tirez sur le pianiste (1960) 105
Touchez pas au grisbi (1954) 85
Tous les matins du monde (1992) 14
Trauner, Alexandre 124
37°, 2 le matin (1986) 6, 83, 131
Trintignant, Jean-Louis 88, 91

Trois hommes et un couffin (1985) 6, 9, 141, 145, 147–59
Trouble with Harry, The (1954) 85
Truffaut, François 4, 15, 21, 48, 78–9, 84, 91, 93, 96, 99, 105, 131, 137
2001: A Space Odyssey (1968) 184

Ulmer, Edgar G. 107
Un amour de Swann (1984) 14, 18–20, 22–3, 27–37
Un dimanche à la campagne (1984), 15–21, 26–7, 38–49, 73, 79, 129
Un éléphant ça trompe énormément (1976) 141
Une nuit à l'Assemblé nationale (1988) 142
Une partie de campagne (1936) 41
Une semaine de vacances (1980) 100
Urgence (1985) 75

Van Gogh, Vincent 42
Van Hamme, Jean 111
Va voir Maman, Papa travaille (1977) 100
Valseuses, Les (1973) 145–6, 171, 173–5, 179, 182
Veber, Francis 142
Vengeance du serpent à plumes, La (1984) 142

Verdi, Guiseppe 19, 51, 61, 87
Vertigo (1958) 84–5
Vidor, King 131
Vie de famille, La (1985) 148
Vie est un long fleuve tranquille, La (1987) 80, 145, 159–70
Vie et rien d'autre, La (1989) 7
Vigne, Daniel 14
Vivement dimanche! (1983) 78–9, 84–96, 98, 122, 134, 136
Vivre sa vie (1962) 131
Vuillard, Edouard 39–41, 45

Wargnier, Régis 7
Welles, Orson 111, 131
Where Angels Fear to Tread (1991) 13
Wilder, Billy 131
Williams, Charles 86–7

Y a-t-il un Français dans la salle? (1982) 142
Yanne, Jean 142
Yourcenar, Marguerite 14

Zidi, Claude 6, 141
Zingg, Jean-Pierre 39
Zola, Émile 8, 31